PRAISE FOR CROSSING FIFTY-ONE

"*Crossing Fifty-One* is a powerful saga about midlife experience and changing family dynamics that deserves a prominent place not only in libraries interested in family psychology but also in deep discussions among psychology and book clubs interested in topics of healing, recovery, and physical and mental connections between health, illness, and family relationships."

—D. Donovan, Senior Reviewer, *Midwest Book Review*

"Debbie Russell uses her lawyer brain to delve deep into her family's past and, through that, figures out her own place in the world. It is a deeply satisfying and enjoyable read, and a great tool for anyone embarking on their own journey."

—Julie Klam, *New York Times* Best-Selling Author of *The Almost Legendary Morris Sisters*

"Debbie Russell navigates anticipatory grief over the decline of her father by embarking on a quest to preserve his legacy, inadvertently uncovering hidden family secrets along the way. She skillfully utilizes her investigative and litigation experiences to weave a persuasive multigenerational account that reads more like mystery than memoir. I consumed it in one sitting and can highly recommend this captivating debut!"

—Nita Sweeney, best-selling author of
Depression Hates a Moving Target

"The generational threads that can bind us together or tear us apart take center stage in this raw and honest mid-life reckoning. A universal tale of family secrets and love in the face of dysfunction—and how the lessons from the past can come back around to save our futures."

—Deborah Burns, award-winning author of
Saturday's Child

"A story of intergenerational inheritance and choosing what we keep, the author's journey to discover what happened in earlier generations is the catalyst for empathy for her family and for herself. Cheers to author Debbie Russell for unlocking the door that had seemed firmly shut for too long."

—Lizbeth Meredith, award-winning author of
Pieces of Me: Rescuing My Kidnapped Daughters

“This debut author has created a replication of a flawed and bruised family dynamic that reads like a novel and carries a universality that is quite human, and extremely well developed.”

—Greg Fields, award-winning author of
Through the Waters and the Wild

“Former trial lawyer Debbie Russell tackles midlife in an entirely unique way, by turning her attention to her paternal lineage. Every family has secrets, and Russell faces them head-on while in the throes of anticipatory grief. This book will resonate with anyone who has dealt with the loss of a loved one or who is facing an identity crisis in midlife.”

—Maria Leonard Olsen, Civil Litigation Attorney, Journalist, Mentor to Women in Recovery, Author of
50 After 50: Reframing the Next Chapter of Your Life

“The author’s father is wonderfully painted – supportive and optimistic, even as he is placed on hospice care. Readers intrigued by genealogical research, or who are facing the realities of aging parents, will find the work to be edifying and engaging.”

—Booklife Prize

“I started reading and I simply couldn’t stop! The story is beautiful and will help so many people.”

—Tracy C. Ertl, Publisher, TitleTown
Publishing LLC

Crossing Fifty-One: Not Quite a Memoir
by Debbie Russell

ISBN 979-8-88824-003-8

Publisher's Cataloging-in-Publication
(Provided by Cassidy Cataloguing Services, Inc.).

Names: Russell, Debbie, author.
Title: Crossing fifty-one : not quite a memoir / Debbie Russell.
Description: Virginia Beach, VA : Köehlerbooks, [2023] | Includes bibliographical references.
Identifiers: ISBN: 979-888824-003-8 (hardcover) | 979-888824-005-2 (paperback) | 979-888824-004-5 (ebook) | LCCN: 2023902917
Subjects: LCSH: Russell, Debbie. | Fathers and daughters. | Anticipatory grief. | Adult children of dysfunctional families. | Family secrets. | Genealogy. | Substance abuse. | Loss (Psychology) | Middle age. | Dysfunctional families. | Love. | Perseveration (Psychology) | Resilience (Personality trait) | LCGFT: Autobiography. | BISAC: BIOGRAPHY & AUTOBIOGRAPHY / Personal Memoirs. | FAMILY & RELATIONSHIPS / Family History & Genealogy. | FAMILY & RELATIONSHIPS / Life Stages / Mid-Life. | PSYCHOLOGY / Psychopathology / Addiction. | BIOGRAPHY & AUTOBIOGRAPHY / Women.
Classification: LCC: BF723.P25 .R87 2023 | DDC: 155.9/24--dc23

Published by

köehlerbooks™

3705 Shore Drive
Virginia Beach, VA 23455
800-435-4811
www.koehlerbooks.com

CROSSING FIFTY-ONE

Not Quite a Memoir

DEBBIE RUSSELL

VIRGINIA BEACH
CAPE CHARLES

For my father . . .
and his father

TABLE OF CONTENTS

Part 1 1

Chapter 1 Now: Christmas 2015 3

Chapter 2 Now: January 2016 19

Chapter 3 Then: December 1951 28

Chapter 4 Now: February 2016 38

Chapter 5 Now: Christmas 2016 45

Part 2 53

Chapter 6 Then: 1900 55

Chapter 7 Then: January 1952 60

Chapter 8 Then: 1930 70

Chapter 9 Now: February 2017 81

Chapter 10 Then, January 1952 85

Chapter 11 Then: January 1952 93

Part 3 105

Chapter 12 Now: March 2017 107

Chapter 13 Then: February 1952 111

Chapter 14 Now: March 2017 116

Chapter 15 Now: March 2017 120

Chapter 16 Then: February 1952 126

Chapter 17 Now: March 2017 135

Part 4 139

Chapter 18 Then: February 1952 141

Chapter 19 Now: April 2017 146

Chapter 20 Now: May 2017 160

Part 5 ... 163

Chapter 21 Then: February 1952 ... 165

Chapter 22 Now: July 2017 ... 172

Chapter 23 Then: March 1952 ... 179

Chapter 24 Now: July 2017 ... 190

Chapter 25 Now: August 2017 ... 193

Part 6 ... 199

Chapter 26 Then: March 1952 ... 201

Chapter 27 Now: September 2017 ... 207

Chapter 28 Then: March 1952 ... 212

Chapter 29 Now: October 2017 ... 217

Chapter 30 Then: 1988 ... 225

Part 7 ... 237

Chapter 31 Then, March 1952 ... 239

Chapter 32 Now: October 2017 ... 247

Chapter 33 Then: April 1952 ... 252

Chapter 34 Now: November 2017 ... 255

Chapter 35 Then: April 1952 ... 259

Chapter 36 Now: Christmas 2017 ... 263

Chapter 37 Now: January 2018 ... 269

Chapter 38 Then: April 1952 ... 274

Chapter 39 Now: Mother's Day 2018 ... 277

Chapter 40 Then: 1959 ... 284

Chapter 41 Now: Father's Day 2018 ... 287

Epilogue ... 296

Acknowledgments ... 297

Resources ... 300

Discussion Questions for Book Clubs ... 301

A NOTE TO MY READERS:

Wikipedia defines a memoir as "any nonfiction narrative writing based in the author's personal memories." Of course, my personal memories may differ from those of others who lived and experienced the same events. In writing this book, I relied on notes I maintained contemporaneously, clinic records from my therapists, written communications and consultations with people who appear in the book, and extensive research on addiction and treatment in the 1950s. In some places, I recreated dialogue. When requested and when I deemed it appropriate, I changed the names of those mentioned to protect their privacy.

DEBBIE RUSSELL PATERNAL FAMILY TREE

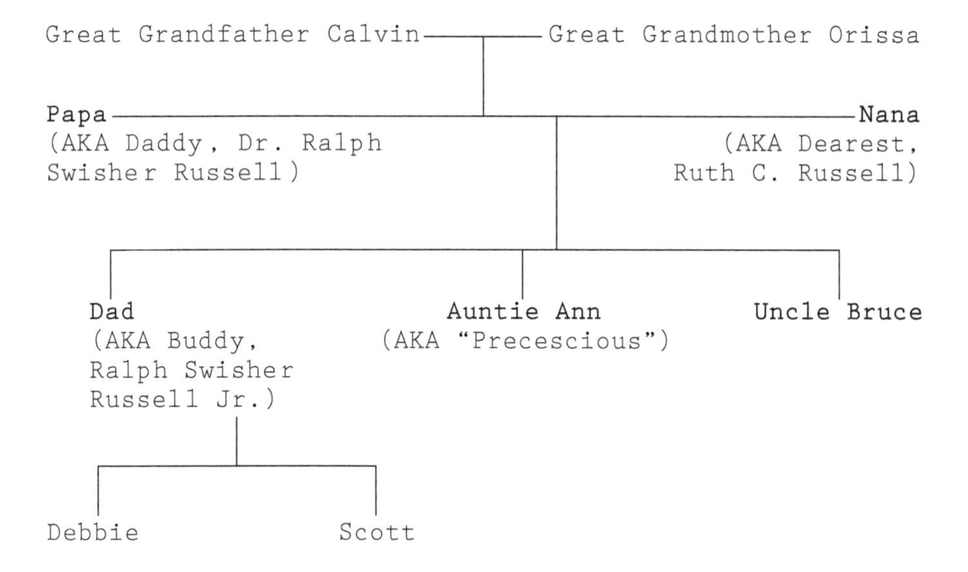

PART ONE

"All the world's a stage, and all the men and women merely players . . ."

William Shakespeare

CHAPTER 1

Now: Christmas 2015

"Should I call 911?" The server smiles politely, her eyes locked on Dad.

"Let's give it a minute," I respond, attempting to project a pleasant, calm demeanor I don't actually feel. The last thing Dad wants is to be responsible for lunch being called off.

Miraculously, Mum nervously agrees.

Nodding, the server glides away.

Slumped in his chair, eyes closed, Dad does not move. At least he's not thrashing around on the floor. That would draw too much attention.

The muted sounds of conversation and clinking silverware blend seamlessly with Nat King Cole's "Have Yourself a Merry Little Christmas." The upscale St. Paul restaurant, a lovely relic of the Victorian era, is decked out in holiday splendor, appealing to Mum's heightened need for that certain aesthetic. My reservation has secured us a cozy table near the fireplace. We are tucked behind one of several glittering Christmas trees scattered throughout the restaurant. Table placement is key. Mum cherishes her privacy even when dining out.

However, despite all my efforts at concealment, a young woman makes her way over to our table. "I wasn't meaning to eavesdrop," she begins, "but I work in a nursing home, and this happens pretty regularly."

Her gentle voice calms me, but glancing at Mum and seeing the fake smile she dons like a mask, I feel my heart beat a bit faster. We have been exposed.

The young woman continues. "One little trick I've learned is to put a Kleenex or napkin in front of the person's face to monitor their breathing."

I could see Dad was breathing, but now I struggle to control the slight panic that has crept in and taken its place in my chair at our table.

I suppose there are worse ways to go.

Since Dad's Parkinson's diagnosis over a decade ago, I've had a front-row seat to his slow disappearance. Once the buffer and the glue for our little family, he now struggles to fulfill his most important role: keeping Mum happy. This morning, he insisted that he could manage the holiday lunch outing, but just getting from the car into the restaurant was touch and go.

I exhaled once we were seated at our semi-secluded table. We ordered our food, and Mum immediately began prattling on about how lovely everything looked. I nodded and smiled, playing my role of a dutiful, devoted daughter. When Mum finally paused her soliloquy, we both glanced over at Dad.

He was out cold.

That was about ten minutes ago. Or was it ten hours? I can't tell.

Mum keeps talking. I guess it helps her take her mind off her unconscious husband. I keep smiling while monitoring Dad's breathing out of the corner of my eye. The restaurant staff hovers in as nice a way as possible. Finally, we agree that 911 should be called.

After what seems like forever, three burly paramedics make their way back to our table. By this time, Dad is coming around.

"What did I miss?" He smiles weakly.

His smile fades as he glances over at Mum.

"I'm so very sorry."

The paramedics check his blood pressure. It is low. They want to take him to the ER. He declines. This becomes a bit of an issue, as it is against medical advice.

"I just want my lunch," Dad says firmly. He can be stubborn, but I know what's really driving this refusal. He can't disappoint Mum. Not again.

The server smiles kindly. "I'll put your order back in right away."

The paramedics put me on the phone with the ER doctor after Mum demurs. Despite her powerful and opinionated outbursts, it always comes down to me to "handle" the situation. As the eldest child—who also happens to have spent the last two decades prosecuting violent criminals—I know my way around my own family conflict.

"I love having our lawyer right here with us." Mum crinkles her eyes at the EMTs.

Is she flirting with them?

A certain smugness, to which I have grown accustomed, accompanies her statement. I try not to cringe. My value as a lawyer replaced my value as a daughter around the time I hit my early thirties. Single, with no children, I remain acutely aware of how deeply I have disappointed a mother whose dreams for me aligned more closely with an episode of *Real Housewives* than an episode of *Law and Order*.

Ignoring Mum, I explain Dad's wishes to the random ER doctor on the other end of the phone. Then, because Mum balks at the responsibility again, I sign the "against medical advice" form, and we finish our lunch. This will leave me firmly on the hook if this decision leads to Dad's ultimate demise.

Afterward, as we make our way somewhat laboriously back to the car, I silently predict that this will be the last time Dad eats a meal in a restaurant.

Upon arriving home, I call my brother, Scott, to give him an update on Dad's condition. As usual, it goes to voicemail. Two years younger than me, Scott takes after Mum in how fiercely he protects his privacy. He was just in town for Christmas. He brought his girlfriend. It was exhausting. They brought with them a roaster and a bread maker and took over Mum's kitchen. I'm sure they thought they were being helpful, but it only served to push her into a corner, which she proceeded to occupy like a petulant toddler. Then they were gone, leaving me to pick up the pieces. It's what he does. It's what I do.

Christmas has always been a source of anxiety for me. My earliest memories of the holiday revolve around a big, glittery production staged for geriatric relatives and friends. Behind the scenes, underneath the ostentatious decorations and fancy clothes, Christmas exacerbated the wild fluctuations of my mother's moods. She worried about the food, how we looked, and inevitably, how much appreciation our guests demonstrated for all her efforts. I, in turn, worried about how she would react to whatever gifts Dad had picked out for her.

Nowadays, I focus on just getting through it. With no children of my own, I concentrate on meeting Mum's childlike expectations for a festive time. Dad does the same. Scott shows up if he can make the time. And if he feels up to it.

Since he didn't feel like taking my call, I leave a brief voicemail, after which I sit alone with my thoughts. I replay our lunch in my mind and then conjure up ghosts of Christmases past. At some point, I remind myself that no Christmas we've ever gone through—or are likely to ever go through—could top what Dad's family endured during the Christmas of 1951.

◆ ◆ ◆

Mrs. RS Russell
3204 Goldsmith St.
San Diego 6 Calif.

Ralph S. Russell, MD
P.O. Box 100, Fort Worth, Texas

Dearest:

Did not sleep a wink on the plane but as we flew over Fort Worth and put down at Dallas, I did some thinking. I decided that since I was so close to this facility, that I would give it the "once over." It was so cold, 19° or 20° that I figured Lexington would be at least 10° colder so – after seeing the installation and meeting Dr. Osberg, the psychiatrist who is my Doctor I decided to save the extra fare and stay here. I will request that the ticket be sent to you to get a refund. This will help with the heavy expense you are having with no income. Incidentally I made out no check on First National on account of the no income situation while I am not working.

Please call Dr. McCoy (the doctor who was instrumental in having me treated) and tell him that I am very happy with Fort Worth. There are 24 in this ward and I have a private room. There is TV, an Admiral 17". From my window I see the 1,400 acres and the town in the distance. Room is nice and cozy warm. More in a few days – Daddy

Will telephone tonight.

Over a decade ago, I realized that a life—any life—can be reduced to the contents of boxes. When my parents vacated the home where I grew up, they packed my childhood bedroom into several of those boxes that hold reams of paper for office printers. They also passed along to me boxes from their prior lives, lives lived before they met each other and became my parents. Several of these boxes also contained lives even further removed from my own—those of grandparents and more distant ancestors I had never met or barely remembered.

At the time, I accepted them with very little thought. I owned a darling bungalow with a basement and was far too busy living my own life to concern myself with other lives relegated to musty cardboard cartons. Eventually, though, my curiosity got the best of me. As a kid, I had always been interested in my lineage, and for good reason. It was exciting and colorful. My great-grandfather on Dad's side had penned his memoirs, entitled *Life Story of Calvin Parker Russell: Western Pioneer and Ranchman, as told by himself.* The hardbound book exceeded three hundred typed pages. My great-grandfather had gifted a copy to each of his sons, which in turn was passed down. Dad received one such copy.

I was delighted to take it off his hands when he and Mum downsized.

Poring through it eagerly, I devoured three hundred pages of fascinating information about my great-grandfather. His younger son, my grandfather, took up less than ten of those pages.

I never met Dad's father. He died of asthma at the age of fifty-nine, six years before I was born. Yet he abruptly sprang to life one day when I went down to the basement and lifted the cover of one of the boxes marked "memorabilia" in Dad's easily recognizable scrawl. A plain manila file folder, bound with a rubber band, lay nestled among newspaper clippings, scrapbooks, and photos. Curious, I opened it. Within was a neat stack of letters, some handwritten, some typed. The first one immediately grabbed my attention:

Earp, California
September 18, 1951

Harris Isbell, M.D.
U.S. Public Health Service
Lexington, Ky.,

Dear ~~Sir~~ Doctor:

An article abstracted in the Modern Medicine caught my attention yesterday and prompts this inquiry today.

The last five years of my 26-year practice have been beset with bronchial asthma and a too frequent use of Demerol, barbiturates, and M.S.* The last least of all and the first, most of all. I have been off and on Demerol six times, and this month have used 15 Grams 1 V along with 6mgms ACTH** a day. No Demerol this week but have been fighting withdrawal symptoms with barbiturates and some M.S. although I seem to be allergic to M.S. To say the least, I have been quite miserable.

On account of the asthma, I have spent the last three years on the Colorado River desert, near Parker Arizona and Blythe California as Dist. Surg. For the Metropolitan Water District. This is rather an inactive job and the area is very isolated. My family have been in San Diego. Where my real practice (what there is left of it) is located. This has not helped my morale. I have given notice to go back to my practice the first of November. Now I wonder if it had not better be a trip to Lexington.

My asthma does not bother me as long as I take ACTH. That is, not a great deal. I do not know what it will be if I get real active, as I was during World War II. The bulk of my practice is obstetrics, having specialized in it in 1944 by P.O. at Columbia.(Margaret Hague Hospital, Jersey City)

May I have the benefit of your experience, by your comments?

Yours Truly,
Ralph S. Russell M.D.,F.A.C.S.
Dist. Surg M.W.D.
Earp California

---

* Morphine Sulfate

** Adrenocorticotropic Hormone

This first letter of introduction was followed by an official-looking response:

FEDERAL SECURITY AGENCY
PUBLIC HEALTH SERVICE
LEXINGTON, KENTUCKY
SEPTEMBER 27, 1951

DR. RALPH S. RUSSELL
DISTRICT SURGEON
METROPOLITAN WATER DISTRICT
EARP, CALIFORNIA

DEAR DR. RUSSELL;

YOUR LETTER OF SEPTEMBER 18, 1951, TO DR. ISBELL HAS BEEN REFERRED TO THIS OFFICE FOR REPLY. THE CONTENTS HAVE BEEN DISCUSSED WITH THE CLINICAL DIRECTOR OF THIS HOSPITAL, AND HE ADVISES ME THAT THE PATIENT WOULD REQUIRE A PROLONGED PERIOD OF HOSPITALIZATION, AND NO ATTEMPT WOULD BE MADE BY THE MEMBERS OF THE STAFF OF THIS HOSPITAL TO PRESCRIBE TREATMENT FOR A PATIENT NOT ACTUALLY HOSPITALIZED HERE.

THERE IS ENCLOSED AN APPLICATION FOR ADMISSION, TOGETHER WITH A PAMPHLET WHICH DESCRIBES THE TREATMENT AT THIS HOSPITAL.

IT IS SUGGESTED THAT YOU COMPLETE THE APPLICATION, AND RETURN IT TO THIS HOSPITAL, AND IMMEDIATELY UPON RECEIPT OF IT, IT WILL BE EXAMINED AND IF ELIGIBLE FOR ADMISSION, YOU WILL BE NOTIFIED WHEN TO REPORT.

SINCERELY,
W.K. MCCURRY
ADMINISTRATIVE OFFICER
CLINICAL RECORDS SECTION

Dad rarely spoke of "Papa," as my grandfather was referred to posthumously. I knew that he had been a doctor and had suffered from asthma. My Grandmother Ruth, or "Nana," I knew mostly from letters and cassette tapes that we would record and mail back and forth. Dad was the eldest of their three children, seven years older than my Uncle Bruce and nine years older than my Auntie Ann.

When these letters were written in 1951, Dad, or "Buddy," as he was known in the family (he was a "Junior"), was twenty-three, attending Boston University, majoring in speech communication, and aspiring to be an actor. Bruce was sixteen, about to turn seventeen, and a senior in high school. Ann, or "Precescious," as Papa affectionately called her, was fourteen years old.

A quick glance through the folder showed me that it contained approximately eighty letters. The great majority of them were written in Nana's hand and addressed to "Dearest" or "Daddy," when she wrote on behalf of the family. There was also the occasional letter directly from Dad or his siblings interspersed.

This stack of letters established that shortly before Christmas 1951, at the age of fifty-one, Papa made the consequential decision to seek treatment for his dependence on Demerol and other narcotics. When I first read through the letters, I couldn't help but think that this decision was entirely unexpected by the rest of the family, as well as somewhat unilateral. That first handwritten letter, undated and in a very shaky scrawl, seemed to support my theory.

Another initial reaction was disbelief, inspired by the line at the bottom of the letter, "*will telephone tonight*." The fact that Nana wouldn't receive this letter until after she had already spoken with Papa by phone jarred me. These days, a change in plans is conveyed immediately via phone or text. As someone who relies on information as an internal steadying device, I found myself unnerved, thinking about Nana's reaction to an after-the-fact announcement that Papa would not be home for Christmas.

Changing plans is frowned upon in my immediate family.

Advance notice is expected in all things.

In 1951, personal news traveled only as fast as the US Postal Service. The next letter in the stack, on Boston University stationary, was from Dad. The frantic, exaggerated scrawl revealed the emotions of an anxious son:

Dec. 18, 1951

Dearest Dad –

I received yours and Mothers letter and I thought it best to call home for further details. After talking to Mother I decided to get this letter right off to you. First of all, I want to know if you are allowed to have visitors. If so, I want to plan to come and see you sometime during Xmas vacation Dec. 20-Jan 2. If not then, maybe between semesters Jan 15-22. Don't worry about the expense as it is all taken care of and no one is being inconvenienced by it. Besides, it is very necessary for me in order to put my own mind at ease; to talk to you and to see the surroundings and also the circumstances that you are in.

If visitors are not permitted, I want you to write me a detailed account of everything giving as much information about Ft. Worth U.S.P.H.S. Hospital as possible. Mother was a little upset when she had found out that you went to Ft. Worth instead of Lexington. What's the difference?

Above all Dad, remember you are the most important person in my life and I love you with all the heart and soul that's in me. Please don't blame or denounce yourself for what has happened. It was accidental. Your family and your friends are behind you 100%. May God bless you and be with you.

All the love from my heavy heart.
Your son, Ralph Jr.

The first time I read this letter, the words blurred through my unexpected tears. I struggled to understand my emotional reaction. I felt an overwhelming bond with my then twenty-three-year-old father. Dad's words of comfort for his struggling father foretold the father and husband he would become. But now, this person who has been my primary source of support throughout my life is fading away, increasingly overshadowed by a debilitating condition, and a wife who can't manage to interact with or support him emotionally. Dad has always been in my corner, even when my corner was messy. But of late, my corner feels lonely.

I have spent a lifetime repressing tears, only allowing them to appear in private. Instead, I absorb frequent bouts of Mum's tears. She cries at the drop of a hat. When this happens, I can usually maintain a calm, comforting presence, while my stomach churns. Her tears repulse me, as I find them manipulative. Dad, on the other hand, has made caring for Mum his number-one priority for as long as I can remember.

I fight an overwhelming sense of emptiness, as I contemplate the stark differences between Dad's family of origin and my own. Dad is the common thread in both, and that thread is quickly fraying. Is this what anticipatory grief feels like? Inexplicably, I find myself back in the basement searching for a folder of letters that may be the only thing that can keep my heart from shattering into a million pieces.

TO Mrs R S Russell

Ralph S Russell M.D.
P. O. Box 100, Fort Worth, Texas

STREET 3204 Goldsmith St

CITY & STATE San Diego 6 Calif.

Dearest: Did not sleep a wink on the plane but as we flew over Fort Worth and put down at Dallas, I did some thinking. I decided that since I was so close to this facility, that I would give it the "once over". It was so cold, 19° or 20° that I figured Lexington would be at least 10° colder so - After seeing the installation and meeting Dr Osberg, the Psychiatrist who is my Doctor I decided to save the extra fare and stay here. I will request that the ticket be sent to you to get a refund. This will help with the heavy expense you are having with no income. Incidentally I made out no check on First National on account of the no income situation while I am not working.

Please call Dr McCoy (the doctor who was instrumental in having me treated) and tell him that I am very happy with Fort Worth. There are 24 in this ward and I have a private room. There is T-V, an Admiral 17." From my windows I see the 1400 acres and the town in the distance. Room is nice and cozy warm. More in a few days.

Will telephone tonite. Daddy.

Earp California
Sept. 18, 1951

Harris Isbell M.D.
U.S.Public Health Service
Lexington Ky.,

Dear ~~Sir~~: Doctor:

An article abstracted in the Modern Medicine caught my eye yesterday and prompts this inquiry today.

The last five years of my 26 years practice have been beset with bronchial asthma and a too frequent use of Demerol, barbiturates and M.S. The last least of all and the first, most of all. I have been off and on demerol six times, and this month have used 15 Grams 1 V along with 6mgms ACTH a day. No demerol this week but have been fighting withdrawal symptoms with barbiturates and some M.S. although I seem to be allergic to M.S. To say the least, I have been quite miserable.

On account of the asthma I have spent the last three years on the Colorado River desert, near Parker Arizona and Blythe Califo as Dist. Surg. for the Metropolitan Water District. This is rather an inactive job and the area is very isolated. My family have been in San Diego. where my real practice(what there is left of it) is located. This has not helped my morale. I have given notice to go back to my practice the first of November. Now I wonder if it had not better be a trip to Lexington.

My asthma does not bother me as long as I take ACTH. That is, not a great deal. I do not know what it will be if I get real active, as I was during World War 11. The bulk of my practice is obstetrics, having specialized in it in 1944 by P.G. at Columbia. (Margaret Hague Hospital, Jersey City)

May I have the benefit of your experience, by your comments?

Yours truly,

Ralph S. Russell M.D.,
F.A.C.S.
Dist Surg M.W.D.

Earp California

TWX CODE NO
LEX KY 477

IN REPLYING, ADDRESS THE
MEDICAL OFFICER IN CHARGE
PUBLIC HEALTH SERVICE HOSPITAL

FEDERAL SECURITY AGENCY
PUBLIC HEALTH SERVICE
LEXINGTON, KENTUCKY

September 27, 1951

28328

Dr. Ralph S. Russell
District Surgeon
Metropolitan Water District
Earp, California

Dear Dr. Russell:

Your letter of September 18, 1951, to Dr. Isbell has been referred to this office for reply. The contents have been discussed with the Clinical Director of this hospital, and he advises me that the patient would require a prolonged period of hospitalization, and no attempt would be made by the members of the staff of this hospital to prescribe treatment for a patient not actually hospitalized here.

There is enclosed an application for admission, together with a pamphlet which describes the treatment at this hospital.

It is suggested that you complete the application, and return it to this hospital, and immediately upon receipt of it, it will be examined and if eligible for admission, you will be notified when to report.

Sincerely,

W. K. McCurry
Administrative Officer
Clinical Records Section

WKM:ESH

BOSTON UNIVERSITY FACULTY CLUB
147 BAY STATE ROAD
BOSTON 15, MASSACHUSETTS
TEL: CIRCLE 7-9347

Dec. 18, 1951

Dearest Dad—

I received yours and mothers letter and I thought it best to call home for further details. After talking to mother I decided to get this letter right off to you. First of all, I want to know if you are allowed to have visitors. If so, I want to plan to come and see you sometime during Xmas vacation Dec. 20 – Jan 2. If not then, maybe between semesters Jan 15 – 22. Don't worry about the expense as it is all taken care of and no one is being inconvenienced by it. Besides, it is very necessary for me,

(over)

in order to put my own mind at
ease; to talk to you and to see the
surroundings and also the circumstance
that you are in. If visitors are not
permitted, I want you to write me a
detailed account of everything giving
as much information about Ft. Worth
U.S.P.H.S. Hospital as possible. Mother
was a little upset when she had
found out that you went to Ft. Worth
instead of Lexington. Whats the difference.

Above all Dad, remember you are
the most important person in my life
and I love you with all the heart
and soul thats in me. Please don't
blame or denounce yourself for what has
happened. It was accidental. Your family and
your friends are behind you 100%. May God bless
you and be with you. All the love from my
heavy heart. Your son
Ralph Jr.

CHAPTER 2

Now: January 2016

The pleasant warmth that accompanies a second glass of Malbec has just settled over me when my cell phone buzzes, interrupting my conversation with cousin Jim. Caller ID informs me that the call is from "Mum and Dad." Given that it's 6:30 on a Monday evening and the phone calls between me and my parents are religiously regimented, this does not bode well. On the other hand, Mum often calls with lengthy requests for odd, non-urgent tasks.

I let it go to voicemail.

A week or so prior, I'd welcomed Jim's text suggesting dinner and drinks. Jim is just two months younger than me, and we are easily taken for siblings, thanks to our large dark eyes and healthy eyebrows.

Twenty-five years ago, Jim and his wife, a Minnesota native, settled in the Twin Cities area to pursue their doctorate degrees at the same university where I attended law school. For one period a day during the first semester of my second year, I babysat their infant daughter in an empty classroom at the law school. Given my admitted limitations as a caretaker, it turned out to be a relatively easy task, as baby Alex didn't yet have the means to escape her bucket-type car seat.

Back then, I enthusiastically looked forward to lots of face time with Jim and his growing family, but as the years passed, such contact was constrained to a few scattered events like holidays and high school graduations. Due to the size of these gatherings, there was rarely much opportunity for intimate conversation. Thus, after twenty-five years, I wasn't sure whether I knew my cousin very well, even though every prior get-together had always been warm and a lot of fun.

So now, when Jim made a point of reaching out and seeking a get-together, I was surprised, but very pleased.

Settling comfortably into a small table tucked away in the corner of a cozy neighborhood bar, we quickly launched into a conversation about our shared familial connections. I felt an easy connection with Jim that is missing with my own brother. As we discussed our common lineage, I soon realized that, over the years, I'd accumulated a large cache of information about our ancestors that may not be widely known throughout the family.

"Did you know that our grandfather admitted himself to a federal hospital for his Demerol addiction?" I inquired, somewhat dramatically.

Jim's eyes widened. "Had no idea!"

I then spill the beans about the stack of letters, neatly placed in a manila folder, that somehow came into my possession many years ago.

"I keep thinking I should write a book about the family and how they managed during the four months he was away," I say. "The letters are quite a testament to fortitude and how Nana kept everything afloat until he came back."

Jim wants to hear more, but at that moment, my phone buzzes again. Ugh. Mum has left a voicemail. I'm trained not to ignore voicemails. There's no excuse for not being readily available when Mum needs something.

"Oh, hi there, dearie. Just the mum here. Say . . . we have a little situation here, and I'm wondering if you might be able to come over and help me get your dad off the floor. He's had a little fall."

I relay the message to Jim, dismayed at having to cut short our very pleasant evening.

"I'll come with you." He cheerfully offers his assistance without an ounce of hesitation.

I'm momentarily taken aback, as this is unexpected. I then shift to predicting Mum's reaction when Jim walks through the door with me. She won't like it one bit. Even though he is family, he is *Dad's* family, not to be liked nor trusted. But Jim will be another voice of reason if Mum decides to be unreasonable.

Around the time Dad turned eighty, Jim, then a partner in a medical device firm, advocated for Dad to get hearing aids. Mum didn't want to pay for them. She historically maintained a tight grip on the purse string, loosening it only if she saw some sort of shiny object that captured her fancy. When I was in high school, that shiny object was a weeklong time share in Florida in the middle of August. Nobody wants to be in Florida in the middle of August, so they got a pretty good deal. When she demurred on the hearing aid issue, Jim moved heaven and earth to make it affordable for them.

As Dad became weaker, Mum balked at making the drive to Jim's business to get the devices periodically adjusted. In response, Jim came to their place, despite it being on the opposite side of the metropolitan area from his home and business. When Mum tried to put him off, he insisted. It became a routine. She would try to dodge him, and he would always win out.

"I don't get to see my aunt and uncle very often, so I appreciate the opportunity," he would respond cheerfully as Mum tried to talk him out of it.

She never seemed convinced. "I don't get why he does this," Mum would say to me after each visit. She's always harbored suspicion about the motives of others. In Jim's case, she probably thought he was spying on them to report back to his mother, Dad's sister, Ann.

With all this in mind, I quickly balance two potential outcomes: 1) the likely blowback from Mum for bringing Jim into her inner sanctum with no advance warning; against 2) the also likely feeling of relief at having someone else in my corner for when the blowback occurs. The choice is an easy one.

We make a quick stop at my house to take care of my dogs and then drive the twenty minutes over to my parents' townhome.

"Anybody home?" I call out as Jim and I enter.

At my parents' place, you can either go up six steps to the bedrooms or down six steps to the main living area. Mum's placed bedsheets on the steps to preserve the off-white 1980s carpeting that runs throughout the townhouse. She now stands at the bottom of those steps to the main level, dwarfed by the cathedral ceiling, also 1980s in origin. Dad's sitting on the floor at her feet, his back resting against the bottom step.

"Here we are!" Mum's cheerful voice is like a punch to my stomach. "Why Jim, what a lovely surprise!" she chirps.

Surprise indeed. Lovely? Unlikely. But here we are. Jim and I make our way down to Dad, who looks up at us in bewilderment.

"What's happening here? Is that my favorite nephew?" Dad always tries to keep things light. It's how he copes with discomfort.

"Uncle Buddy, what happened?"

"I wish I knew. I'm just so weak."

"I just need you to help me get him up off the floor." The urgency in Mum's voice cuts through the chitchat. Her tone makes it clear that there will be no negotiating. I look at Jim. He shrugs almost indiscernibly.

"Looks like Dad is sleeping downstairs tonight," I say cheerfully, hoping that I've sufficiently masked the rage that's beginning its slow boil. I'm momentarily taken aback by this feeling.

Then I remember. Almost a decade ago, just as Dad's hearing was beginning to fail, Mum decided that she and Dad would move to Savannah to be closer to her sister. I remember the familiar pit opening in my stomach as my brain scrambled to make sense of this announcement. *Is this my fault?* She dropped this bombshell on the Fourth of July. I'd begged off a get-together with *my* friends to entertain my parents, who had no friends of their own. Besides, I'd been trained to regard the Fourth of July as a family holiday.

"I'm just so lonely," she'd stammered through her tears.

Rather than risk an ugly scene, I held my tongue.

My parents would go on to spend a few months running around Savannah with Mum's sister, looking at houses they couldn't afford. They ultimately made a low-ball offer on one, which was promptly rejected, causing them to reluctantly abandon this plan.

Mum was devastated. I couldn't get a read on Dad, but that was not unusual. I tried not to think about the fact that he seemed willing to abandon me because Mum wanted to be close to her sister.

As Mum's restlessness continued, though, I could no longer keep my opinions to myself. I suggested that, at their age, they might want to start thinking about the future when looking at living arrangements.

"Have you considered some sort of senior community?"

My question, though well-intended, was anything but well-received. "You want us to live in some sort of garbage can?" Mum screamed at me.

This was a prime example of Mum hearing something entirely different than what I'd said. Nonetheless, her response frightened me. We had just finished Easter dinner at my place, and she came at me, as if she might slap me upside the head. Ultimately, Dad had to physically guide her out the door and into the car. We didn't speak for several months after that.

Eventually, we simply picked up as if nothing had happened.

The problem with those kinds of non-resolutions is they sit with you, fermenting for the next blowup. The Savannah episode from a decade ago now bounces around inside my head as I contemplate how Jim and I will get Dad into the next room where at least there's a pull-out couch. I shake the memory off. Jim and I each take an arm and gently pull Dad up and escort him to the couch.

Within twenty-four hours, Dad is hospitalized with a bladder infection. The next day, the attending physician informs us that Dad will not be able to return home; instead, he will need to spend some time in rehabilitation. While Mum and Dad are shocked, I'm totally prepared for this development. I've been prepared for months, if not years.

"Of course," I respond in an all-knowing tone, as if this is totally typical. It is, in fact, to be expected, but my parents are currently unable to comprehend that. They sit silently; their discomfort at the news is palpable.

"The social worker will work with you to select a facility that will work for your family," the doctor continues kindly. His delivery goes a long way, particularly with older people in general and my parents in particular.

Two days later, Mum calls, interrupting my preparations for heading out and picking her up for our daily hospital visit. She is frantic.

"I just got off the phone with the social worker, and they want to discharge your father *today*!" she shrieks. "I've been all through our insurance coverage, and unless he stays in the hospital for *three days*, the nursing home will not be covered *at all*!"

"Mum, I really need you to calm down. This is about Dad and what's best for him."

"How dare you speak to me like that? I know this is about your father!" The conversation, which was not great to start with, is rapidly deteriorating. Must. Not. Escalate.

"Alright, I'm going to finish getting ready, and then I'll be by to pick you up. We can figure this all out when we get to the hospital." Hanging up, I breathe deeply, trying to quell the pounding in my head.

I call Scott. It goes to voicemail. Of course it does. I muster a non-confrontational tone.

"Hey, it's your sister. I really need you to come up here and help me deal with Mum. Things are getting a little out of hand with Dad's situation, and she's losing it. Please call me as soon as you can."

I then send him a text: *"Listen to your voicemail. Need you to come up ASAP."*

In hindsight, maybe that was a bit confrontational . . .

I finish getting ready and head out the door. I still need to actually *talk* to someone. Maybe Jim will answer?

He does. "Cousin! How's it going? How's Uncle Buddy?"

Relief washes over me at the sound of Jim's cheerful greeting. Finally, a port in the storm!

"Well, here's the situation. Apparently, the hospital wants to discharge Dad today, but their insurance won't pay for a nursing home stay unless he's been in the hospital three nights, and he's only been there for two nights. Mum is apoplectic over the money situation, and I'm heading over to pick her up and take her to the hospital. Oh, and I can't reach Scott."

"Of course you can't." Jim understands my brother's innate ability to stay under the radar. He then describes an incident where his wife's family had to enlist the help of a patient advocate. "All hospitals have them. So, when you get there, just ask for one and talk through what's going on. Do you think he's ready to be discharged?"

"Well, he was still awfully weak yesterday, so it's hard for me to imagine that he is."

"The advocate will help you. Keep me posted!"

With that, I have the two things I need most—support and a plan.

Thankfully, Mum's pulled herself together by the time I pick her up. Her hair, dyed a shade darker than mine, is ratted into its usual frizz, and her bright red lipstick liberally applied. She's ready to face the world.

"We'll get this figured out," I say soothingly as we drive the ten minutes to the hospital.

Upon our arrival, there is, of course, nobody available to talk to us, so we make aimless chitchat with Dad. He still seems out of it. Then, my phone rings. It's Scott. I put him on speaker so he can say hello to Mum and Dad, after which, I dip out to a stairwell to talk about the current crisis.

"I can't come up," he says flatly. He's in the middle of starting up a new coffee shop with his girlfriend, and he must get all the permits and inspections scheduled. He goes on and on until I'm tired of hearing about it.

"Okay," I respond. "I need to go." *What else can I say?*

The doctor who wants to kick Dad out of the hospital has arrived. Despite not having met with a patient advocate, I decide that I can handle it.

"Could we step outside for a minute?" I ask, beckoning for Mum and the day nurse to join us.

"Here's the thing," I say once we are all in the hallway. I look straight into the doctor's eyes, which are framed by narrow, wire-rimmed glasses. "If you discharge my father today, he will be going home, because my parents cannot afford a nursing home, and insurance will not pay for one if he has not spent three nights here. From what I can tell, he can't yet walk on his own and he is extremely weak. But if, from your standpoint, he is well enough for discharge, then he will probably fall again at home, and we will be right back here. My guess is it'll most likely be within a week."

The doctor bristles. "I don't have any control over what insurance does," he mutters, looking away, unable to meet my defiant gaze. "I can't provide false information."

"Okay, you do what you need to do, then."

I've thrown down the gauntlet. He and Mum return to the room, while the nurse hangs back with me. "I just wanted to tell you that I spotted a rash on your dad's back. I think we might be able to add that as a new condition that will require continued monitoring," she said.

I resist the urge to hug her—as well as to burst into tears.

She continues, smiling conspiratorially. "I'm pretty sure your dad won't be discharged today."

The remainder of the afternoon passes before we receive word that Dad won't be discharged after all. Things, it seems, move at a glacial pace in the health care world.

So much anxiety over nothing.

After dropping Mum off, I head for the sanctity of home. The dogs are waiting, as is a nice glass of wine.

And the blinking of the message light on my landline.

Scott has left no less than *three* blistering voicemails. How *dare* I *demand* that he drop everything to come up here? I must really think he has absolutely no life of his own that requires his time and attention. It just goes to show how ridiculous and self-centered I am. And on and on.

Each voicemail maxes out at two minutes. By the third, I simply hit *Delete.* This is not the first time he has berated me in painfully personal terms. I'm sure it won't be the last.

CHAPTER 3

Then: December 1951

The upending of Christmas 1951 astonished me. How would Papa's rather abrupt, unplanned, and quite consequential decision impact the rest of the family?

Tuesday afternoon –
Dec 18

Dearest Daddy,

I had so hoped your letter would arrive in today's mail but because it didn't, I can't wait any longer to get word to you-

Bud called last night and we had a fine visit which did me lots of good – He wants to see you during his vacation so I do hope it will be possible –

You are on our minds so much I can hardly complete all I should before Christmas –

Naturally we are all wondering why you didn't proceed to Lexington as you planned – of course you are closer home which is a factor but naturally we are anxious to know if the treatment is the same and your care etc. as it is written up in the pamphlet about Lexington –

Could you send me a similar one about Fort Worth.

Your sweater was in the car – I will wait to send it to you because I want to send whatever else you may need or want – could you use a radio – may I send more pajamas – Is there a library there and can you get the Post?

Don't worry about a thing here we'll get along fine – Just write as often as possible and let us know anything we can take care of or send you to help out there –

Did you tell me over the phone that you felt optimistic – my mind was so thick - I can't recall - whatever we send may not arrive on Christmas because we are waiting to know what you want or need –

Loads and loads of love from all of us – R

Nana's response confirmed what I first suspected when I read the second line of Papa's very first letter to her. He'd originally planned to travel to the narcotic farm in Lexington simply to check it out. He had a return flight booked. He hadn't packed enough clothing for an extended stay *anywhere*. His sweater was still in the car. I also gleaned Dad was called upon to support his mother during this difficult time, and he rose to the occasion.

Nana's next letter seemed anxious. Or was I projecting? Having struggled with feelings of abandonment my entire life, I've had to learn not to expect immediate responses from people, no matter how much I'd prefer them. In this age of texting, I cannot fathom having to rely on the mail service of the 1950s.

Thursday evening-
Dec 20

Dearest Daddy –

Have just written Ralph Jr. – he is anticipating seeing you at Christmas time and I wanted a Christmas letter to reach him –

I keep looking and waiting for the letter you said you sent Saturday or at least wrote Saturday – we still have only delivery of mail once a day and the mails are so full I'll hope for it tomorrow – It bothers me very much that you took so few things with you and I have sent some briefs and pr. of pajamas and that's all waiting to hear what you are in need of –

Dr. McCoy called and said he knew we'd done the right thing and didn't want me to worry about anything –

We were downtown all day today I hope for the last time – our hearts are not in it all as nothing has too great appeal.

This television is the greatest comfort for us – as we can be here by ourselves and yet be entertained – I hope you think of us that way

I want to send you anything you need – your Christmas things we've waited until we know what you can use there – Do write twice a week – and I do hope Bud is able to spend some time with you – He called me Wed. eve and we had a wonderful visit – it did me lots of good - and I know his visit with you will if it works out –

I'm going down to mail this so you'll get it –

Hoffmans invited us for dinner Christmas and Edalens in the evening but all decided we would rather just be home quietly together –

Loads and Loads of love dear

R.

Could I order one of the newspapers for you?

When I started to read these initial letters from Nana, my first response was disbelief. Surely, she must be angry. Resentful. Frightened. How could Papa do this to her? Or maybe she *was* furious but needed to be civil on the written page. After all, my frame of reference was a mother who would blow up if Dad was fifteen minutes late for dinner.

Reading Nana's letters forced me to look at family dynamics from quite a different perspective. Even though Papa made the decision to admit himself to the narcotic farm in Fort Worth, unilaterally—or even selfishly, in my opinion—this event did not seem to have a catastrophic effect on the rest of the family. Try as I might, I could find no traces of anger or resentment from either Nana or Dad.

Were they repressing it, as I had learned to repress my own anger? Or could it be that they simply took it in stride because that's how they were wired? I found myself debating this question repeatedly as I imagined Christmas of 1951.

Meanwhile, Papa meticulously documented his schedule, physical condition, and surroundings.

Dec 15, 17, 24, 27th

Dec. 15 Fort Worth and Dallas are shivering. Three days ago, men were sweating in their shirt sleeves. Today they are thawing out their car radiators. No snow however, just a brisk breeze of 20°. I am getting along very well except for asthma. Last night 16th was better than the nite before. I awakened every 2 hours on the dot, even without a watch and got adrenalin. They have started A.C.T.H., the same dose that I was on. Isn't that fine. Only a light wheeze this morning. Some nurses from somewhere else are putting up Xmas decorations in our large day room. I would be helping them except that I was told to wait for the Dr.

It is nine o'clock and past. I have cleaned my room, made my bed, done my community work, breakfast, shave, clean clothes, requested air travel tickets be sent to you and am writing this letter. Later a physiotherapy or rather, a social service worker is visiting to see what we want to work at. I may do some leather work now until the library is open to me. Later I may try to wrangle a teaching job, to teach nurses obs. like I used to if they want or need a class. This would give me a good review beside filling time and feeling that I am doing something worthwhile.

In December 1951, two locked drug rehab facilities operated in accordance with the Federal Narcotic Farms Act of 1929. This federal statute was officially entitled "An Act to establish two United States narcotic farms for the confinement and treatment of persons addicted to the use of habit-forming narcotic drugs who have been convicted of offenses against the United States, and for other purposes." In 1935, the first facility opened in Lexington, Kentucky. The second opened 1938 in Fort Worth.

Upon his arrival, Papa would have been issued an identification card and number, strip-searched, and given several forms to fill out, wherein he would have described the extent of his drug usage. He would then have been placed on a detoxification ward, where he would remain for thirty days.

Never having done this type of therapy I find it very interesting to watch. There are interesting people from all over the country. Interesting problems. The personnel are very nice. All are civil service except the Drs. The employee (aid) who did my work stint with me this morning was a resident of San Diego 31 years. His mother had been a janitor at Loma Portal school. Knew Mrs. McKim. Can you beat that? He wondered if she still lived over the drug store.

A mere day or two after his arrival, Papa had embraced his situation with an open heart and mind. His ability to acclimate was astounding, his curiosity even more so. If he was suffering through detox, he wasn't letting on.

After describing the folder of letters to Jim, I agreed to lend it to him for a couple of weeks—but only for a couple of weeks. I was very clear on this condition. My interest in Papa's experience was reignited. Russell curiosity runs deep. After getting the folder back from Jim, I bought a book entitled *The Narcotic Farm: The Rise and Fall of America's First Prison for Drug Addicts*. From the introduction:

> The Narcotic Farm's goals were audacious: nothing less than the complete social rehabilitation of America's drug addicts and the discovery of a permanent cure for drug addiction. Today this dual mission seems hopelessly naïve. But for decades, these hopes animated the federal government's quest to solve the problem of drug addiction by confining the nation's addicts in one institution and transforming them into productive citizens.
>
> "Narco," as it was known locally, housed a coed cast of strange bedfellows: heroin-addicted jazz musicians, opiate-abusing MDs and nurses, street hustlers and prostitutes

> from New York, and Dilaudid-addicted drugstore cowboys from the rural South were all in the mix.*

The phrase "opiate-abusing MDs" caught my eye. That was my grandfather.

The book offered a comprehensive and fascinating account of the narcotic farm in Lexington. I was unable to find much information specific to the one in Fort Worth, but there was some information relevant to both facilities:

> Of the two, Lexington was the larger and more prominent. It was to remain the single most important treatment and research facility in the country well into the 1960s. From the beginning Lexington had a mixed institutional character. Federal prison and narcotic officials saw it mainly as a penitentiary where troublesome addicts could be isolated and confined; Public Health Service physicians saw it as a hospital where mentally disturbed addicts could be treated and rehabilitated. Architecturally, Lexington reflected the official ambivalence: its beds and wards were secured with massive gates and intricate locks. As one doctor remembered it, Lexington was "more like a prison than a hospital and more like a hospital than a prison."**

If it felt like a prison to Papa, he was not about to let on to the family. He wrote:

---

* Cambell, Olsen, Walden, *The Narcotic Farm: the Rise and Fall of America's First Prison for Drug Addicts, p.12 (2008)*

** Institute of Medicine (US) Committee for the Substance Abuse Coverage Study; Gerstein DR, Harwood HJ, editors. Treating Drug Problems: Volume 2: Commissioned Papers on Historical, Institutional, and Economic Contexts of Drug Treatment. Washington (DC): National Academies Press (US); 1992. A Century of American Narcotic Policy. Available from: https://www.ncbi.nlm.nih.gov/books/NBK234755/

Dr. Neu was just in making "rounds." He is a commander U.S.P.H. He was very nice, changed my orders only slightly and gave me the impression that I was doing all right. I wish I could help dress up our own X-mas tree.

All my love – Daddy

Merry X-mas (as possible) (copied as per instruction of mail censor on two sides of paper 12-17-51)

Papa's mail was read and censored before it could be sent. I located a single typewritten page, entitled "INCOMING MAIL REGULATIONS (Addict Patients)" among the letters in the folder. This sheet spelled out, in painstaking detail, how correspondence with those on the "outside" was regulated. I marveled at how quickly and easily this physician-father-husband had adapted to what could be considered massively chafing and restrictive rules.

P.S. Send District checks to Mrs. Young Box 100 Fort Worth. I have been assigned to Dr. Osberg, the Dr. who admitted me. There is a good library. Sunday night went to church service. Mostly X-mas music. Send a small radio – no pajamas.

P.S. A good letter came from Buddy, seems he wants to come to visit. I would like it very much but it is expensive and unnecessary. Love R

N.B. Asthma much better. Please write Edgar. Send me his address. No medicine since Friday nite. My hands look much better. R.

Dr. Ralph S. Russell

I wasn't sure what "no medicine since Friday night" meant. Perhaps Papa's detoxification was on the right track.

Saturday eve –
7:20
Dec 22

Dearest Daddy –

Have just returned from taking Ann to a party out on the point – all the trees lighted and houses decorated – we have a small tree but won't put it up until Sunday- Bruce has worked every day since vacation and so can help us only on Sunday –

I feel so much more relieved tonight as we received your first letter to us about 4:30 this afternoon. Each day we'd think surely tomorrow we'd hear – but not until today and it was mailed the 18th. But the mails are terribly crowded and it's taking 3 and 4 days for local letters to arrive at their destination I find.

Well to say we were so happy to hear is putting it mildly. I called Dr. McCoy who said he'd had a card from you and hopes you write him from time to time.

Ed stopped in and I let him read it and I called Hoffmans – they are so interested and have been so kind –

I hope you are receiving my letters and Buddy's – I am wondering if it's possible for him to complete his plans to be with you a little at Christmas – I hope it can be arranged. He is so enthusiastic about his school and does want to see you.

A few questions I would like answered are –

1. Don't you need some shirts of some kind – or a robe – or anything in that line-
2. Are you interested in any of the Christmas mail – Naomi wrote also Amber – Naomi wants more professional advice on her aches and pains and a letter from Mrs. Weeks wants medicine for her brother
3. May I send these compensation checks from the Water District for you to sign-

That's all I think of right now. Everything is going well here – and very smoothly – it won't be very Christmasy around but we are quiet here together hovering over that television. Bruce hasn't been out a night yet – he loves it so – glad one is available to you and you can see the Rose Bowl game perhaps – or other programs-

We were thrilled to hear and your writing was so steady and fine – Do write the two times a week – we wait from letter to letter – will be thinking of you all the time and send loads of love – Mother says so for her too – she's lost 5 lbs – we haven't written any of the family will wait till after Christmas – Ruth

Nana's relief was palpable, even to me, reading her words decades in the future.

With that, the family retreated to the comforts of home and a new television. Christmas 1951 was scrapped, as Papa, abruptly and without warning, decided to not make the return trip home. For all the decades my family spent worrying about pulling off the "perfect" Christmas, I can honestly say we never experienced one quite like the one I was now reading about. Both Nana and Dad were prepared to support Papa in his effort to rehabilitate himself, and the trappings of Christmas became completely irrelevant.

Is it a coincidence that as Dad's health continues to decline, my desperation to hang onto all that he was is ratcheting up?

CHAPTER 4

Now: February 2016

Nobody wants to be in a nursing home, and Dad is no exception. It was pitched as a rehab facility, but every time I visit, I find it hard to ignore the unconscious old people slumped in their wheelchairs throughout the hallways and common areas.

It's the last stop on the train ride to death.

While Mum complains about the staff, I do my best to elevate Dad's morale.

He was diagnosed with Parkinson's twelve years ago, when he was seventy-six. At the time, his symptoms were limited to a slight tremor, a stooped posture, and a shuffling gate. He was referred to a neurologist and started taking the medication carbidopa-levodopa.

I immediately shifted into fix-it mode. It's who I am. I bought books, did extensive research, and tried to understand the nature of the disease. These days, I wonder if it was mere curiosity or an intense need to control outcomes. Either way, it didn't matter. My parents decided that denial was the route they would take. They dutifully saw the neurologist every six months, as directed, but their overt skepticism regarding the diagnosis stymied any desire on their part to do more. Sometimes, I would go along.

Good daughters go along.

One such time, as we were driving to the appointment, I asked Dad how he was feeling that day.

"I just don't seem to have much motivation these days—" His voice trailed off.

I encouraged him to share this with the neurologist.

She put him through his paces, tapped his knees and feet with her little hammer, and observed his gait. She then asked for any additional information.

Dad glanced at Mum. She smiled graciously and answered for him. "No, I don't think so."

I gritted my teeth. "Remember, Dad, you mentioned on the way over here how you just don't seem to feel motivated lately."

Mum's smile faded as her eyes shot daggers at me. Clearly, that was confidential information.

"That's actually very common with Parkinson's patients," the neurologist responded. "Fortunately, there's an antidepressant on the market now that has been shown to be quite effective for people in your situation."

She gave Dad a "sample" twenty-eight-day supply. I was ecstatic. It was free, so the biggest impediment to my parents giving it a try had been removed.

I should have known better. Mum refused to let Dad even try them.

"He doesn't need them," she declared emphatically. "Besides, we aren't going to risk any side effects."

It didn't help that Mum disliked the neurologist. She had let me know that within the first couple of appointments. Mum doesn't like quiet, studious people, and this doctor was both quiet and studious.

Feeling more desperate, I asked around and found an amazing place with top-notch doctors and programming. One of only forty-eight facilities in the country to be named a "Parkinson's Foundation Center of Excellence," its unique approach to treatment involved all aspects of care – mental, physical, and emotional. And best of all, it was right here.

"Let's give this a try," I found myself practically begging.

Dad underwent a battery of tests there and came out the other side with all sorts of recommendations for occupational therapy, exercise, and reading material, all designed to ease the journey through the Parkinson's experience. But Mum couldn't—or wouldn't—manage the twenty-minute drive to the facility, effectively shutting Dad out from opportunities to enhance his quality of life.

Now, he's stuck in a nursing home, and Mum splits her time between visiting him and complaining to me about all of it. As per usual, I don't share her perspective. There are many great things about this place. It offers lots of therapy, good food, and plenty of stimulation: bingo, prayer services, current events updates, books, TV, and my absolute favorite, an aviary, where a dozen or so beautiful little birds flit about, filling the room with their unique songs.

Dad's goal is to improve his strength so he can return home. Papa set a similar goal for himself when he entered the program at the narcotic farm. However, unlike Papa, who documented his impressions of his surroundings in meticulous detail, Dad is much more circumspect. He perseverates on getting out and getting home. I talk with him by phone daily and visit a couple of times a week. In the evenings, I endure lengthy phone calls with Mum, where she describes in excruciating detail every little thing she dislikes about the place and the staff. I'm losing energy for the dogs and even my job. Thankfully, I'm out of trial work and into community engagement, a gig that suits my problem-solving skills. At least the people at work seem to appreciate my ideas and input.

After what seems like forever, Dad's release date approaches. The facility dispatches a team to my parents' place to check out its safety. It fails. Miserably. This is no surprise to me, but Mum is outraged. I wonder if at some point, she might choose to keep her home intact and leave Dad in the facility. In the end, she relents and hires movers to relocate their twin beds downstairs to the family room and the old sofa bed, where Dad spent his last night before going to the hospital, to the garage. A handyman installs grab bars in the adjoining bathroom. The team instructs Mum to purchase a raised toilet seat and bath chair. I once again call upon Jim to make recommendations and email Scott to see if he will share the cost with me, as Mum is predicting financial ruin over these expenses.

"Just send me the receipts," is Scott's curt reply. He and I have not spoken since he buried me in vitriolic voicemails. Just as well.

Mum hates how it all looks. I hate how Dad's world is shrinking. His swallow function was evaluated, and the result is that he is no longer allowed to eat the foods he loves, as everything will have to be of a "nectar" consistency (whatever that means). These new restrictions send Mum into a panic and me to the internet, where I discover "pureed bread." I order supplies. It calms Mum, thereby calming me.

Upon being discharged for home, Dad, through Medicare, qualifies for several weeks of home health care. Both Mum and I worry that two-to-three weeks might not be enough. Dad is still pretty weak, and Mum, at age seventy-nine, standing four feet eleven inches and weighing not quite one hundred pounds, is not an ideal caregiver, despite her strong opinions to the contrary.

Over lunch, a friend plants the idea of hospice care. The word *hospice* always suggests someone with terminal cancer and three weeks to live. However, insurance covers this care for an initial six-months, which can then be extended if the patient is still alive, but actively declining. The kinds of things that are included in hospice care are amazing and what all elderly patients and their families should be entitled to: 24/7 access to medical care; social workers; speech, physical, and occupational therapists; clergy or other counselors; and trained volunteers. These things are all fully covered through Medicare if, and only if, a doctor certifies that the patient has a terminal illness with less than six months to live.

After mulling over this newfound knowledge, I come up with a new plan; get Dad certified for hospice. I spend about half an hour talking with a wonderful nurse who works with Dad's GP. We go through the criteria for hospice care, one of which is a 15 percent decrease in weight. I figure this will be an easy one to clear, as Dad's quite unimpressed with his new restrictive diet.

But one of the things I most wish for is emotional and psychological support for my parents as they go through the last chapter of Dad's life. And who knows how long this chapter might last? That type of support is covered by insurance through hospice care, but not anywhere else. And Mum certainly will not agree to pay for it.

A week after Dad comes home, his doctor summons him to the clinic to sign a Physician's Order for Life-Sustaining Treatment, or POLST. As it turns out, the nursing home never had one on file, which may have been illegal. A POLST is a universal document, understood and accepted by all healthcare providers, from primary-care doctors to paramedics. With it, there is never confusion about what a patient wants to happen if the patient is unable to communicate his or her wishes.

On the drive to the clinic, I bring up the subject of hospice.

"*What*?!" Mum hisses at me from the back seat. "What are you talking about?"

"Mum, it's an insurance thing. It's a way to get services paid for. You know we're running out of time for the in-home help that you're getting now."

"I can't believe what I'm hearing! We just got your father back home, and you're talking about hospice?"

"I'm just going to ask a couple of questions. Would that be okay?"

"I think that would be useful," Dad weighs in. I'm surprised. And grateful.

"I don't want to talk about this anymore," Mum retorts.

With that, we finish the drive in silence. Once in the doctor's office, Dad executes his POLST, declaring that he will never go back to a hospital. Mum is nonplussed. She does not want him dying in the house. We ignore her protests. This is Dad's choice, and I will empower him to stick with it.

I then take a deep breath and launch into a hypothetical situation involving hospice care.

Dad's GP is remarkably understanding. He gets exactly where I'm going with this line of questioning. I feel a rush of adrenaline. For a moment, my parents aren't even in the room, and my plan for Dad is moving along smoothly.

"Ralph, just so you understand, certifying you for hospice in no way means that I think you only have six months to live," the doctor says. "I've had several patients in hospice for years. But your daughter is right, there are so many services that you can access through hospice that you would otherwise be ineligible for."

Both Mum and Dad shake their heads in disbelief.

"Well, this is certainly something we'll think about," Mum says brightly. "We don't need to decide today, do we?"

"Of course not. Just know that the services are available if you decide you would like to take advantage of them."

While I privately rejoice, I must acknowledge that being certified for hospice also means being certified for death. I can't blame Mum and Dad for postponing their decision for another day. I lend them my copy of *Being Mortal: Medicine and What Matters in the End* by Atul Gawande. But the more I try to plan for a peaceful final chapter, whether for Dad or for me, the more I seem to be swimming upstream.

An unexpected source of comfort is Dad's younger sister, Auntie Ann—*Precescious* in Papa's letters from the narcotic farm. During Dad's incarceration in the nursing home, and following his discharge, I keep her apprised via email of his condition. Then, in the fall, she and her husband come for a visit. This just about puts Mum over the edge. While she sets a pretty table and smiles through gritted teeth, Dad honestly loves every minute of it. His memory is mostly intact, and he regales us with stories of his youth, including the one where he and his friend visited Ginger Rogers. It's an oldie but a goodie. Mum rolls her eyes when she thinks nobody is watching.

When the evening finally comes to an end, Mum is at the front door saying the final goodbyes and I'm back in the family/bedroom helping Dad with the buttons on his pajama shirt.

"It feels like the end," he whispers.

"Not at all," I respond brightly, not sure if I believe what I'm saying.

Two weeks later, Dad's care team convinces him to enter hospice.

CHAPTER 5

Now: Christmas 2016

CLINIC NOTE: Client stated that three weeks ago she started crying daily, has trouble sleeping, difficulty concentrating, and experiences feelings of guilt. She reports overwhelming sadness and stress over the anticipated loss of her father from Parkinson's Disease. Client would also like to create stronger boundaries with her mother due to their tumultuous relationship.

◆ ◆ ◆

I'm going to be late. Of course I am. Even though I put the clinic's address into my phone's GPS, I manage to take the wrong exit and set myself up to arrive late for my first therapy appointment.

Let the self-loathing commence.

I am not the type who arrives late or who gets lost.

Or, at least, I didn't used to be. The irony is not lost on me that, today, I am the very stereotype of the tardy, unglued person who needs therapy.

I turned fifty-one a couple of months ago. The exact same age as Papa when he walked away from his medical practice and requested admission into a locked federal facility, seeking treatment for a Demerol addiction.

This must be what a midlife crisis looks like in my family. What is it with us type A overachievers?

Rather than dabble in drugs or take up *more* drinking, I decide to give therapy a try. Except that finding a therapist is a bit more complicated than picking out a nice bottle of Chardonnay or deciding which Netflix series to binge. It's not like I can just ask someone for a recommendation, like I would for a landscaper or car mechanic. Besides, nobody I know is in therapy. Everyone seems to have their lives well in order, with lots of Facebook posts to prove it.

To be fair, I post my share of happy events or thoughts of gratitude or whatever I think might generate enough likes to make me feel better about myself. I also had myself convinced that I could land the plane for Dad in a way that would be supportive and helpful.

Until the day when, much like Humpty Dumpty, I fell off the wall and couldn't seem to put myself back together again.

Or find my way to a therapy appointment.

Deep breath.

When I finally arrive, I stride purposefully into the newish building and am momentarily distracted by the view of a wooded area with a trail behind the building, courtesy of floor-to-ceiling windows. A sense of peace washes over me.

The building seems empty, save for the clinic. I open the door into the lobby and am welcomed by scents of freshness and coffee. A small water feature burbles, accompanying soft, smooth jazz. The tightness in my chest eases.

After completing the insurance paperwork, I am escorted to a room straight out of a Pottery Barn catalog: muted earth tones; soft, comfy furniture; and a long-piled area rug.

Jennifer is a lovely creature, petite, impeccably dressed and coiffed. I imagine she's in her thirties. *What does she even know about life?* I wonder. She is warm, engaging, and just a bit more animated and intense than I was expecting.

Researching therapists online was a total crapshoot. I picked Jennifer off the psychologytoday.com website primarily because she seems to know a thing or two about borderline personality disorder.

I've declared myself a newly minted expert on mothers with BPD, having recently consumed a book on the subject. I have come to realize that maybe, just maybe, I'm not the crazy one in my family. Although today, I certainly feel like I've got at least one or two screws loose.

Why am I here? I need a therapist to help me deal with my volatile, gaslighting mother.

Oh, and to help me navigate the other, not-insignificant fact that my father—my hero, my advisor, my biggest fan, and my very favorite person in the entire world—is slowly but surely exiting stage left.

Shouldn't be too much for a trained professional, right?

"I'm so sorry to be late." I sink onto Jennifer's plush loveseat. With that introduction, I promptly burst into tears. Mortifying.

Jennifer's eyes widen. She seems kind.

I try to muster a smile, hoping my tears don't render me a doppelganger for Alice Cooper.

"I sure can't seem to keep it together anymore." I may as well start things off by demonstrating that I have a good mastery of the obvious.

"Tears represent an excess of grief that has nowhere to go." Jennifer nods empathetically.

Wow. Did she go to school for that?

I don't know that I can take her seriously. For a moment, I consider how quickly I can gather my things, slip out the door, hop back into my car, and return home. I know that route, so it should be a lot easier than getting here was in the first place. There's wine in my fridge and dogs who will listen. I can manage, really, I can.

Except I'm already here. I made it this far, so I should probably stick around to see how it plays out.

"I'm not really sure what's happening to me. I've spent the last twenty years as a trial lawyer prosecuting violent crimes. I've seen the worst of the worst. You may have even read about me in the paper."

"I only moved here a couple years ago. Was it a recent case that made the news?"

She's trying to be nice, but now I don't even want to talk about the one thing I'm really good at—trial litigation. Somehow, none of it seems to matter at the moment. Right now, I'm reduced to little more than an emotional mess. My thoughts and words tumble out disjointedly. I'm so disconnected from my real self, the self that is always organized, efficient, helpful, and courageous. Or is this blubbering fool my real self? Ugh.

"My mother is giving me the silent treatment," I explain sheepishly. Fifty-one years old, and I'm getting the silent treatment from my mother. All because I had the audacity to suggest my parents loosen their purse strings and pay for extra in-home help. It was yet another desperate suggestion on my part to stop Mum's crying and complaining.

That was a whole three weeks ago. It feels like an eternity. As I sink deeper into the plush loveseat in Jennifer's space, I realize that I have no idea whether Christmas dinner with my parents is still on. Somehow, staying home alone with the dogs feels positively heavenly right now.

"I really thought that once we were able to get the hospice team in place, things would finally begin to level out," I tell Jennifer earnestly.

Who was I kidding? When you're playing a game of Whack-A-Mole, there is no *leveling out* until the time has expired. And after just a few weeks in the hospice program, Mum's grievances had ramped up again. It was all wrong; the people were terrible, the help inadequate. In an effort to get a handle on things, I spoke with the social worker in charge, only to be told that this was my parents' journey.

"*Their* journey," I emphasize between sobs. "It's as though I've been erased from the family. And nobody wants to hear about how *I'm* feeling."

I then tell Jennifer about my Humpty Dumpty moment.

A couple days after Thanksgiving, I discovered, in a box of old Christmas decorations, a little doll I'd created when I was nine or ten. Her dress was of the same material as a Christmas necktie I'd made for

Dad around the same time. He'd wear this tie faithfully every Christmas for the next forty years. I hadn't seen this doll in a while, though, and as I pulled her out of the box, a dagger went right through my heart.

I then made the mistake of sharing this with Mum and Dad a couple days later.

Mum's response was startling. She smiled—coyly, it seemed. "I think I should get a little credit for letting you have the space to do your crafts in your room and nurturing your creativity."

I was dumbfounded. "Mum," I said, "this is not about you."

She recoiled. "Well, just cut my head off, why don't you?"

Forging ahead, I volunteered that I was struggling. Struggling at work, struggling at home. Struggling.

Mum's jaw tightened.

Dad sighed. "This is all my fault."

Great. A heaping serving of guilt for all of us. Or at least two of us. I mustered the strength to not scream at them both and left. Once in the car, my tears erupted into full-blown jagged sobbing.

There's a famous quote attributed to Albert Einstein, "The definition of insanity is doing the same thing over and over again and expecting different results." It's probably applicable to me. After enduring more complaining and weeping about how hard it was for Mum to get Dad up in the morning, I decided to broach the idea of paying for supplemental in-home help. Forgetting that money issues triggered extraordinary and frightening outbursts in my mother, I somehow managed to convince myself that this time would be different. Yes, Albert, the very definition of insanity.

Sure enough, Mum's fury quickly exploded. She stomped out of the combined family room/bedroom and went to the kitchen to prepare dinner. I followed.

While we stood in the kitchen, she raged at me, as if my suggestion was a personal insult. "Look at me! Look at this house! You want to say that this house is a mess? That I'm a mess? That your father is a mess? How dare you?"

Her face was flushed; her fists clenched. I had a fleeting thought that she might actually hit me. After all, she'd tried it before. This time, Dad wouldn't be there to stop her.

I started to respond quietly and carefully. "No, Mum, this is only to give you some respite. This is really hard work for you."

"You're not going to tell us how to spend our money!" she shrieked as she burst into tears—typical for her outbursts.

The kitchen was rapidly closing in on me. I had to leave. Head and heart pounding, I felt as though I might pass out right there. I went back to where Dad was.

"Sorry, Dad, but I have to go." I don't recall his response. I probably didn't wait for one.

And with that, the last block holding the Jenga tower of my inner strength was pulled out, and the whole thing came tumbling down.

Tears bottled up for years now spilled every morning as I got out of the shower.

They spilled as I walked to the bus stop.

They spilled as I sat in my office.

They were sending me a signal, letting me know that I couldn't keep faking my way through my life. I also came face-to-face with the fact that I would not be able to endure Mum without Dad. I needed a plan for myself.

While Papa, at age fifty-one, spent four months at a narcotic farm, leaving his family to fend for themselves, a similar option is not available for me. It's not like I can take an extended vacation from my life and expect anyone else to pick up the slack. There *is* no one else. The dogs have not mastered the art of feeding themselves or letting themselves out. I am engulfed in a sense of abandonment.

And now I'm trying to convey all these jumbled up feelings—grief, fear, anger, abandonment—to a complete stranger, with whom I feel little, if any, rapport.

Is this really how it's supposed to go?

As I conclude my rather incoherent presentation of how I landed, blubbering in Jennifer's office, I glance out the window. I grew up in the woods, a haven when things inside the house became too much for my child self to bear. Now, half a century later, for a moment, I feel a similar reprieve. There's no judgement here, at least as far as I can tell.

"In your email, you mentioned that you thought your mom was borderline personality disordered," Jennifer says. "What makes you think that?"

As a seasoned litigator, I'm prepared to make my case. I pull out the book that I recently consumed—home alone on a Friday night. Tabbed in about twenty places, it contains information that mirrors my own experiences in a way I find oddly comforting. There's a reason behind Mum's behavior, and it's not that I'm imagining it all.

The gaslighting was a primary indicator. And the isolating behavior.

My words spill out. "My earliest memories of my mother involve her throwing huge, volatile tantrums over things Dad said or did. There would always be the sound of her yelling and then his muted response. Mum has a permanent list of all the ways Dad has disappointed her, which she likes to revisit periodically, lest we go off thinking he's a great guy. Over the years, he's developed a habit of not always telling her the truth about things for fear of these outbursts."

"Now, she gets angry at Dad if he doesn't stand up straight or speak clearly or if he starts coughing in the middle of a meal. She has conditioned herself to always feel betrayed by him, and now she views his current shortcomings as just another example of intentional failures on his part."

"What's been most difficult for me is how I feel like I'm losing my mind when she frames an interaction or situation in a way that's not at all how I saw or experienced it. She has no friends, and even though my dad is the only one close to her, she treats him terribly."

"What about your dad?"

What about my dad?

These days, I struggle to remember Dad as a vivacious person. I know that he has always been silly. He has always been kind. A college theatre professor when I was a child, Dad was denied tenure, and as far as Mum was concerned, the family never recovered. He subsequently held different jobs over the years, the last one as a trainer for a big bank. He traveled for business a great deal, and as luck would have it, one of his trips to Minneapolis coincided with my twenty-fifth birthday when I was going to law school. He took me out to dinner and bought me a small cake with *2* and *5* numeral candles. He was a man of small, thoughtful gestures. Most importantly, he was my number-one fan at each and every significant juncture in my life.

"His mind is still pretty much intact, which is almost the worst-case scenario because he is aware of all his limitations. He still has a sense of humor, which breaks my heart."

More tears. Sitting in Jennifer's neutral-toned office with immense windows and the smell of new construction, I feel as if I will never regain my composure.

"I really can't take this anymore," I sniffle, reaching for my twelfth Kleenex. "I've never been a crier. My mother is the crier. She cries all the time."

Jennifer nods. "You've reached the point where all the grief you've been storing up inside yourself has nowhere to go. It's coming out through your tears."

She then asks the requisite questions about whether I feel like harming myself and whether I have access to guns. For some reason, I laugh. Nope, I'm not ready to check out quite yet. We schedule another appointment for the week after Christmas.

Papa took four months to rehabilitate himself. I suppose it was somewhat unrealistic of me to think I could get everything figured out in one session.

PART TWO

"Act the part and you will become the part."

William James

CHAPTER 6

Then: 1900

Although I feel some sense of relief after unburdening myself to a total stranger, I find even greater comfort in further unpacking Dad's box of memorabilia. Previously ignored in the basement, I have now deemed it worthy of being brought upstairs. Prior peeks have revealed captivating stories about my ancestors. Now, I need to dig deeper.

My curiosity about my heritage first emerged in eighth grade. Around that time, Dad's Uncle Edgar (Papa's brother) sent us a genealogy chart. Using this chart, I meticulously typed up a name plate for each family member, complete with birth and death dates, and places. I then affixed these to a sprawling hand-drawn family tree and turned it in for a social studies assignment. In addition to being created decades before Ancestry.com, it was a lovely work of art.

In the preface to his egocentric and lengthy autobiography, my great-grandfather wrote, "I have written this true story of my life primarily as a record for my descendants and incidentally for the pleasure and information of any who may care to read it; also, as a diversion and occupation for the otherwise idle moments of my retirement from actual business. If it gives any food for thought or a better knowledge of pioneer days in the Western United States and Mexico, in addition to the diversion I have received in the writing of it, my object will have been accomplished."

Along with chronicling his own adventures, Calvin Parker Russell had himself been an avid researcher of the Russell family. In an application to the Sons of the American Revolution, he wrote that he had viewed records at the Genealogical Alcove in the Congressional Library. These records verified that the Russells descended from Private Abraham Parker, who fought at the Battle of Bunker Hill. Just like eighth-grade me, my great-grandfather had done his research!

Because Calvin Parker Russell was larger than life, it only made sense that his funeral service was described in the Lincoln, Nebraska, newspaper in January 1944. His obituary celebrated him as a great man of the American West:

> Calvin's father, Joseph A. Russell, was an Episcopal missionary to the Indians, and the frontier life and parsonage environment made a lasting influence on the boy . . . In 1887, Calvin purchased a herd of cattle and settled on a homestead in Kansas, sold the cattle and started in the lumber business in Atwood, Kas., sold the lumber business and opened a bank in Voltaire, Kas. In 1889, a new enterprise beckoned and Mr. Russell took his family to Mexico, where for ten years, he engaged in coffee and cattle ranching.
>
> In 1903, they came to Lincoln, where . . . in 1905, Mr. Russell became connected with the Lincoln Telephone and Telegraph company. In 1912 he was made auditor, and in 1918 was elected secretary-treasurer in which office he continued until his retirement on December 1, 1937, at 80 years of age.

Despite the wild adventures this obituary promised, Great Grandfather Calvin's actual autobiography makes for dense reading. Clearly, he had not the benefit of Strunk and White, as it assails the reader with excessive details. Or perhaps, I'm just that sort of reader who is easily overwhelmed by such minutia. In the interest of time,

I skip the sprawling descriptions of weather and countryside and try to focus on the named players. By doing so, I learn that one of his brothers, Howard Hyde Russell, was a lawyer-turned-preacher who played a major role in American politics in the late nineteenth century. He makes a brief appearance on page 194: "Howard Hyde Russell was the founder and at that time National Superintendent of the Anti-Saloon League and was fighting hard for a sober nation, and the family always felt that his efforts and those of his associates were largely responsible for the writing of the Eighteenth Amendment into the Constitution of the United States."

I immediately Google Howard Hyde Russell and quickly fill a file folder with printed information on this formidable advocate for Prohibition. Quickly, it hits me; did my great-grandfather's death impact Papa in a way that might have contributed to his eventual dependance on narcotics?

My impatience grows exponentially as I continue paging through the autobiography. It would have been so much easier to just put Papa's name in a search engine.

Finally! Papa is mentioned on page 294, almost as an afterthought:

"[I]n January 1903, a telegram from Hunter was mailed to them saying, 'Come to Tampico at once to take position in bank as accountant, and in charge of weekly reports to headquarters.' Their joy was unbounded. They loaded their pack animals and two large mules hired of Mr. Potter with furniture, bedding, sewing machine and other household goods they would need and, undaunted, started on horseback for the 150-mile ride along the coast with Ralph, their two-year-old son, straddled on a pillow on the saddle in front of his father."

The only other reference to Papa is on page 298, seemingly as the impetus for the family to leave Mexico and return to the US for good:

In April Ralph contracted a very serious case of dysentery. A Doctor Lipencott, the only American doctor in Tampico, and strongly addicted to the use of liquor, was called and advised them that to save his life, he must leave Tampico and be taken to the United States at once. In the night Calvin called to Rissa and said, "How soon can you be ready to take Ralph to the States."

She said, "Can we go? I will get us ready tomorrow."

She did, and the following day at 10:00 a.m. they were on the train. As Ralph waived goodbye from the car window, his father, on the platform, felt that he would never see the boy again. Today, thirty-seven years later, the boy Ralph is a successful, practicing physician and surgeon in the city of San Diego, California, with a wife and three lovely children of his own.

"The boy Ralph . . ." What a detached way to refer to one's own son. In December 1941, my great-grandfather gifted a copy of his massive memoir to my grandfather, along with a note of explanation:

I write to let you know that we mailed you under a separate cover a day or two ago a book for Christmas. On the fly leaf it says to Ralph Swisher Russell, but it is also for Ruth, Ralph Jr., Calvin Bruce and Ann and I hope you will get as much pleasure in reading it and looking at the illustrations as I had in writing it for you and giving over in memory those past active times.

Many incidents and experiences that would have been interesting have of necessity been left out as the memories of over 80 years of an active life could not be contained in a paltry three hundred pages. Nothing has been said of our many vacation experiences, our detours into the ditch and consequent hospital experiences and our lovely visits to you in California.

I can't help but wonder about Papa's reaction when he received the sprawling memoir that contained only two references to him.

Including his countless letters, my great-grandfather likely produced close to five hundred pages about his myriad experiences and adventures. These memoirs ranged from the family's excitement on the frontier and in Mexico, to mundane depictions of everyday life. In 1932, he wrote a four-page *Appreciation* about the flower garden that my great-grandmother created at their home in Lincoln, Nebraska. Yet over the course of his remarkable life, he wrote next to nothing about his two sons and his experiences as a father. In the end, my great-grandfather was a man for whom fatherhood simply was not an accomplishment worth writing about.

As I continue digging through Dad's box, I spot the front page of the San Diego newspaper from the day I was born. I also discover a certificate from the hospital where I was born, honoring him as my father. Entitled *Diploma – Magna Cum Laude,* it recognized that "Ralph Swisher Russell, father of Deborah Lange Russell, has survived the rigors, hardships and perils of the Ancient Craft of Fatherhood and is this day certified to that select group, the Fraternity of Fathers Who Lived Through It, and may from this day forward be fully entitled to all accrued rights and privileges thereto."

Dad saved this tongue-in-cheek award all those years, along with all his scholarly and professional accomplishments. Unlike my great-grandfather Calvin, fatherhood meant a lot to my father. I have countless wonderful memories to prove it.

At some point in the not-so-distant future, those memories will be all I have left.

CHAPTER 7

Then: January 1952

On the first day of the new year, Papa wrote:

Dearest and All:

I intended to write this after seeing Buddy but he evidently did not make it. If you could, I would like him to not come. It is a long ways, he can only see me for 1 hour on two different days. I am practically in quarantine for the first 30 days. It is sort of an observation period to see what is best for our planned occupation for the next few months. I am optimistic. I am well. I have had more recreation per day than most any time in my life. I did not realize double 6 dominos could be such a difficult game, much cribbage, ping-pong, shuffleboard and T.V. orchestra, books – just finished Caine Mutiny – enjoyed it. I will be an expert in the above games by the time I graduate.

◆ ◆ ◆

Two weeks into his stay, Papa seemed to be in fine form, maybe even thriving.

According to the book, *The Narcotic Farm*, "Patients were kept busy with vocational therapy, group or individual psychotherapy, religious services and indoor and outdoor recreation. . . . Recreation was also promoted as healthy and morally therapeutic for the addicts there, all of whom were encouraged to live by social norms embraced by mainstream society."*

Papa also wrote:

My doctor (Osberg) is away for a few days leave so I do not have any news on my occupation while here. There are 6 or 700 patients here and these are bed patient facilities and out patient department. So my guess now is that is where I will land.

I have been in a different room for 3 days. It is a double room. My roommate by mutual choice is a doctor's son from Alabama. A fine fellow in his 30s. He is under the Veterans Administration Program, has had three severe operations elsewhere and needed much pain killers for that and now, like me, he is getting well from it. Neither of us need any sedative now.

Papa, having just crossed fifty-one, found himself housed with someone two decades his junior. They were both going through detox, which, I've heard, brings out the worst in a person. Nevertheless, Papa determined his roommate to be a "fine fellow" who was making progress, just like him.

Bed is not as comfy as home, but it is a clean healthy bed. Food is wholesome and adequate. I'll take your cooking every time. Do you realize what a fine table you set?

Now- I don't want any of this isolation business. It will be especially hard to be "as usual" but there is nothing to be ashamed of in this case. No crime has

---

* *The Narcotic Farm, supra, a*t 14

been committed. My explanation as I gave it to Bruce is honest and adequate. I took certain medicines to relieve my asthma and now I have to get well from the medicines and this is the best way to do it.

Love Daddy

Papa's closing paragraph revealed an understanding of the effect his sudden absence would have on the family. Nana previously wrote that she had begged off some invitations around Christmas, preferring to just stay home. Papa was encouraging her to go on "as usual," despite recognizing the challenge this would present.

As I read, I keep asking myself: what would it mean to be "usual" when your husband or father has checked himself into rehab and you belong to a certain segment of 1951 society? I already knew from Dad that the family lived comfortably in a well-to-do part of San Diego. I wonder about gossip. I wonder about judgment. Then I pause.

Am I trying to be "as usual?"

Does inhabiting a certain social status compel those of us within its confines to maintain that pretense of "as usual?"

Papa's next letter to Dad, who was twenty-three at the time, provides the guide for how to stay the course in the midst of what some might consider a calamity:

Jan 2 1952

Dear Ralph,

I have held off writing to you, (1) expecting to see you, (2) and not being able to get word to you not to come. Your letter was so fine, and I will always cherish it. Your handwriting rather indicated that you were agitated about the situation. There are several things to be made plain, and I hope you share the news with the family. This is no calamity, although it is sudden. My life is not endangered, my health is good and is improving. My medical practice is bound to suffer some, but it will pick up again. Financially we will be hard up. I will not be an expense thank goodness and there will probably be enough assets to borrow money to see the family through. Your mother had a good advisor in Mr. Hoffman. Your plans are to go ahead as is and Mother will be able to send you the usual.

Papa seems so stoic. My initial impression of him as an addicted deadbeat dad may have been slightly off the mark.

See if you can get Uncle Edgar to start Bill Ralph making payments on a boat I sold him. And Uncle Edgar can see if Metropolitan Water District has paid for the medicine in the Field office dispensary. They are called "First aid Medicines."

A striking difference between Dad and Papa's relationship and my relationship with Dad and Mum is the openness around the issue of family finances. When I was twenty-three, I had absolutely no idea about my parents' financial situation. To hear Mum go on, we were always on the brink of poverty. But then again, there was enough money to buy that timeshare in Longboat Key, Florida. It was always contradictory and confusing. As soon as I left home, I ignored it all.

If you wish, you can send to Medical Officer in Charge at this address and/or at Lexington Ky and ask for pamphlets of information. The one I had at home was for Lexington. I thought that I might get more relief from the asthmatic background here at Ft. Worth. It turns out to be less expensive as it is only half as far to Lex. That is another reason for you to save your money and not spend it on transportation which I tried to save.

You could only have an hour with me and $150.00 or more is too much to spend when after all I'm all right.

I'm optimistic and quite well. I'm entirely off the medicine that had "got my goat." Set your mind at ease. I believe I can take the rest of the program in my stride. Remember that I can <u>get</u> any number of letters, although I can only send out 2 a week. One has already gone to San Diego this week. These letters coming in will help my morale – which is not so bad anyway.

As ever – your loving father – Daddy

U. S. PUBLIC HEALTH SERVICE HOSPITAL
Fort Worth, Texas

This is a government hospital operated by the U. S. Public Health Service which treats people who are addicted to the use of drugs and others suffering from nervous and mental illnesses.

The hospital is south of Fort Worth and hasseveral modern fireproof, brick buildings with the newest equipment for giving medical and psychiatric care.

<u>Treatment Program</u>: On arrival, each patient is assigned to a doctor who is responsible for his care and treatment here. Shortly after admission the patient is given a physical checkup, has a talk with his doctor and begins his medical treatment for discontinuing the use of drugs. When the patient is physically well he begins to take part in a hospital program which will help him in his cure. The hospital treatment plan includes regular hours for rest, meals, work and recreation. Work assignments of individual patients are based on their past work experiences and interests. The hospital has a library, gymnasium, canteen and an active recreational program. We also have a farm which adds to the many interesting activities in which our patients may take part. There are three Chaplains with weekly Catholic, Protestant and Jewish religious services.

<u>How You May Help</u>: Friends and relatives may do a lot to help our work here. You can help us to understand the patient at the time you visit and talk with the Social Worker or doctor or when you write to us. We may ask you to talk with a Social Worker from an agency near by who will send to us, in confidence, any information you wish to share with us about our patient. The home to which our patient will return, his plans for the future, including work, have a lot to do, we feel, with how well he will be able to get along after he leaves the hospital. It would help us to know, if you will write the Social Worker, about any plans you may have for our patient.

<u>Letters and Visits</u>: According to hospital rules patients may write two letters a week to persons with whom they have told us they wish to keep in touch. However, anyone who wishes may write to them as often as they wish. It will help us to deliver these letters to patients as rapidly as possible if you will give their full name at the beginning of the letter and address the envelope to the patient at Post Office Box 100, Fort Worth 1, Texas, also showing your own address on the envelope.

(Over)

Some kinds of things cannot be supplied to patients. If you wish to send him a package won't you let us know so that we can tell you whether this will be suitable?

Patients may have two visitors every 30 days, each for an hour at a time. The usual visiting hours are between 1:30 and 4:30 p.m. on Sunday, Monday, Wednesday and Friday Afternoons. Extra visiting hours may be given to patients whose visitors come from a long distance from the hospital and who can remain in Fort Worth for only a few days.

Money for Patients: Patients can spend as much as $12.00 a month for such items as cigarettes, candy and soft drinks which may be bought in the hospital canteen. Money for this is deposited at the hospital and may be sent for a patient's use by money order addressed to the Agent-Cashier, Post Office Box 100, Fort Worth 1, Texas.

We hope you will feel free to call on us whenever we may be of help either at the time of your visit or through letters.

THE SOCIAL SERVICE DEPARTMENT

By my calculation, Papa had been at the narcotic farm not quite three weeks at this point and declared himself "entirely off the medicine that had 'got [his] goat.'" I wonder if Papa knew exactly how long he would need to be there. Was his self-prognosis overly optimistic?

In 1953, M.J. Pescor, chief of medical programs in the regional office of the U.S.P.H.S. in Dallas, described the necessary steps for treatment in an article entitled "The Problem of Narcotic Drug Addiction":

> Addicts who become physically dependent on drugs cannot be treated at home or in a general hospital. They must be in a special hospital or institution which has custodial precautions to provide a drug-free environment such as certain private sanitoria, some State hospitals, and the two Federal hospitals located at Lexington, Kentucky and Fort Worth, Texas.
>
> The first step in treatment at such an institution is withdrawal of the drug which usually takes about ten

> days. . . . The next step in treatment is the removal of psychological dependence on the drug. This is much more difficult and involves a number of approaches such as the correction of physical defects, psychotherapy, recreational therapy, occupational therapy, vocational training, education, religious instruction, and the like. An important factor is time, time enough in a drug free environment to become accustomed to living without drugs. The optimum period appears to be about four to six months. This may be because the body of a physically dependent person does not return to complete physiological normal for approximately six months after withdrawal.*

Several weeks into his treatment, Papa had already gritted his way through the unpleasantness of detoxification and was able to convey optimism to his eldest son.

Although I'm still not convinced he wasn't just posturing to make Dad feel better, I must give him credit for expressing himself in such straightforward terms.

It reminds me of Dad in those rare moments when we could be forthright without Mum flying off the handle.

Dad wrote back immediately:

January 3, 1952

Dearest Dad:

I just received the letter which you sent Mother. She sent it along with her letter to me. The reason you haven't heard from me recently is due to the fact that I was planning to fly down and see you. I had my plane reservations and everything but after discussing the

* M.J.Pescor, The Problem of Narcotic Drug Addiction, 43 J.Crim.L.Criminology and Police Sci. 471 (1952-1953)

matter with my advisors, I decided to postpone the trip until between semesters. With the arrival of yours and Mother's letter this afternoon I guess I will postpone it indefinitely. However, if things get critical and if I can help you any, even if it means just being with you, I will be down there on the next plane. Otherwise I will try to do the next best thing and write to you as often as I can.

Shame creeps over me as I read Dad's words. I think back to when I was twenty-three; I really couldn't be bothered by anything to do with my own family. I was living it up in Washington DC and completely focused on my own life.

I am sending along the MWD checks which Mother sent me thinking that I would be seeing you. Now then, let me tell you a little bit about my vacation. First of all, I worked for a week at S.S. Pierce Co. as a drivers helper. They are a very fine grocery outfit like Hamilton's in SD, specializing in imported and rare delicacies. It was quite an experience for me. The work was a little hard on me at first because I was a little soft but I soon got back in shape. My job consisted of loading a truck with cases of goods and then driving to some part of Boston where they were distributed. I had a different section each day so I got to see a little more of Boston that way. I finished working on the day before Xmas.

Just like Dad, I've held a job since I was fifteen years old. In fact, Dad was the one who helped me get my first job as afterhours cleaning crew in a dentist's office. My heart swells reading his description of what might otherwise be considered mundane work.

I also called Oscar Hammerstein II to thank him for my scholarship. He said that he had heard good reports on my work and he wants to see me in New York if I can get down between semesters. I am to write him and let him know. What do you think of that? I was very thrilled but I am not allowing myself to get too excited until something actually happens. I returned to Boston in time for New Year's Eve which I spent at a little party given by some friends of mine from school.

In reviewing this vacation for you I am realizing how very lucky and fortunate I am and how much I have to be thankful for. However all this seems very minor compared to the gratitude I feel each time I think of how fortunate I am to have the Dad that I have. For anyone who is able to endure the hardships, sufferings and heartaches that you have and still remain strong and optimistic is truly a great man. My heart goes out to you. Keep up the good work. We have licked tuffer problems than this. I must close for now but I will try to write again real soon.

With all my love, Ralph Jr.

Tears escape again as I read and reread the closing paragraph of this letter. I think about Dad, who, as a very young man, possessed an extraordinary ability to express such open love and support for his own beleaguered father. If Dad felt let down by Papa, he did not show it. Instead, he expressed gratitude for his own good fortune. Gratitude is all the rage these days, and Dad was ahead of his time.

This is the Dad I know, the Dad I grew up with. Despite all he has weathered, particularly over the past few years, his cheerful, optimistic disposition has never wavered. I'm also realizing that I know next to nothing about Dad as a young man, beyond a few cursory data points. He played sax in a jazz band and started his professional life as an actor and director. Reading a newspaper clipping from early 1952 that is also housed in this box of memorabilia helps me flesh things out a bit.

Dad started out as a pre-med student at Menlo Junior College, but early in his college career he was bitten by the theatre bug. He then transferred to Los Angeles City College, where he received an Associate in Arts degree. He worked as a radio announcer and started acting with small theatre groups. He won the first-ever Rogers and Hammerstein Scholarship from Boston University and transferred there, moving far from home for the first time in his life. He was just finishing up his first semester at Boston when he got the news that Papa was checking into rehab in Fort Worth.

Digging deeper in Dad's box, I pull out his high school diploma from 1945. Dad had taken six years to get a two-year degree. Papa was struggling with a "too frequent use" of Demerol, barbiturates, and morphine sulfate for five years, according to his letter of inquiry to Dr. Isbell at the narcotic farm.

I can't help but wonder if these two facts were linked in any way.

CHAPTER 8

Then: 1930

"I'm optimistic and quite well," Papa wrote to Dad. "I'm entirely off the medicine that had got my goat. Set your mind at ease. I believe I can take the rest of the program in my stride."

This passage from Papa's first letter to Dad strikes me as exactly how a parent should comfort his child. And while Dad practiced this kind of comfort with me, Mum thrust me into the role of comforter every time she felt the slightest bit of anxiety. It's a role I've struggled with my entire life.

I was born in San Diego where Dad's family was established and where he had met Mum when they were both working the reservations desk for United Airlines. I was three when we moved to Wisconsin to be close to Mum's family. As far back as I can remember, Mum's loathing for Dad's family was on full display. It didn't matter that her relationship with her own mother, "Gamma," could charitably be described as turbulent. With the benefit of hindsight, I can now recognize that Mum pretty much loathed everyone, including Dad.

As a child, however, it was simply bewildering.

One morning during the summer following second grade, Mum announced at the breakfast table that she and Dad were getting a divorce. I was in the middle of a week of Girl Scout day camp. Head pounding, I announced I was not going to camp and retreated to my room, where I spent the day obsessing over where I was going to live. To this day, I don't remember how Dad responded to this announcement. Did he respond at all?

The divorce never happened.

Another time, when I was in the fourth grade, after Mum verbally berated Dad during one of her epic meltdowns, I found myself sincerely wishing the divorce would happen. The sooner the better. I asked Dad why he didn't leave her.

"Because I love her," he said.

I was stunned. From my perspective, Mum was tolerable at best and entirely unlovable at worst. She was a housemate of sorts who was better off left alone. I avoided her by spending lots of time with books, crafts, nature, and my imagination. Every so often, when Mum played the piano or strolled around the woods on our acre of property, I'd catch a glimpse of an artistic, imaginative woman. Much of her time, though, was spent walking around the house with a hand-held mirror to aid her in rearranging the furniture, knickknacks, and wall hangings. Apparently, it gave her a different perspective. If only she could have procured such a mirror for life in general.

Dad's love for Mum, like his love for us kids, was never in doubt. He expressed it in a steady, quiet way, serving as the perpetual haven from life's trials. He also *did* things with us, like taking us swimming and roughhousing with us on the floor, much to Mum's dismay. While I have specific memories of these activities, I have none like that with respect to my mother.

As young kids, Scott and I accompanied Dad on his weekly trip to the local landfill. Because we lived in the country before the era of rural trash pickup, we disposed of our own trash. Dad had the procedure down pat. For us kids, these trips were the perfect opportunities to share what was on our young minds.

I think I was in first grade when I asked, "Dad, what does 'fuck' mean?" on one such trip. I had heard it at school, and the only context had been secrecy and snickering from the older kids.

"Well, when one horse gets on top of another horse—"

I still remember my confusion following that feeble attempt at an explanation. And so, our family bumped along in fits and starts. Dad changed jobs, Mum threw tantrums, and we took trips to Disney World. The very first trip was by car, and Mum's mother, Gamma, accompanied us. The two of them got into some sort of fight, and Gamma flew back home early. Looking back, they seemed to fight a lot. Ironically, Mum continually declared that Dad's family was pretentious and unlikeable. She rarely concealed her disdain for Nana and the rest of "that" family, including my cousins, except for the few occasions when we were in their company. We certainly didn't spend any time talking about them and their very rich family history.

Thus, I knew precious little about Papa, beyond the sparse information that he had been a doctor, had suffered from asthma, and had died at fifty-nine. Dad was only thirty-one at the time and hadn't yet married Mum and started our family. Because we never talked about Papa, I never comprehended what that loss meant to Dad. How much did he grieve? Did he still grieve?

After I left home and no longer felt the constant pressure of Mum's reactions, I bought Dad a small spiral-bound book entitled *Dad, Share Your Life with Me.* I can now see how self-serving that gesture was, but at the time, it felt like it was for him. It was a book of questions—365, to be precise—for each day of the year. If Mum wasn't going to let us talk about the past, this book would at least give Dad the opportunity to record the things he deemed important.

Now, as I look through Dad's box for clues about his father, I realize that I need to find that book. Had Dad ever written in it? Was there anything there that could help me learn about Papa? I ask about it when I'm visiting them. As it turns out, it's still at their house, and Dad knows exactly where it is. He sends Mum to retrieve it. I'm elated.

Once back home, I page through it eagerly. Dad put forth a good effort! His childhood and his relationship with Papa come alive on the pages. I learn that Papa would tie their big sled to the back of the car and drive around because they had no hills to sled down. I learn about how they celebrated the Fourth of July when Dad was a kid:

Each 4th was special in its own way when I was growing up in Nebr. My dad and I would each have a small firecracker and a match that we would take to bed the night before the 4th. The first one up would light the firecracker under the bed of the other. Our 4ths always started with a BANG. I don't know how my mother stood it.

I learn that Dad and Papa shared a love of fishing:

I went fishing many times with my dad when I was young. We caught mostly crappies, perch, bass, bullheads and blue gills in the local rivers and the Sutherland reservoir. My biggest catch was a 40 lb. Bonita (tuna)which I caught on a deep sea fishing outing with my dad off the coast of San Diego. I think I was 13 or 14 at the time. To be the center of attention while I reeled the fish in under my Dad's instructions was very exciting.

I learn that at some point before he turned twelve, he and Papa built a boat:

Back in Sutherland I helped my Dad build a Class C racing sailboat. We built it in the attic of the hospital. We had to take it apart in order to get it out of the attic and reassemble it outside. We sailed it on the reservoir which was a few miles south of town. When we moved to Calif. we used the boat as a trailer, stuffing it from stem to stern with anything that would fit. After we had arrived in San Diego and settled in, we decided to take the boat out on San Diego Bay. As we backed the boat down the ramp into the water, it immediately sank!! The seams had all opened up on the hot dry trip out.

Little by little, I get an idea of who Papa was, as well as his many talents:

My dad, your grandfather, was a very creative and inventive man. Although we had electric fans all over the place, Dad rigged up a system of hoses so that he could run cold water through the radiators. I don't think it helped much but he thought it did.

Through the little stories he recorded, I can picture Dad's life as a young boy living in the hospital Papa built:

The hospital had several rooms on the third floor that were rented out to single schoolteachers during the school year. The teachers would also have breakfast and supper with us around a long oblong table in the hospital dining room on the first floor. There were usually 7 to 10 people at each meal including us, teachers, and various hospital staff. There was always interesting discussion and conversation at mealtime.

Dad's answers to the book's pre-printed questions depict Papa as a loving father who spent plenty of time with his eldest son. Until he was seven years old, Dad received all the attention as an only child, since Uncle Bruce and Auntie Ann did not come along until he was seven and nine, respectively.

At some point, though, my imagination around Dad's early years runs out. The little memory book has failed to bridge a gap between the family's experience at a rural hospital in Sutherland, Nebraska, and the move to a very different life in

San Diego, California. It was when the family was in San Diego and Papa was working in Blythe, four hours away, that he ended up with a "too frequent use" of Demerol, barbiturates, and morphine sulfate. This gap is begging to be filled.

One day, while I am again rummaging through Dad's box, I discover what I initially assume is merely another typewritten essay about some adventure or musing by my great-grandfather Calvin. The document is on the same kind of paper. However, the title and first paragraph immediately reveal that it is something else entirely:

PSYCHIATRISTS CALL IT STRESS: I CALL IT DAGGER POINT

In the mind of every physician are stored away many human-interest situations. These have to do with past experiences in his practice. Some circumstances may have been steppingstones in, or may have changed the course of, his career.

I've hit a jackpot of sorts. By comparing dates mentioned within the essay, I conclude that Papa authored this piece around 1955, after completing a routine Cesarian section on a Native American woman. This experience prompted him to recall the first such operation he ever attempted:

By contrast, my mind went back to another Indian case which had occurred in the early part of my medical experience, just twenty-five years ago. I was trying to take care of a budding medical practice and finance and build a hospital at the same time. A Psychiatrist would call it a stress situation . . .

There were no adequate hospital facilities within twenty miles of the town where I had chosen to practice. No Building and Loan Association would risk money on a hospital. 'There is no profit in hospitals,' they said. So, I mortgaged my inheritance and built the hospital myself. In May of nineteen thirty, the new hospital was ready for the care of patients. The middle west was in the beginning of the depression.

I already know a bit about this hospital from Dad's entries in the little book I had given him. The family had lived in the basement apartment below it. Dad was two years old when the hospital opened, and patients paid their medical bills in livestock. The family rented out the upper level to schoolteachers. Now, in Papa's "Dagger Point" essay, I learn that a "small but sure source of income was the migrant beet worker." Papa described one such worker, "Buck Chatto":

His six-foot stature was topped by black thatched hair partially hiding a jagged scar at his left temple. His somber eyes and chiseled features were reminders of his royal Navajo ancestry. His father had been a chieftain of the Navajos of Arizona. Buck had separated himself from the politics of the pure Indian by marrying Maria. Maria was a Mexican girl.

Buck finally brought Maria in to see me. Maria was a healthy girl of twenty-two. Examination revealed a deformed pelvis which resulted from an almost fatal accident when she was only seven. She had been run over by a low rock truck in Arizona. I realized at once that only by means of a Caesarian operation, could this child be born.

If I took this case, it would be my first Cesarean operation, a fact which only added more to my concern. 'Should I attempt it myself or should I send the case to the State Hospital in Omaha?' For me to operate or not operate, that was the question.

My surgical chief in Omaha had advised me to go to a small-town community. 'Start in a small town,' he had said, 'You will be close to the people that you will have in your practice. You will have ideal conditions to start your own family life.'

The next two sentences were crossed out in pen. To me, it was the most revealing thing my grandfather wrote:

~~Then he added on a sour note, 'It will be a good place to bury your mistakes.' He had inadvertently given me a severe inferiority complex as far as surgery was concerned.~~

Otherwise known as "imposter syndrome." I wonder why Papa crossed this out. I also wonder if most high-achieving people suffer from it. I know I have. Papa's dilemma was very real. He could choose to send the woman elsewhere, thereby eliminating any risk to himself and his reputation. Or he could choose to perform the surgery himself for the first time in his professional life, doing so without the staff and equipment needed to ensure that it would go smoothly.

If this were not enough pressure, when the day of the surgery arrived Buck refused to allow the procedure:

The situation demanded that I use kid gloves before I could use the rubber gloves. I launched into a desperate sales talk. I used pictures in the anatomy book. I drew sketches of Maria's deformed bones. I showed him the x-ray pictures of Maria's body. I concluded by emphasizing the necessity for this immediate operation if the lives of his wife and baby were to be saved.

The fire in the somber eyes cooled. The proud head bowed for a moment. Then he spoke.

"You work hard! You help my woman! If she killed, you look out!"

This was the dagger point that I felt between my shoulder-blades as I started my first Cesarian.

The writing is mesmerizing, even from more than sixty years into the future.

My wife had never seen me operate. Of all times, this happened to be the one that I had invited her to be present. I took a last look around the room. On one side was a glass cabinet with a great variety of instruments. Were there any that I should have sterilized? In a corner was a pressure sterilizer that I had made. It was a large hot water tank with top and bottom cut out to house a large pressure cooker in the top and a gas plate in the bottom. Over the operating table was my homemade shadow proof spotlight. I had made it from a hundred-watt lamp circled by concentric bands and six rear-view truck mirrors angling the light in from the sides.

The patient lay on the table. She was a good surgical risk. The fetal heart sounds had just been checked and were found to be strong. That was just it. Under my hand was a healthy mother and unborn child. What would I have on my conscience an hour from now?

Papa, in addition to being an accomplished surgeon, was a skilled storyteller with an extraordinary amount of insight into his own psyche. Thanks to that insight, I am now peering through a window into his soul.

The exhilarating moment came for the incision. With the scalpel in my hand and a prayer in my heart, I began.

In ninety seconds, there was a small choking wail.

"It's a boy!" almost shouted the anesthetist.

"Wonderful," breathed my wife.

A peculiar thumping sound was heard out in the corridor. The Navajo had gone into a victory dance. If I had not been so busy putting in the closing sutures, I would have joined him. It was my victory too!

Insecurities have a weird way of settling deep within us. Papa wrote this essay a good twenty-five years after the event it describes and still captured, in minute detail, all the tension and pressure that existed within him on that day.

As my fingers trace the edges of the pages, I see vividly how I've been managing my own stress up until now. Or haven't. I've simply moved through it, going from crisis to crisis, some of my own making, others involving my friends and relatives. I competently manage and compartmentalize each one and then put it behind me. Professionals call it "functional freeze." But now, at the age of fifty-one, my fear of losing Dad has intensified to the point where I can't simply move through and put it behind me. Instead, I fear it is my own dagger point.

Then, out of nowhere, it dawns on me: Papa was not treating his asthma with Demerol, barbiturates, and morphine sulfate.

He was treating his dagger point.

1

PSYCHIATRISTS CALL IT STRESS : I CALL IT DAGGER POINT.

In the mind of every physician are stored away many human interest situations. These have to do with past experiences in his practice. Some circumstances may have been stepping stones in, or may have changed the course of, his career.

Several weeks ago, the receptionist introduced me to a new patient. Her name was Helen Moonglow. This was definitely a name derived from indian ancestry. Her conditions was easily diagnosed and the management of her case was routine. My nurse made the necessary arrangements at one of the metropolitan hospitals. She reserved a room and scheduled a place on the surgical calandar. She arranged for another doctor to assist at the operation and she called on the Anesthesia Service to designate a doctor to administer the anesthetic. Every step in the procedure went smoothly and the woman has recovered.

By contrast, my mind went back to another indian case which had occured in the early part of my medical experience, just twenty five years ago. I was trying to take care of a budding medical practice and finance and build a hospital at the same time. A Psychiatrist would call it a stress situation.

I had finished eight years of College and University work to get my medical degree. In addition, I had finished eighteen months of internship and a year of ~~assistantship~~ preceptorship with one of the best surgeons. ~~of the middle west~~. There were no adequate hospital facilities within twenty miles of the town ~~that~~ where I had chosen to practice. No Building and Loan Association would risk money on a hospital. "There is no profit in hospitals," they said. So, I mortgaged my inheritance and built the hospital myself.

CHAPTER 9

Now: February 2017

CLINIC NOTE: The patient has a very strained relationship with her mother, and a father in failing health. She is a strong intelligent woman who is trying to establish healthier boundaries with her mother, which has shown to be very difficult. She often feels she is not being authentic with her mother, yet when she does there is almost inevitably an argument. Therefore, she wants to keep the relationship with her parents as functional and happy as possible due to her father's illness. The whole situation causes her great frustration and sadness at times.

Processed the patient's feelings about her mother and initiated a discussion about her childhood.

◆ ◆ ◆

It's my seventh therapy session, and I feel like I'm on some sort of hamster wheel with not much hope of getting off. Jennifer is very nice and a good listener, but I have friends for that. I talk to the dogs all the time, and they are excellent sounding boards, even when they're asleep. Additionally, I've completely mastered the art of overthinking things.

The newness of the therapeutic experience has worn off, and now I just feel stuck. Isn't Jennifer supposed to help me get unstuck?

She wants to talk about Mum, but Mum is really the last person

I want to spend any energy talking about. For most of my adult life, she has found countless opportunities to remark, "I don't have a relationship with my daughter."

Just like that. Usually, it's in the context of her telling me that she had mentioned this "phenomenon" to a third party. It's incredibly disconcerting. Every time she says it, I feel sick. How did I screw up this time? I always feel like I'm chasing something elusive—being the daughter she always wanted me to be. Compounding the issue is the fact that this is precisely how I feel about her. As a child, I spent much of my time avoiding her. As an adult, I cringe when I hear other women describe their mothers as their best friends. I can barely handle being in public with mine.

My friends all think Mum is so cute. She has always played cute extraordinarily well. As she enters her eighth decade, her quest for cute clothes, jewelry, scarves, and shoes shows no sign of relenting. Despite years of chemicals wreaking havoc on her hair, she insists on a permanent and color every six weeks, leaving her with a ratted "style" that is the color of dark chocolate. Coincidently, she has a weakness for chocolate. She wears lipstick every day, whether she plans to leave the house or not. You never know who might show up.

Image has always been of paramount importance to her. When I was a child, she bought several wigs, despite having no hair condition that might instigate such a need. Having no access to Botox, she would, on most mornings, affix a piece of Scotch tape to the crease in her forehead. She was always dieting, which seemed odd because Gamma, her mother, was a few pounds shy of morbidly obese and could be counted on to make the best food from scratch.

When I entered kindergarten, she ruminated over my long, narrow face and decided that ponytails would help. Because my natural hair wasn't up to the task of providing "fullness," she sent me to bed each night with several sponge roll curlers in each ponytail. Each morning, she would then festoon them with yarn bows. Even today, my scalp hurts just thinking about it.

Growing up, I continued to rack up ways of disappointing her, many of them due to my exhibiting little interest in homemaking. After being out of college for a couple of years and not getting that diplomatic position I'd expected would be handed to me based solely on my degree and outgoing nature, I decided to go to law school. It was a kind of last resort made easier by my outstanding LSAT scores and interesting post-college experience in a small international trade law firm in Washington, DC. However, my ultimate choice of schools necessitated a relocation away from my boyfriend and our two-year relationship.

Mum expressed her dismay in her unusual way. "Gamma was hoping you'd be getting married by now."

First off, Gamma had never even hinted that she'd like to see me hitched. Second, I was not yet twenty-five. Astonished, I chose to let it go, chalking it up to a difference in generational expectations. But now I see it as yet another seed planted in the garden of Mum's disappointment. My choice to become a criminal prosecutor was yet another.

As we stood in my tiny apartment getting ready to go to a law school graduation party, she reacted quite unexpectedly to my announcement that I had accepted a position in the county attorney's office that was going to pay me through the summer while I studied for the bar.

"You don't want to come back to Milwaukee and work in a nice firm?" Mum chided.

It was another gut punch. Clearly, she had not been paying attention. Law school had been pretty much the lowest point in my journey to find a career. Starting out, I aspired to be an entertainment lawyer, but once I realized that the job entailed contract review and negotiations, I knew I didn't have the chops for it. I have extremely limited attention to detail and sometimes a zero-sum approach to negotiating. However, following a lackluster first year in which I carried a solid 'C' average, I took criminal procedure, and the sun finally shone bright through the dirty window of my existence as a law student. Coincidentally, it was also my first 'A' in law school.

Fast forward to my third year. I scored a clerkship in the county attorney's office and walked right into an episode of *Law and Order*. I was ecstatic. Dad already knew. He had listened to all the "in-between" stuff when I despaired of ever finding a job that clicked for me.

For Mum to think that I was, a) going to return to Wisconsin, and b) work in a law firm, was truly mindboggling.

The conversation escalated to the point where I was in tears.

Looking at photos of that party and my graduation the next day, there is no trace of tears, no trace of the pain generated by that conversation.

Nor do those photos reveal my reaction to Mum's comment after she perused the graduation program. "Looks like half the class graduated *cum laude*."

Death by a thousand cuts.

Any mother-daughter relationship Mum could have hoped for was never going to survive under these circumstances. Instead, she set the stage for me to spend the rest of my life playing the role of dutiful daughter, destined to never quite get it right.

Jennifer listens, her eyes wide with attention until our time is up.

"I'm really glad you shared that with me today, Debbie."

Honestly, if this is the way therapy is supposed to go, I'm not sure how much more I'm going to be able to endure.

CHAPTER 10

Then: January 1952

On January 13, 1952, Papa wrote:

Dearest and All:

Here another week is almost gone. I had expected to move out of quarantine this week but the week starts with Friday and I got here Saturday. I just finished wrapping Bruce's birthday present in the censor's office and I hope it gets off today.

Yesterday I was interviewed by the chief of the educational programs. He believes the best plan for me is to assist in the clinic. Dr. Lewis is the surgeon in charge. There is a doctor patient that is leaving very soon and I will take his place. He follows through on certain cases and assists in surgery.

Whoa. This seems huge. An addict patient assisting in treating his fellow patients? But that was the mission of the narcotic farms—to help recovering addicts also recover their places in society.

I have signed up for a Spanish course Tues. and Thursday evenings. Last night I got into a red-hot bridge game. I was amazed at the sharp bridge players around here. I needed instructions. The buildings here are very comfortable. So far the temperatures have been good, in spite of the outside weather. My roommate has been transferred. I saw him yesterday. He looks better.

I am sleeping much better. Lights are out at 10:00. I generally get up once for toilet and to use the vaporizer. I do not use any more A.C.T.H. I have more strength and am on the go most of the day. I avoid heavy exertion and do not go to the gymnasium. Hot and cold shower at 6:00. Awake when the alarm rings.

Radio came and is a dandy comfort. Buddy's letter was a "lift." Can Ann write to me? If Edgar does not write soon, I will have to spend one of my precious 2 letters a week on him. Tell him so please. "Lord Jim" it's in the library here.

All my love for my little family – Daddy
Ralph S. Russell

The very next day, Papa had more to share:

Jan 14

Dearest and All:

Sunday afternoon and it is about 65 outside and humidity 95% that's what the radio said while looking outdoors in the morning. The ground looked like it had been raining but they say it's because of the humidity, so the ground has been sweating. Your air mail the 9th got to me on the 11th. I like your old stationary better. I believe I have been receiving all of your letters. You would not be writing anything unacceptable. I have also applied for the Honor Ward which I will explain to you if I make it.

I had another conference with Dr. Osberg. He is not

going to be able to give me as much time as I had hoped for. I am a very complex personality and to find out what makes me tick in an asthmatic way would be like taking a complex watch apart. Maybe I should have been an Ingersoll or an alarm clock which are easier to fix.

Papa's concern over his own drug use propelled him to write directly to Dr. Isbell in September 1951. Dr. Isbell was, at the time, the director of the Addiction Research Center, located at the Lexington Narcotics Farm and had authored an article entitled "What to know about drug addiction," which was published by the US Government Printing Office in 1951.

While I cannot be certain that it was the one to which Papa referred in his letter, the article's concluding paragraph leaps off the page at me. "Since most addicts have some sort of personality disorder, it follows that the basic attack on the problem of addiction is to prevent the development of such disorders. It is the current belief that most of these result from frustrated drives for security, recognition, and affection, particularly during childhood. Granting this, attention must be focused on preparing parents and prospective parents for their roles in shaping the personalities of their children."*

I catch my breath after reading that conclusion from all the way back in 1951—that personality disorders "result from frustrated drives for security, recognition, and affection, particularly during childhood." It's all starting to make sense. While I may not be able to prove my theory beyond a reasonable doubt, I believe it highly likely that Papa did not receive security, recognition, and affection during his childhood. Great-grandfather Calvin's autobiography, in which Papa is merely "the boy Ralph," is Exhibit 1.

My heart goes out to my sensitive, intelligent, and insecure grandfather. Once he was situated in Fort Worth and completely detoxed from narcotics, Papa realized that it was going to take some

* Isbell, H. *Clinical Research 1944-1963 pp 27-41 in Martin and Isbell (1978)*

time to figure out why his asthma and stress compelled him to abuse those drugs.

Similarly, I wonder how long it will take me to figure my way out of my present quagmire.

Next Friday I will be moved to other quarters. I'll not know 'till Friday, so will not be able to tell you next week. Mail does not go out or in on Saturdays or Sundays. My present to Bruce will probably go out Tuesday. It is packed and weighed, but I don't know the routine to obtain the stamps. The chief nurse on this floor is taking a few days sick leave on account of a cold. She is very helpful in such things. I received the letter that you forwarded from Buddy. Fine.

My health is good. I do have little touches of asthma which soon subside with the vaporizer. I believe that I have run across something which is going to help. It is something that I ran across in a psychopathology book that I picked up in the doctor's office while I was waiting to see him about my asthma. It is a sort of a throat exercise.

Psychopathology—the scientific study of mental illness or disorders. Papa is looking beyond the physical causes of his asthma, just as I am considering a similar conclusion six decades later.

I realize that I am jumping around a good deal in this letter. I did not plan it out. The radio is a comfort. Sunday is the slowest day. Had a little nap after dinner. Dinner was sliced ham, mashed potato with gravy, a little celery and carrot, milk, turnips and strawberry ice cream. The Red Cross comes around about three times a week with cake or popcorn.

I do hope that you are making out all right. It's a terrible big load that I have thrown on your shoulders. Mother being there is a help, thank goodness for her. It sounds like Bruce is working very hard. Well, idleness never produced a good man. But he has a right to his senior activities.

All my love, things are smoothing out here,
Daddy

"Things are smoothing out here." After thirty days, Papa seemed to have gotten past the detoxification process and was transitioning into a new routine that was heavily scheduled and focused primarily on recreation.

In his next letter, he wrote:

Dearest and Buddy:

There is a librarian here who comes to our section once a week with a little cart. She selects books which she thinks the boys will like to read, also papers and magazines. The important ones from all over. I enjoy the Christian Science Monitor very much.

Papa's letters remind me that he is housed with men young enough to be his sons.

Since writing you last, I have gone before the classification board, which consists of the head of each department occupation, education, medical and security and the chief of the ward. They want me to work in the clinic and live close by to the clinic. The position in the clinic is not yet vacant and there is a delay in placing me in living quarters to go with the job. Consequently, I will continue here for a time. Everyone is in my corner, and it made me feel good and I am continuing in my optimistic attitude. I am comfortable here and all is for the best.

As a former criminal prosecutor for over two decades, I've developed an uneasy familiarity with criminals and victims who suffer from addiction, personality disorders, and mental illnesses. The recuring theme among all of them is the ruination of lives and relationships. But Papa does not seem to fit that mold. He is remarkably steadfast in his quest to get better. I also marvel at his acceptance of responsibility, something most addicts I've encountered struggle to do.

The more I dig into and research my grandfather's life, the more I identify an inner strength that permeates every corner of it. He's locked up *voluntarily* and is bound and determined to make the best of it. He's also parenting to the best of his ability, from a distance, and is openly and honestly describing his experience for his family.

For as dramatic an event as his decision to not come home for Christmas in December 1951 likely was, I cannot identify any subsequent drama after Papa settled in.

Here are things that you can now send me: my windbreaker jacket, my crepe-soled shoes the brown pair that Bruce cannot wear. The radio is working well.

New faces come and old ones go, which continues to make life interesting. The photographer could not stick it out. I do not know what he expected.

Papa must have been referring to another voluntary patient. Those individuals could leave at any time. They made up a small percentage of the overall population. Most of the inmate/patients were serving out a federal probationary sentence with drug treatment as a condition of that probation.

A number of young men are here and of course, have the best chance for the future than the older ones which are more established. This does not apply to me because I think that I am going to be all right. I can leave at any time, you understand that, but it would be what they call A.M.A. Against Medical Advice, which I am not going to do unless something serious happens out there that demands my present. The clinic has done without me for so long that a few more months should not make too much difference. Mother's letter was very encouraging. I read the letters over and over. My asthma is present but under control.

All my love – Daddy.

Papa understood what "against medical advice" meant, and he appeared to possess the perfect blend of optimism and pragmatism that would see him all the way through this experience. After about forty-five days at the narcotic farm, he had risen through the ranks of patients and was allowed to perform surgeries at the institution, as he wrote in a letter dated January 28, 1952:

I began my new duties yesterday by assisting Dr. Lewis with an emergency stomach operation. He then took me on ward rounds and introduced me to the surgical cases that he wants me to watch while he is away for 2 or 3 weeks. One of the Internal Medicine doctors is temporarily ill so it seems that I may come in handy. The doctor who I was to replace is still here but he will stay in lab and clinic while I will be in surgery and hospital wards. An operation is scheduled for tomorrow morning on a doctor. It will be done by a civilian consultant urologist. Dr. Lewis and I will assist. It is helping me and I am sleeping better. Also am getting a little aminophylline twice a day. I will continue to live in these same quarters where I am comfortable and the hospital wing is on the same (second floor) about 100 yards away. Surgery is 50 yards away. It is a very nice set up. I saw the X-ray set up today, it is fine too.

Dr. Lewis was trained at Philadelphia General and knows his stuff. More recent surgical stuff than mine so will get smartened up a bit.

Arrangements were underway today for me to be under minimum custody so that I can get to the hosp. ward and medical library any time I need to.

All my love – save my letters.

Daddy

Minimum custody after just six weeks. Is getting better just that easy?

CHAPTER 11

Then: January 1952

Winter in Minnesota can be brutal. Fortunately, it can also provide the ideal set of circumstances to hunker down and do family research. At this point, I'm obsessed with figuring out what happened to Dad's family during the period between Sutherland, Nebraska, and Papa going to the narcotic farm. Auntie Ann has provided a note Nana wrote as an introduction for a scrapbook bursting with photos and newspaper articles.

According to this note, upon their arrival in San Diego, Papa took over an existing practice, "one of the largest in the city." Nana further remarked, "Due to overwork, his asthma was aggravated to a serious degree." Then, in 1946, Papa obtained a position with the Metropolitan Water District, located at Parker Dam in Blythe, California. This position was approximately four hours away from San Diego, but the desert provided better air quality. Papa worked three weeks out of the month and then returned home to San Diego for a week. During that week, he would work at his own practice, which had grown to a point that he had two other partners.

In November 1951, Papa had committed to returning to this practice full-time. But by September of that year, this plan seemed untenable, as he wrote in his initial letter to Dr. Isbell. Based on his self-reported drug usage, I wonder whether it was the fear of getting caught or some other motivation that led to his decision to admit himself to a locked prison type setting.

On January 7, 1952, he wrote to my uncle Bruce:

Dear Bruce:

This letter may get to you a little ahead of your 17th birthday but if it does, that is all right too. I hope to be home long before your graduation. Even in time to see you on the basketball floor. Or at least to see one of the games with you. Now I realize that we did not have much time together in the last few years. Either you were busy or I was busy with other things. We did have one hunting trip and did play a little golf. The fishing was not too good.

Uh oh. I wonder about how Papa's absence affected Bruce as an adolescent. Dad was seven years older, and doing his own thing, presumably . . .

Now for a little council for you. If it is worth writing at all then it should be as legible as possible. Do not write so you just get by. I am so glad that you have a good job and that you are so well thought of at the store. It really is a feather in your cap. I do not want you to miss out on too much of your high school activities on that account. But I'm glad that you are not lazing around like some of the boys are doing. I have hopes that you will take up medicine. Do not be afraid that it will be too hard. I think that I know how much brain you have, and believe me, it is enough.

Going into medicine is intimidating enough, but without some fatherly guidance, it might feel unattainable.

I would like you and mother to save all my letters so that I will have a record of some of this that I am doing.

The tidy file folder is proof of the family complying with Papa's wishes. Except, nobody ever looked at them again until they arrived at my bungalow basement.

I've developed a mite of a cold. The A.S.A. and Antihistamine will probably knock it out. I have several people that I call my patients. They bring their problems to me and want my advice. One comes to me several times a day and wants to know if he should take the medicine that the doctors here have ordered for him. I get a big kick out of encouraging him. The doctors here are fine. I had a physical Exam Saturday, one of the best that I have ever had.

Well, may you have many happy returns.

Daddy
Ralph S. Russell

I am Papa's granddaughter in more ways than I ever could imagine. While I embrace those personality traits like dedication and perseverance, I'm also realizing how overachieving and striving for perfection can be incredibly debilitating. Reading this letter to Uncle Bruce, I think back to when I was seventeen. I cannot fathom what it would have been like if Dad had suddenly informed our family that he would be going to a facility for an extended stay for drug addiction.

Perhaps it's my frame of reference. Mum is nothing like Nana, whose early January letters demonstrated how she was coping with the situation:

Dr. Ralph S. Russell Jan. 9 1952

Dearest Daddy –

Your letter written New Year's Day certainly gave us a nice boost – we wondered if you had heard or seen any of the New Year activities.

It is also fine to know you are feeling well and best of all – optimistic. That surely gave us a lift – our confinement at home was because of our colds – and the adjustment we had to make once again – though not from any chagrin – not at all – understand that – but I had a very bad cold which of course was slow in getting better because of my nervous state. All is fine again – Bruce still has a cold – but he said today he was better.

It's been cold here the last two weeks – the top of the garage had quite a white coat on it when I closed the window this morning.

Did you receive the radio I sent – I sent it in care of Mrs. Manning. Have you been receiving all my letter – I am using different paper – do you believe the airmail paper too thin – I hope you received Bud's last letter – it was so fine.

Bruce and I worked outside all day Sunday – I cleaned or rather straightened the service yard and he trimmed the front hedge – we just finished when we had a nice rain.

I don't seem to have any news in particular as we have been doing routine things here at home cleaning – putting Christmas things away etc. –

Our thoughts are with you so much of the time as well as all our love.

Will be looking for your next letter –

Loads of love from each of us -
Ruth

Apparently, this was not the first time the family had to make an *adjustment* of some sort. Papa had, by his own account, engaged in a too frequent use of Demerol, barbiturates, and morphine sulfate for *five years*. What did that mean, though? What effect did his drug use have on the family, especially Nana?

Having only been in her presence a handful of times over the course of my childhood, I knew her mostly as a voice on a cassette recording. When I was growing up, we communicated via recorded cassette tapes that we dutifully mailed back and forth between Wisconsin and California. When I went to college, we exchanged letters regularly, and she always expressed pride in what I was doing.

The letters between Papa and the rest of the family reveal a family laboring to keep it all together. But unlike the family in which I grew up, this group was attempting to paddle in the same direction.

Jan. 10, 1952
Is the new radio alright?

Dearest Daddy –

This is about the first night we haven't been glued to the television – but Bruce has his "K" club here so we have all gone to our rooms upstairs – so to speak –

It's just as well as I wanted to write to you and Buddy and when I've watched for a couple of hours I'm generally ready for bed and too sleepy to write –

I had to tell you the big news – I started to work last Tuesday – as a librarian in the library at the Naval Training Center – I learned of it through Mrs. Wiggins and after an interview with the librarian I decided to take it – I am only working 20 hours or part time – that is all that was opened to me but it is an "in" and a very pleasant place to work-

There is the large main library and several branches – tomorrow I am at one of the branch libraries from 4:30 – 8:30. The hours are all jumbled together and not the best in the world for the family – but I found the more I looked around – that besides consolidated – much of the other work is under civil service and after you take the exam then there is a wait of several months before you know whether you have passed or not – once I said I'd do the work – I was in so fast – being finger-printed – picture taken etc. I can hardly believe it's true–

Mother is most willing to carry on here at home so it's going to work out very well and I am very happy to do it. I get $87.50 and full time $175.00 This part does not please me so much but then it all helps-

The check for the medicine came – $288.53 and also for the refund on the plane ticket – so that was very nice – we are managing very well and will continue to do so –

We keep track of the weather there pretty well – as when we get the graphic description all over the U.S. about the weather Fort Worth is mentioned very often.

My schedule for the rest of this week is Friday 4:30-8:30, Sat – 9-5:30

I'll send next weeks later –

Loads of love from us all -
Ruth

Nana got a job! In 1952, women, particularly doctors' wives, didn't work outside the home. The calm and reassurance I feel from Nana's words differ starkly from anything I ever experienced with my own mother. Nana was picking up the slack, and quite capably, if I do say so myself. She also had the support of *her* mother, who had come to stay and lend a hand.

On the other hand, given that Papa had been living and working away from the family in Blythe for the past three years, perhaps this was a routine that was not as foreign as I initially guessed. Nana seemed determined to convince Papa that there was nothing to worry about as far as the family in San Diego was concerned. But did her words reflect reality? Or did they mask a functional freeze that was only betrayed by headaches and colds? I doubt I'll ever know. All I have are her letters. Perhaps, once again, I am projecting my own stuffed-down suffering onto others. Maybe not every family is burdened with stuffed-down suffering.

Growing up, I had no idea that Nana had ever worked outside the home. It was a big part of the reason why Mum resented her. Now as I page through these letters, it becomes clear that this perception was incorrect. It's also likely we never spoke of it because Mum didn't want us talking about it.

In his next letter, Papa responded to the news that Nana had gotten a job.

Thursday

Dearest and All:

You could have knocked me over with a feather when I saw by your letter that you had taken a position. The pay is not too hot but as you say, it is an in. What would we do without Mother to pinch hit at home.

I saw a new doctor yesterday, my doctor being away. It was about my asthma, which cool damp weather and a slight cold had aggravated. Feel much better and had a good night last night.

The weather is nice today. It would be nice to take an outside walk, which will be possible after Friday. That is when I leave the hospital department and get an outside pass. That does not mean Fort Worth or Dallas but does mean 40 acres or more which is quite enough to walk around.

The circulation in my hands is quite better, in fact, normal. The cracked areas at my thumb and fingertips are all smooth and pink. I want to know what shows Buddy saw in N.Y. I see the New Yorker regularly.

Love to all – Daddy

The more I try to attach meaning behind his letters, the more I get the sense that Papa's asthma, coupled with his tendency to overwork himself, created his dependency on narcotics. Being away from home for three weeks out of the month, he was able to use (and ultimately abuse) those narcotics without drawing anyone's attention—namely members of his immediate family. While Nana was certainly aware of the asthma, perhaps she was not aware of the extent of Papa's "dependence" on narcotics.

Or was she?

Now that he was away and not earning any income, Nana revealed just how challenging the situation was for her and the family, but how capable she was of managing it.

Jan. 23, 1952

Dearest Daddy –

I have Ann home in bed – she called me from school Monday afternoon and I went up and got her – She's had a temp. from 100-102° - She is so sorry to be away from school – as the communities were to have their pictures taken today also tomorrow and Friday she plays the piano part with the school orchestra – for both assemblies – of course if you were here you could get her right over this – but I'm giving her fruit juices – a.s.a. and aureomycin so hope it's right –

I work today from 2-6 – Mother is going to P.E.O. You hardly said a thing about my working – one way or the other – any way it's been a life saver – mentally – I couldn't be where my surroundings are more pleasant and I am fortunate to have it – although the pay provokes me

– several have said they would like something similar – so things work out – and they will for us also –

Here I see a glimpse of what Nana might *really* be going through. That glimpse expands as I read her next paragraph:

I was awfully tired when I wrote last time and feel much better today in fact am feeling more like myself this week – it's taken all this time since Dec. 14 to get myself in hand – I'm sorry to say. Everything is going smoothly and we are getting along fine.

Bruce did a fine job on the lawn Sunday and I worked out back for 3 hrs. yesterday a.m. and things look fine. Bruce appreciated the billfolds – they arrived in good shape – you certainly did nicely.

By now you have more freedom and I'm glad the first part is over for you.

All send loads of love –
R –

Taking a month to get herself in hand? Maybe things were not as easy as they initially appeared. Reading between the lines, I now believe that Nana knew what was going on with Papa for quite some time. When she wrote, "We have gone through just about all we can," her apprehension practically leaps off the page.

Having grown up with a mother who rarely seemed to have herself *in hand*, I struggle to picture what that would look like. Yet judging by the letters before me, it seems that in the month since Papa unexpectedly left the family, Nana managed to get a job, pay the bills, take care of the children, and not have a nervous breakdown herself. Unless the month of getting herself *in hand* was her version of a nervous breakdown. Either way, her inner strength shined.

Papa experienced another dagger point in September 1951 when he was faced with the prospect of returning to the practice and life that had fueled his addiction. Then, his unilateral decision to seek treatment had created a dagger point for his family.

My mind drifts to my family's first dagger point.

I'd not yet turned ten when Dad failed to get tenure at the university where he was a speech and communications instructor. He was also the faculty director of the plays put on by the theatre lab. I like to think of this period in our family's history as the golden era. Mum excelled at mimicking the women in town who were married to executives and threw fancy cocktail parties.

A couple years after Dad was denied tenure, she went to work for the first time in my life, taking a position as a paraprofessional in the junior high school. I remember her coming home one afternoon, sobbing that the kids had called her "Dragon Lady." It may have had something to do with her hair. Or maybe it was because she was overly strict in the lunchroom. Either way, the effect on her was the same.

Mum had never wanted to work.

I remember finding out why when I was about twelve. I was sitting in her bathroom with her one day while she ratted her hair. Despite it being 1977, she still insisted on maintaining some version of the beehive style that had been popular during the previous decade. As she styled her hair, she told me that she and Dad had met while they both worked the San Diego reservation desk for United Airlines. I remember expressing shock that she would give up that job before I was born, especially after I learned about the travel benefits for employees.

"I wanted to be a housewife," she explained.

Even at the tender age of twelve, I couldn't imagine anything more unfulfilling. I already knew I didn't want to be a mother, and I wasn't even sure what a housewife was, beyond what I knew of June Cleaver.

My mind bounces between 1952, 1977, and the present. I think about Dad, who lived through all of it. I pull a newspaper clipping with the headline, *Ralph Russell Directs 'Oh Dad, Poor Dad,'* out of his box. It reads in part: "Russell picked the play because he thought it would have an impact on the audience and provide a challenge for cast and crew. He describes the play as a 'marvelously, fantastically, zany, farcical, absurd comedy.' Russell's varied background includes stock company work, acting and directing films, television, and off-Broadway."

I remember my brother and me belting out the full title of the play: *Oh Dad, Poor Dad, Mama's Hung you in the Closet and I'm Feeling So Sad.*

As I left childhood behind, this line became etched on my heart.

Ralph Russell Directs 'Oh Dad, Poor Dad'

A man with broad dramatic experience is the director of "Oh Dad, Poor Dad" upcoming production of West Bend's Musical Masquers and the theatre lab at The University of Wisconsin Washington County Campus.

Director Ralph Russell of West Bend, speech instructor and theatre lab director at UWWC, believes the play's author, Arthur Kopit, is "one of the best contemporary playwrites around." The production, with a cast of 11, is set for March 26, 27, 28, and April 2-3 at the UWWC student union theatre.

Valley," "The Gondolieres," and "The Red Mill."

Russell has been in two films: "Visual Aids in Education" and "Julius Ceasar." He appeared on Arthur Godfrey's Talent Scouts; was on the network UN Anniversary Drama with Louise Rainer, Basil Rathbone, and Eleanor Roosevelt; Omnibus; and Theatre Guild on the Air. An off-Broadway appearance was at the Bleeker Street Theatre in "The Girl on the Via Flaminia."

April 2-3 at the UWWC student union theatre.

Russell picked the play because he thought it would have an impact on the audience and provide a challenge for cast and crew. He describes the play as "a marvelously, fantastically, zany, farcical, absurd comedy."

Russell's varied background includes stock company work, acting and directing films, television, and off-Broadway.

Stock company experience has been with the Globe Shakespearean Festival in San Diego; the Brattle Theatre in Cambridge, Mass.; the Plymouth Rock Center of Music and Drama, Duxbury, Mass.; the Timberland Playhouse in Pottersville, N.Y.; and the Barter Theatre in Abingdon, Va., a professional repertory touring company.

Acting and directing duties include the plays "Life with Father," "Seven Year Itch," "Glass Menagerie," "Romeo and Juliet," "As You Like It," and "The Taming of the Shrew." He has also performed in the musicals "Annie Get Your Gun," "Good News," and "The Telephone," and was in the chorus for "Down in the

Ralph Russel

Russell's high estimate of Kopit is shared by the drama critics. Kopit has won numerous awards including the Leverett House Playwriting contest for "Oh Dad" in 1956, the Adam's House Playwriting Contest in 1959, the Vernon Rice Award in 1962, and the Outer Circle Award in 1962.

Kopit was born in 1937 in New York and graduated from Harvard in 1959. His list of plays includes "The Questioning of Nick" which he directed and adapted for television, "Gemini," "Don Juan in Texas," "On the Runway of Life You Never Know What's Coming Off Next," "Across the River and into the Jungle," and "Sing to Me Through Open Windows."

PART THREE

"If your heart is broken, make art with the pieces."

Shane Koyczan

CHAPTER 12

Now: March 2017

After two months of dutifully showing up every week to perform what felt like some sort of monologue, I've informed Jennifer that I feel well enough to space out our sessions to once a month. What I don't disclose is that I cannot remotely identify any sense of progress. Hell, I don't even know what progress would look like. After a month, Papa was humming along in his program, gaining more privileges and insight into what got him to the narcotic farm in the first place. In sharp contrast, I spin my wheels, rambling on for an hour mostly about my interesting life and terrible mother. Jennifer sits at rapt attention, and when the hour is up, I get in my car and drive home, wondering what the point of it all was.

Meanwhile, I struggle mightily with the dull ache I carry every minute of every day. Some might call it anticipatory grief. Whatever it is, it's aggravated every single time I find a new scrap of interesting family information that I want to share with Dad. Knowing that I will first need to read Mum's mood and get past her resistance makes everything that much harder and sadder.

One such tidbit was discovering that the University of Michigan was a repository of the writings of Howard Hyde Russell—my great-granduncle who had helped bring about Prohibition. His writings filled no less than *seven* boxes. I enlisted the help of my college friend Paul, who lived in Ann Arbor, to run over, check it all out, and give me a report. His mission was a resounding success. He sent me photo after photo of the boxes, and he even pulled out a document here and there to take a close-up so I could get a flavor of all that my great granduncle had left behind. It was possibly the coolest thing that had happened to me in quite some time.

When I phoned Mum and Dad to share my excitement, though, Mum snapped back at me, "Why would he do that?"

"What do you mean, why would he do that?" I was momentarily confused by such an unexpected response.

"Doesn't he have a family?"

I paused, wondering if I'd heard her correctly. What did Paul's family have to do with it? I felt the familiar heart rate increase. I had no idea how to answer that question. Yes, Paul was married with a teenage son. When I had reached out with my request, he responded enthusiastically, suggesting that he might even bring his son along. I know I'd have reacted the same way if our roles were reversed.

I stalled, battling defensive feelings, which resulted in a slight headrush. What was she getting at? Was I not supposed to have asked him for help? Was our friendship inappropriate? *What the hell?* As I bumbled my way through some sort of innocuous response, she cut me off.

"We're not going to talk about this anymore."

And so, we didn't. Instead, she pivoted to an update on Dad's incontinence. Or maybe it was the minutia of the most recent visit from hospice workers, who were inevitably not up to par. Whatever it was, it was important to *her*.

A week or so after that unsettling experience, my brother called. He and I are currently in a truce. It may be temporary, but at least he isn't lobbing grenades. He even managed to find the time to come up last fall to help facilitate the meeting with the hospice providers. I reflect on that meeting and marvel at my naivete in believing that we were going to turn the corner into smoother sailing for Dad's final chapter.

"So, I just got off the phone with Mum and she was pretty unglued about that conversation she had with you, last week was it?

It was about some ancestor, I can't remember, Howard something or other. She was crying so hard; I couldn't always tell what she was saying." Scott sounded weary. In the past, he'd always managed to avoid these types of episodes.

"What?" I was incredulous. "Unglued?"

"That's what I couldn't understand. I even asked her how talking about Howard Hyde Russell and Prohibition had anything to do with her. And that's when she blubbered that just the mention of Dad's family brought back all these awful memories of how his mother treated her and all the bad things he had done all those years ago."

"Wow!" I was so stunned that it was about all I could come up with. Reading Nana's letters, I find it hard to believe that she would have treated Mum with anything other than civility, if not kindness.

Mum was either exhibiting some type of narcissism, or she truly had some kind of PTSD that was triggered by any mention of Dad's side of the family. Regardless, I decided that I would no longer tolerate these reactions. Onward. I had lots of questions for Dad. I'd found a few new things in his box of memorabilia that I wanted to show him and talk to him about. I could not bear the idea of my mother denying me these opportunities.

During a subsequent phone call with them, I share what I have learned about my pioneer/rancher great-grandfather Calvin. I'm again taken aback by Mum's reaction. "Seems the Russell men started going downhill after that generation," she responds dryly, barely masking her contempt.

Dad, right there on the line, is silent.

I ignore the snarky comment and plow ahead, asking Dad to fill in some blanks with dates. His memory is not great. He can't remember the year he graduated from high school, but he is able to provide details about his time at Los Angeles City College, as well as how he went to Boston University on the Hammerstein scholarship. For some reason, Mum perks up at this topic. Following her moods can be like inhabiting a pinball machine.

We ultimately spend a couple hours on the phone, Dad talking, me taking copious notes.

After hanging up, I get back to work.

What starts out as yet another routine Google search, culminates in something for which I couldn't have been less prepared.

CHAPTER 13

Then: February 1952

Feb. 8 1952

Dearest Daddy –

Buddy just called from Boston – He was homesick, and I hadn't written for a week. He had not had your last letter so he was worried – He also had seen "Death of a Salesman" and he couldn't get you off his mind – so had to assure himself – so I was happy I had your last letter which was optimistic of your new responsibilities – articles about him receiving the scholarship appeared in recent N.Y. Times also Christian Science Monitor and the Union called and are writing quite an article. I took his last pictures down today for them to use – I didn't realize this is the first scholarship Rogers and Hammerstein have given and it was a Calif boy and not N.Y. who won it.

Reading Nana's words, my heart goes out to my sweet, sensitive father, who was so anxious about his father.

It's late so I'll turn in to be ready for tomorrow – all send loads of love – you can see how dear you are to us – when Bud calls because he hasn't heard any news from you for a week – Mother wrote him last week and failed to mention you – she was so excited about the publicity on the scholarship and the play upset him too –

So things are going to be better day by day for us all –

Love – R –

Mrs. R.S. Russell

My throat locks up as I fight back tears. What heaviness Dad must have felt. He was twenty-three years old, away at school, and worrying about his own father, even as he was being recognized in national newspapers for receiving a major scholarship.

Meanwhile, back home in San Diego, Nana continued to keep things humming along:

Dr. Ralph S. Russell
Feb. 10 1952
Sunday

Dearest Daddy –

Am working today from 1-8:30 at this branch. It's too nice to be inside – a beautiful warm spring day – I have most all the windows wide open.

Ann went to church – Bruce to Sunday school – Mother and I stayed home to get things done at home so I could be here promptly – Bruce washed my car and had it ready for me and was mowing the lawn this afternoon.

I worked yesterday from 9-5:30.

I guess I wrote that Bud called up – there will be an article in the paper soon – He said the reason we are hearing about it again is because it was just officially announced from the University and it's the first one Rogers and Hammerstein have given. He was pretty homesick – I had not written him last week – Mother did, but without realizing it was all full of his work and all about the paper calling etc. - and didn't mention about you in any way – He had been to see the picture Death of a Salesman and it was too much so he called to see if you were alright – we had a nice visit and went right up and wrote both of you – Bud and you – I have been working some evenings on income tax figures – and was relieved I didn't have to mail the form for you to sign.

Unlike Dad, I was rarely homesick when I first went away to college. Escaping a mother who threatened to suffocate me was my primary goal as soon as I entered high school. After I was away at college, I felt, first and foremost, an overwhelming sense of relief, as I set out to embrace a new life that was entirely my own.

Did you receive the Post – rather are you getting it regularly – I didn't order Colliers – Did you receive jacket? Did you receive pajamas a while back -

Bud also said there was an article in the Christian Science Monitor and N.Y. Times about him and that he had sent Eliz the clippings and she would send them on – I wished I'd asked him which papers because now I have access to all of them.

Are you being benefited by the aminophylline – hare you handling the surgery alright-

There aren't many boys in today – but there may be more tonight.

All send loads and loads of love – R
Mrs. R.S. Russell

Papa's next letter is more of the same—schedules, meals and so on—but then veers into startling new territory:

Feb. 11 1952

Sunday evening 7 pm

Dearest and All:

I believe that I answered all your questions of the Feb. 4 letter, so I'll just give you some news and a little business. I have just come from church service. Made rounds with Dr. Kogg and helped him as much as I could. He wants to do everything himself and works unnecessarily hard. The surgeon, Dr. Lewis will be off in about another 2 weeks.

Afternoon I went outdoors for the first time in 60 days. I could have gone out sooner only I was getting used to other freedoms and sort of saved this one. It was glorious out in the sun. I feel much better today. I've been finishing my cold with that terrific heavy nasal discharge and bronchial sputum but am pretty well cleared out right this moment. I just this minute got my ACTH shot – 10mg twice a day. Not using vaporizer so much now. Will speak with Dr. Fagen tomorrow afternoon. A Dr. Crawford (surgeon consultant) will see a couple of patients tomorrow and we may operate during the week.

I believe that I missed telling you about my new quarters. They are called 3B2, an open therapy ward where restrictions are minimal. There are about 12 of us. I am the oldest, then there is one man, 40, 6', 180 lbs who in nature is a lot like Bill Hanske. His cerebral connections were bothered by an electric shock off a hair drier. All the rest average between 17 and 24, just our boys ages. They remind me of Buddy when he was going through the stage with the boys at the house while we were in Lincoln. Just too much energy and not well directed. I see how lucky we were that things went no further than they did. These are nice boys. Some that have been placed here by parents others are forced to be here.

I stop short after this paragraph. Papa's fellow inmates reminded him of . . . Dad? And what did ". . . how lucky we were that things went no further than they did" mean?

We should make a definite effort to clear the records for Buddy because it may be very embarrassing to him to leave them as they are. We should not bother him with it till we get results through a congressman. From what I learned here he should never have plead guilty. Old Bob S was never much involved in that type of thing and did not know.

Love to all and enjoyed mother's note

"We should make a definite effort to clear the records for Buddy."

"From what I learned here, he should never have plead guilty."

Wait, *what*?

CHAPTER 14

Now: March 2017

For better or for worse, when there were gaps in the information I pulled out of Dad's box, I filled them with my own imagination. An example: once I looked at Papa's death at the age of fifty-nine through the lens of addiction, I assumed that his death was related to the use of narcotics rather than from an asthma attack. It just seemed more likely. And certainly more tragic.

This assumption is reinforced by the fact that the only obituary I can find for my grandfather is from the *Sutherland Courier* in Nebraska. Why is there no obituary in the San Diego paper, where he and the family had lived for almost twenty years? Was there some kind of shame surrounding the circumstances of his death?

When Nana died thirty-six years later, having never remarried, her obituary took up an eighth of a page in the *San Diego Union-Tribune*. It listed her numerous accomplishments and included a lovely photo of her donning pearls and a fur stole. It was the kind of obituary notable figures in the community received. Papa was mentioned only in passing, much like how he was treated in his own father's memoir.

Where was Papa's San Diego obituary?

After the two-hour phone call with Mum and Dad, I decide to simply enter Papa's full name into Google, *Ralph Swisher Russell,* the name he shared with Dad.

When the search wheel stops spinning, a headline leaps out at me: *DOPE SMUGGLING SUSPECTS INDICTED BY FEDERAL JURY.* Within the thumbnail of the article, I can see Dad's name and bio; *Ralph Swisher Russell Jr., 19 San Diego Musician.*

My heart just about stops.

The opening paragraph of the article, published in the *Nevada State Journal* in 1947, references an international drug cartel and a shootout that left several Mexican law enforcement officers dead. In order to read the entire article, I must pay for a trial subscription. I can barely control my shaky hands as I enter my credit card information. Once I can see the whole article, I'm dumbfounded.

Due to the article's layout, it's initially unclear whether the gang shootout included my dad or whether his indictment was a separate, but related issue. The paragraph in which he was named reads, "Donald Michael Foote, 19 San Diego, Ralph Swisher Russell Jr., 19 San Diego musician, and Russell B D Freeman, 21 Los Angeles musician charged with importing one pound, five ounces of bulk marijuana from Tijuana, Mex."

Ralph Swisher Russell Jr., 19 San Diego Musician, otherwise known as . . . Dad.

My mind spins, my thoughts churning around randomly. I want to laugh, yet it's ONE POUND of marijuana, which I happen to know—from professional experience only—is a lot. So then I'm horrified, yet it's totally stereotypical for musicians, which brings me back to wanting to laugh. I also immediately recognize that, whatever this was, it didn't permanently impact Dad's life—at least the part of his life that included Mum, Scott, and me.

Okay. Now, what am I going to do with this?

Logically, the first person I need to share this with is Scott. I call him, and wonder of wonders, he answers. I reveal what I've found and send him the screenshots and, later, the full article. Again, we debrief. Neither of us recalls ever hearing about this. It's so cool! So funny! So interesting! So . . .

I quickly shift to the realization that talking about this among ourselves is one thing, but bringing it up with Dad is going to be another matter altogether. Given current circumstances, I can think of no way to talk to him about it privately. Mum is rarely out of earshot and never out of the house when I'm there visiting. And because she has been shaming him for as long as I could remember for transgressions, I know little, if anything about, this would certainly provide her with extra ammo.

This is undoubtedly going to require professional assistance. Finally, I have a reason to go back to see Jennifer. Hopefully, she can help me plot a course of action. I'm trying to be sensitive to notions of shame and guilt and whether something like this should be brought up at this stage of a man's life. Especially Dad's life, which Mum has persistently disparaged for as long as I can remember.

To my dismay, Scott doesn't share my thought process about restraint.

A few days later while at work, my parents' number comes up on the work phone caller ID. Whenever I get a call from their home number, my stomach lurches, as I imagine the worst.

"Hi, Mum," I answer in the cheerful falsetto I've learned to employ when answering her calls.

Her voice is jagged. Years ago, I developed an innate ability to discern my mother's mood from just a few words. Sort of like "Name that Tune," but with far more weighty consequences.

"Do you have a couple minutes?" The cheerfulness is obviously fake.

"Sure."

She then reveals that Scott had called and spilled the beans. I feel the familiar pounding in my head.

"You should have left this in the vault!" she hisses at me. Then, in the next breath, she begs me not to be angry with Scott. Huh. So even though it was *his* action that brought this situation to a head, I am the one to be blamed. Of course.

"Well, what did Dad say about it?" I ask, my curiosity getting the better of me.

"He denied it."

Huh. I hadn't seen that coming. Or maybe I had. In our family, the truth is sometimes hard to come by. But at this stage of the game, what or whom is Dad trying to protect? Who the hell cares what happened *seventy* years ago?

For the moment, I need to salvage the conversation and get off the phone. "Mum," I begin soothingly, falsely. Per usual, I feel such rage at her. Because of how she reacts to things, Dad can't even admit that this incident ever happened.

"Here's the thing, even if it did happen, what's the big deal? It's not like Dad was a drug addict or went to prison or caused us to live in a trailer park."

I have firsthand experience with people whose lives went off the rails due to drug use and criminal behavior. I have prosecuted them for ugly, vicious crimes. The more time I put in, the more jaded I've become. When a public defender wants to give me a sob story about the defendant's crappy family life or addiction issues, I can be as cold as ice.

"I don't care about your client," I haughtily respond in those situations. "I only care about what he did." For me, there's rarely been any nuance to it. Right or wrong, it's gotten me through a couple of decades of mostly successful criminal prosecutions.

However, these cases also gave me a perspective that Mum would never see. Perhaps it's why, at this moment, I find her drama so unnecessary. Somehow, I manage to soothe her distress, at least for the moment. Another bullet dodged.

I conclude the conversation by telling her that I want my own crack at Dad, and it would probably be better if she were not in the room.

So much for my previously scheduled therapy appointment. I postpone it for a week. Now, instead of figuring out how to break the news that I know about Dad's criminal past, I will be debriefing Jennifer on what happened. Although at this point, I have no idea on what exactly I will be debriefing her.

Only time will tell.

CHAPTER 15

Now: March 2017

Papa's words haunt me, now that I know what they meant:

"We should make a definite effort to clear the records for Buddy because it may be very embarrassing to him to leave them as they are. We should not bother him with it till we get results through a congressman."

Armed with a plan, I arrive at my parents' tri-level townhome. I am nothing without my plans, and Indictment Discussion Day will be no exception.

Mum answers the door, and I can immediately tell that she's in a decent mood.

Whew.

Making a huge effort to convey my needs gently and pleasantly, I explain that I simply want a chance to talk with Dad about the indictment to see what he remembers. "It's really no big deal, and once we get through it, we can be done with it, once and for all," I say breezily. "He worries about what you think of all this, Mum, so just find something to do for a couple minutes while we talk about it, okay?"

Miracle of miracles, she is agreeable!

I'm remarkably calm as I enter the room that has become the center of Dad's universe.

His eyes light up when he sees me. "There's my Babes!" It's a nickname I share with Dad's younger sister, my Auntie Ann.

"How's it going, Dad?" I try to manage my anticipation—and my expectations.

"No complaints."

He never complains. Ever.

Okay, enough with the pleasantries. I don't have much time.

As a longtime trial lawyer, I know how to work with a reluctant witness. I'm totally prepared. I have my exhibit and questions ready. With Mum (presumably) out of earshot, I hand Dad the newspaper article from 1947. I've blown it up to a very readable eight-by-eleven-inches.

Dad looks at it but says nothing.

I point to the paragraph with his name. "That's you," I prompt.

No response. He continues to look at the article. Finally, he focuses on the word *musician* by pointing it out with his finger.

At last! We're getting somewhere!

"Did you know those guys?" I try to conceal my excitement with a neutral tone.

"We were in a band. We got hired to play for dances and other events."

So, it *was* him.

He's happy to talk about the band, but in my line of work, that's called being *nonresponsive.* I need him to stay focused on my line of questioning. "So, what happened?" I ask.

"I don't know."

"Well, obviously something happened. You were charged."

"I remember my parents got Uncle Lee involved."

Uncle Lee. Also known as J. Lee Rankin, who served as the thirty-first solicitor general of the United States from August 1956 to January 1961. He was married to Nana's sister Gertrude. They visited us once when I was twelve or thirteen—old enough to be extremely impressed.

"We're related to someone famous!" I remember boasting.

"Not really," Mum said. "It's only by marriage."

She seemed intent on devaluing our connection to a man who, along with being solicitor general, had argued before the United

States Supreme Court in *Brown v. Board of Education*, maintaining that the "separate but equal" doctrine was unconstitutional. Later in his career, he served as general counsel for the Warren Commission, the group tasked with investigating the assassination of President Kennedy.

And now, apparently, Uncle Lee had used his power and influence in an entirely different context.

"What do you mean Uncle Lee was involved?" I press Dad.

"Well, there's this thing that outgoing presidents do—" He trails off.

"Do you mean like a pardon?"

"Well, that's not the word, but it's like that."

"Okay, so you must have been convicted."

"No, I wasn't."

"Did you go to court?"

"No, I never went to court."

Thus begins a series of responses I have heard repeatedly over my twenty-year career as a prosecutor when someone attempts to distance themselves from criminal activity:

a) "I wasn't really involved."
b) "I didn't know what was happening."
c) "It was someone else's car."

I recognize the minimizing, but I just want to understand what happened.

"A pound of marijuana is quite a bit," I say gently, trying not to chastise.

"Well, we all chipped in. We figured it would be more efficient to just make one trip, rather than running back and forth all the time."

I can barely contain my laughter. *More efficient.* Dad and his bandmates were aspiring to efficiency.

But Mum is coming back into the room, and my window for information gathering is about to slam shut. "So, you were busted coming back?" I ask, trying to wrap things up.

"I never went to jail."

"I think you must have." I have enough experience with federal laws involving drug trafficking to know that three guys with a suitcase of marijuana aren't going to just be waved through at an international border checkpoint.

This round-and-round, back-and-forth interview goes on for another minute, and then, out of nowhere, Dad blurts, "*Executive clemency*!"

"What?"

"That's what it was called. That's what I got."

As we navigate this challenging conversation, Dad's energy seems to surge, especially when I pivot to our shared sense of the absurd. For some reason, I can conjure a clear mental image of Dad and his bandmates driving back from Mexico in a rickety van with a suitcase of marijuana bouncing around in the back. I make a joke about musicians buying in bulk. Dad cracks a smile, and I catch a twinkle in his eyes. But now with Mum back in the room, we drop the subject. She would not find anything funny about this. I wonder why.

It defies logic that Dad cannot recall the circumstances of his arrest. Perhaps he simply dares not say anything about it with Mum hovering about. Now that she has essentially halted any further discussion of this topic, I need to pivot quickly, before she erupts.

I brought along some other things from a different box in my basement—a box from Mum's side of the family. It's occurred to me that maybe she feels like she hasn't been getting enough attention. Her grandfather wrote some clever stories during the time he spent in a nursing home, and I thought she might want to see them. I'm hoping to even things out.

Thankfully, I'm right on the money with my assessment. Mum is happy to talk about her grandfather and his creativity. The topic then shifts to jobs, professions, careers. Thanks to the letters, I have a real-time account of Dad's journey through college and beyond. Mum's box, while full of photos and trinkets, contains little written documentation of anything. I know that Mum majored in music education at Rollins College in Winter Park, Florida. To keep the conversation going, I ask her what she had planned to do with her degree.

"It was a finishing school, really," she responds lightly. When I press her for more, her response startles me. "My parents wanted me to find and marry a rich man."

Her eyes bore into Dad. "We all know how that turned out."

Time to pull the knife out of Dad's chest, crack a joke, change the subject, do something—anything—to keep my heart from breaking once again. My mind races as I concentrate on packing everything back up. For Mum, talking about the past always leads to uncomfortable moments such as these.

As I bid adieu to Dad and make my way out, Mum grabs my arm. "Listen! You have no idea what I went through with that," she gestures back toward Dad, "family."

Then, she starts to cry and launches into some incoherent story about her engagement photo being published in the San Diego paper and how distraught it made her. By my calculation, this would have been about fifty-six years ago.

I fake some sort of empathy; I certainly don't feel any. "It 'a be okay," I say.

It was a phrase Dad always used when Mum was upset. Not "*it'll* be okay," but "*it 'a* be okay."

Once in the car, tears explode into convulsive sobs. Having read close to fifty letters from and between members of Dad's family—letters written in real time during a real crisis—I have found nothing that could support or justify the amount of vitriol that Mum has been spewing about them for as long as I can remember. To the contrary, this was a family that supported and looked out for one another. A family where genuine love was a primary component.

I weep for Dad, the young man who had gotten himself into a jam, changed course, rebounded into college, and worried for his own father. A man who would eventually spend the rest of his life loving his own children as well as the mother of those children—a woman who openly despised him and the family from whence he came.

Had she ever loved him? Or was she simply in love with the idea of being married to family money?

My next therapy session cannot come soon enough. I know that rage, sorrow, tears, and incoherence will return with a vengeance within the confines of Jennifer's stylish office.

It's time for a new plan.

CHAPTER 16

Then: February 1952

Febr. 13, 1952

To my Valentine –

Since we cannot have all the niceties of life such as an orchid delivered to you at just the right time, I will just write you a letter. A letter sent before the day and received after the day. Your letters are all so encouraging and help me to keep up my morale through this ordeal. The last one came yesterday telling of Buddy's homesick phone call. Well, if we can hang together a few more months, I'll be back as one of the cogwheels in our family unit. I am going to the library this afternoon and try to find the last issues of Christian Science Monitor to see Buddy's notice.

Are you feeling good? Or well? I should say. I realize that you are under so much pressure. You are always so conscientious that you so easily overdo before you know it. Tell me what you weigh? Is your appetite good? Also tell me a little about Bruce. Is he cheerful? Is he moody? Or is he too busy to be either? Is he dating again? Why did he stop for a while? Well this is turning out to be a funny valentine's letter.

I may be mistaken, but this seems like what a loving marriage looks like.

Do you write letters for some of the boys at the library? The "Gray Ladies" do, for some here who are either disabled or illiterate. It is surprising how many there are here. I wrote for "Bucko" the boy that reminded me of Bill Hansen.

Our ward is getting more friendly and the living situation is smoothing out. You see this ward is a new type of thing here, although I understand it has been worked out at Lexington. I am still optimistic and am glad that I stayed here.

Papa, middle-aged, highly educated, intelligent and curious, was housed with others far younger who likely exhibited few, if any, of those characteristics. Add in the fact that they were likely there involuntarily as a condition of a federal sentence, I can imagine most of them being a surly bunch. But it didn't seem to Papa. His response to his situation never ceased to amaze me.

I was first assistant for Dr. Crawford with a stomach operation yesterday. He was very nice. I was called late last night (10:30) to check up three new cases admitted to the hospital. The chief surgeon who had the operation is like all Drs. worry about. I do not know if his recovery is slow or if it is all worry. We seem to be able to handle things here anyway. The Drs. on duty are working very hard.

My asthma is much better but still coughing up a lot.

When I get back I plan to go over the wood work and rejuvenate the old place. They believe in keeping one busy here so make plans and I'll see what I can do. Next letter I want to take up some business.

All my love at the Valentine time of year – R

Send brown sweater

Papa could have left the narcotic farm at any time, but he was determined to stick it out to have the best chance of recovery. That meant, however, that everyone in the family had to stick it out by "hanging together." Even from far away, in a locked facility, Papa was providing a sense of leadership to the family unit.

His second Valentine's Day letter to Nana showed continued improvement and optimism:

Febr. 17, 1952

Dearest and No 1:

Your Valentine letter is at hand for answering. Several questions to be answered but I did not see any hugs and kisses. They were there however, between the lines. Do not be afraid of the censor, she is understanding.

Whenever you mention your hours of work it makes me think that you are being tied down, you always being so free to come and go except for your definite program for the children's meals, routine etc. You see I am following your letter and answering your questions and giving you my reactions to the things that you have written me.

Papa and Nana were partners, through thick and thin. He trusted her judgement and competence, completely. I think of my parents and how different their relationship has been. I start to realize that it's not necessarily all Dad's fault, as Mum has tried so hard to make us believe. A hallmark of her disorder is the inability to trust *anyone.* Perhaps Dad realizes that. Perhaps I'd be better off if I could accept that.

I have felt the best, the last three days that I have felt for a long, long time. Some of it of course is from the freedom from medicine that I had been using. So to go to the end of the letter, I mean, your letter and answer your "wonder how you really are and how you are going to be?" I am optimistic and think that I am going to be all right. I do not have to carry the vaporizer around with me, my cold is almost gone, there is just occasionally a wheeze but it is only when I squeeze on exhalation. Not with every heartbeat like it has been.

Having little familiarity with asthma, I turn to Google for enlightenment and discover that it's awful, plain, and simple. The inability to breathe seems worse than any other condition I could imagine. One can feel as if your life is actually being sucked out of your body. To wheeze with every heartbeat must have been incredibly debilitating.

Now for a little "Boost" to our Boston Genius. I have just finished reading "Good Night, Sweet Prince" by Gene Fowler. In reading it I had Buddy in my mind most of the time. Now I believe it is more than just parental prejudice or familial well-wishing when I say that I believe that Buddy has many of the good qualities that John Barrymore had.

"Our Boston Genius."

Reading that phrase, I picture Dad working through his junior year of college, preparing for a career in the theatre. His father seemed at peace with the fact that his eldest son would not be following him into a career in medicine. Dad was that type of father, too. He never pushed me in any direction, instead providing me with a sounding board for all my hair-brained ideas.

His good memory, his gentlemanliness (when he wanted to be a gentleman), His imagination, his flair for fantasy, his friendliness with all kinds of people (not always so good Ha!), a good voice, which I trust is getting better with cultivation, a good physic, (which Barrymore did not take care of). A better education I think has our Buddy, although he is still in the process.

Now do not get this wrong. I am not trying to sell the stage to our hopeful, it may be some affiliated line that is the right course. "Quien sabe" Bama would never have approved of "Sleeping by the Sun and Living by the Moon," but our generation is different.

Will close before censor crowns me for such a long letter.

All my love and affection ----Daddy

Papa composed this parental assessment four and a half years after Dad had been federally indicted for "importing" one pound and five ounces of bulk marijuana from Tijuana, Mexico. This time, I do not want to let my imagination fill in the blanks. Dad used the phrase "executive clemency," and I need to figure out what that is and what it meant for his case.

I turn to my good friend, the internet, and look up information on the United States Office of the Pardon Attorney website. It's as good a place to begin as any. A contact email address is listed, so I decide to take a shot in the dark.

To Whom it May Concern:

I am inquiring as to whether or not there exists a list of pardons granted by President Eisenhower.

My father, Ralph Swisher Russell Jr. (dob 7/23/28) has recently disclosed that he received "executive clemency" from Eisenhower, through his uncle, J. Lee Rankin who, at the time, was Solicitor General.

I cannot find any lists or statistics online and am wondering if this is something your office could help verify for me?

In all candor, I am not certain if my father has all the details, or an accurate recollection of things, but I do know he was federally indicted in 1947 for importing marijuana from Mexico. He has gone on to lead a productive life, so it is possible he did actually receive some sort of pardon.

Any assistance you could give me would be greatly appreciated.

Thanks,

Debbie Russell

The following day, the hospice team descends on my parents' home to recertify Dad. It is coming up on six months since he was accepted into the program, and they need to verify that he is continuing to decline. How depressing. As much as I would have preferred to skip it, I can't count on either Mum or Dad to provide accurate information on what transpires. I arrive early on purpose; I've located a couple more photos that I want to show Dad.

As she answers the door, I see instantly that Mum is still raw from my previous visit. "We aren't going to talk about any of this anymore," she hisses, scowling at the file folder I'm holding.

"Nothing bad," I chirp. "Just a couple of old photos."

Dad's eyes light up when I show him a photo of him playing sax in a dance band. Whether it was the same band of miscreants that took the ill-fated trip to Mexico, I'll likely never know. When the hospice staff show up, Dad is delighted to tell them all about his skills on the sax, much to Mum's dismay.

The appointment goes predictably. Mum and Dad minimize any issues, and Dad is declared eligible for continued services. I breathe a sigh of relief and go back to work.

When I arrive back at the office, the email I have been waiting for is sitting in my inbox:

Re: Freedom of Information Act Request: FOIA 2017-268504 (Full Grant)

Dear Ms. Russell:

This correspondence is in response to your Freedom of Information Act (FOIA) request dated and received in the Office of the Pardon Attorney (OPA) on 03/27/2017. Pursuant to the Freedom of Information Act, 5 U.S.C. § 552 et seq., you requested a copy of the pardon issued by President Dwight Eisenhower to Ralph Swisher Russell Jr.

After carefully considering your request, I have determined that the attached 2 pages are appropriate for release in full. No fee has been charged for the search, review or production of these documents.

A PDF is attached to the email. I open it and inhale sharply at the sight of the old-school, book-on-the-copier-with-hands-holding-it-down photocopy. Dad was granted "executive clemency" by President Eisenhower through his attorney general, on December 21, 1956, just as he described. He was convicted and received a year of probation and a one-hundred-dollar fine for bringing a pound of marijuana across the border to share with his bandmates.

As if this day doesn't have enough going on, I still have that pesky therapy appointment scheduled for after work. If I'm honest with myself, I must admit that I need to talk to Jennifer about it all.

Fatigue hits me like a ton of bricks. Suddenly, all I want to do is go home to bed.

200.

Dwight D. Eisenhower

President of the United States of America

To all to whom these presents shall come, Greeting:

Whereas

Ralph Swisher Russell was convicted in the United States District Court for the Southern District of California, on an indictment (No. 11253-SD), charging a violation of Section 1593(b), Title 19, United States Code, and, on November fourth, 1947, a fine of One hundred dollars ($100.00) was assessed and the petitioner was placed on probation for one year; and

WHEREAS the said Ralph Swisher Russell paid the fine and successfully completed the probationary period; and

WHEREAS it appears that the said Ralph Swisher Russell is worthy of clemency:

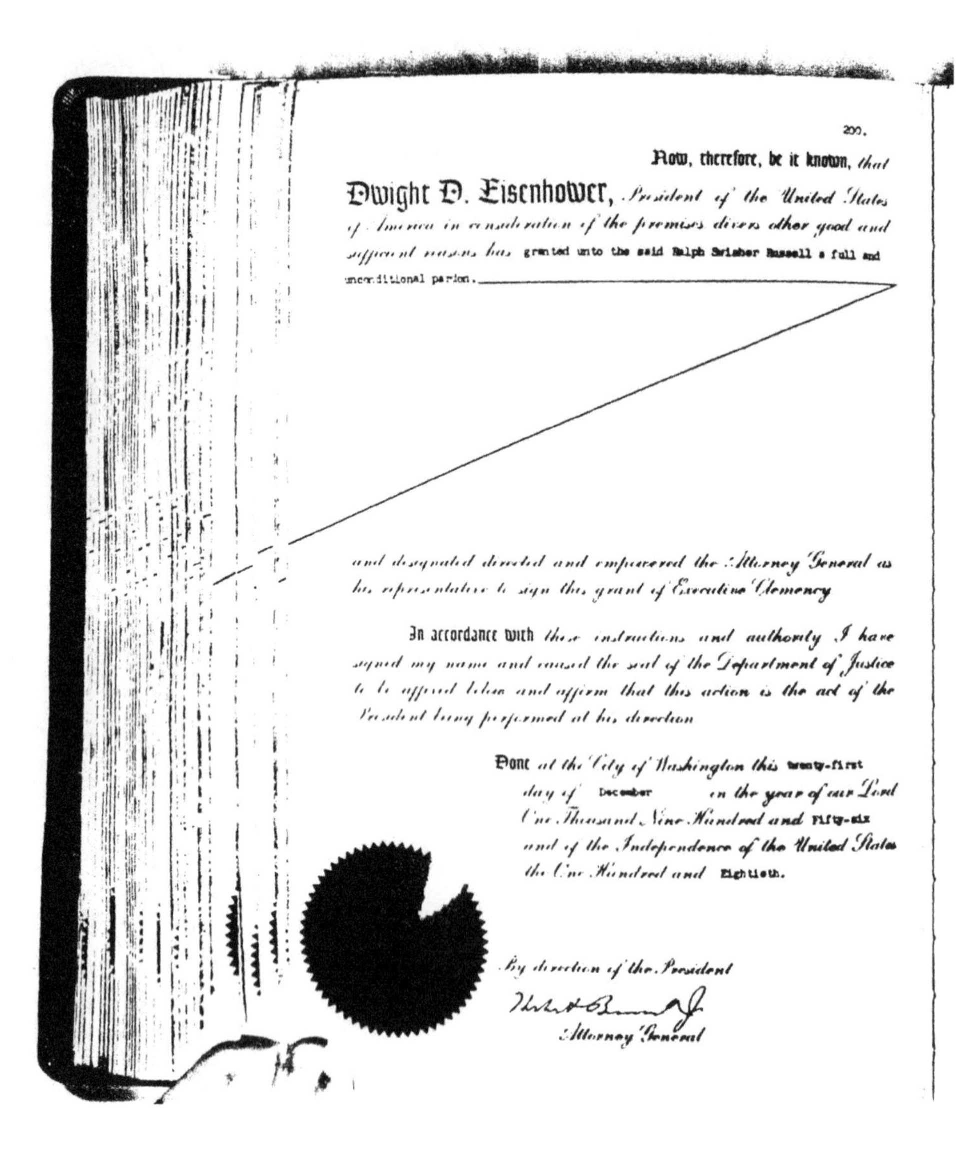

200.

Now, therefore, be it known, that Dwight D. Eisenhower, President of the United States of America in consideration of the premises divers other good and sufficient reasons has granted unto the said Ralph Swisher Russell a full and unconditional pardon.

and designated directed and empowered the Attorney General as his representative to sign this grant of Executive Clemency

In accordance with these instructions and authority I have signed my name and caused the seal of the Department of Justice to be affixed below and affirm that this action is the act of the President being performed at his direction

Done at the City of Washington this twenty-first day of December in the year of our Lord One Thousand Nine Hundred and Fifty-six and of the Independence of the United States the One Hundred and Eightieth.

By direction of the President

Herbert Brownell Jr.
Attorney General

CHAPTER 17

Now: March 2017

CLINIC NOTE: The patient discussed some surprising information she had recently found out about her father. Although she had wanted to discuss this information with her father personally, she indicated that her mother had put a stop to it. She expressed a lot of anger toward her mother, especially regarding her mother's selfishness.

Patient desires strongly to speak with her father alone; to ask questions about his life, tell him how she feels about him, and overall, just have some time to be one-on-one with him. However due to her mother's insecurities and own (probable) mental illness, she does not allow anyone to bring up topics that upset her, and therefore, refuses to allow this interaction to occur unimpeded. Processed patient's feelings toward her mother and discussed ways for her to talk to her father alone.

◆ ◆ ◆

Once again, I have no idea where to begin. Except to say that I'm exhausted. The past week did quite a number on me. Dad is not the bad guy that Mum has made him out to be, but he did lie when confronted about the indictment. He was probably trying to save himself and all of us from yet another meltdown.

Sadness engulfs me. Time is running out to talk to Dad about his life. Mum doesn't want to "glamorize"—her word—all the things he'd done. But is talking about it really glamorizing? Try as I might, I still cannot understand her raw, emotional reactions to things that shouldn't be that big of a deal, particularly those things that happened well over fifty years ago.

I previously tabbed a page in Dad's little memory book. The question on this page was, "If you were to return to your youth, what would you do differently?" Dad had responded:

Cause less anxiety and worry for my parents. A young person rarely realizes how their immaturity and stupidity affects their parents. If I could have settled down to a more focused, career-oriented life sooner, I'm sure my parents would have been much happier.

I don't know exactly when Dad would have written this, but my guess is it was in the last ten to fifteen years. The passage illuminates his insight into himself, as well as his parents. When I look back at the father he was to my brother and me, now knowing how his life almost got derailed completely at the age of nineteen, I feel my heart bursting with pride. And then, the dull ache returns. It always returns.

Mum has spent a lifetime smothering us in innuendos: "You have no idea . . ."

How am I supposed to respond to that?

Scott and I have long since pooled our memory resources and come up with no evidence to support her vague assertions that Dad was truly the worst person ever. But to confront her on the subject would bring forth an outburst like the one I endured right before Christmas. I can't subject Dad to that.

I have two choices; I can let all of this go and deny myself the opportunity to really get to know Dad as the son of Dr. Russell—as the young person he was before he became my father. Or I can push on and risk further abuse from Mum.

Nine times out of ten, I am completely fearless. I've sat across a table from murderers and rapists. I've endured high-profile media cases. But these days, every encounter with my own mother threatens to bring me to my knees. Astounding.

Jennifer, as usual, projects empathy perfectly. It is her job, after all.

"Is there any way you could talk to your dad alone?" she asks.

I slowly shake my head. "She won't even let hospice volunteers sit with Dad for an hour so she could go out and take some time for herself. It would destroy her martyr complex."

Jennifer is silent for a moment. Then she looks straight at me.

"I really think you need to try."

PART FOUR

"Being deeply loved by someone gives you strength, while loving someone deeply gives you courage."

—Lao Tzu

CHAPTER 18

Then: February 1952

Febr. 20, 1952

Sweetheart:

The Hospital will be celebrating Washington's birthday Friday so I will have to write this letter today that you may get it Monday or Tuesday. I have spent the greater part of the afternoon in the education department helping put together the Hospital News. This is the paper the patients put out. I incidentally have an article in it. Now I am back at the Hospital Ward at the typewriter.

I probably have not expressed myself very well up to now. You know how I am. You ask me how I feel or what I think about such and such and I can't say right away. I have to wait a little while before I come up with something. In this hospital, they probably call it delayed conduction or some such diagnosis. Anyway, I think that it is about the most wonderful thing that a woman could do for a man, a wife for her husband or a mother for her family. I feel deeply about it. So many of the patients here have a heck of a situation "Outside". Nothing to look forward to but more of the same. But I feel that "you-all" as they say here in Texas, are all pulling together for me. I know that things are going to be fine when I get home. I see now that I spent more time and energy on the practice where it was not appreciated so much and not enough time and thought at home where it would have been appreciated. Even if I cannot spell the word.

I love this—my physician grandfather expressing his feelings in such a genuine way, even if it sometimes veers toward the analytical. Also, I'm beginning to understand my own emotional reaction to reading these letters. There's a gentleness with each honest sentence that is a salve to my heart. Whether from Papa, Nana, or Dad, they all convey a soft kindness. It is the same soft kindness that I have always gotten from Dad; many times, without even realizing it. I don't know that I've ever felt it from Mum. Perhaps, when I first saw it shine through in Nana's letters, I struggled to believe it to be real because I knew my own mother would never act in that manner.

Well, into other topics. My day now is something like this. Up at 6:00. Shower, dress, clean up my room and go to 7:00 mess. In order to do this, I go down two flight of stairs and through a tunnel about a block long. From breakfast I go another block and up an elevator to the second floor where the medical and surgical ward is located. I say this, because they are all together. The sickest patients are in private rooms. I check any new patents if they come in without the doctor examining them first. I do the surgical dressings which are rather few, right now. The nurse sometimes asks me to start an intravenous or give some aminophylline or things of that kind. Dr. Kozy comes on the ward and makes rounds. He likes to make his rounds alone but frequently we talk over some of the problems that come up. About eleven, the food cart comes up and the patients and the working patients eat in the diet kitchen. No – correction – the patients eat at their beds and we, the working patients, eat in the kitchen.

About noon, I return to my home ward, lie down and read till 1:30 or so. Then I may go to the medical library, (1 block), occupational therapy dept., (1 block), canteen, or there may be something at the hospital for me. (1 block) 4:00 to 5:25 PM clean up, change clothes, rest, read. Supper at 6:00 in cafeteria. (1 block) Evening either Occupational therapy or show. (1 block) About twice a week there is a stage show of some kind but I have not gone to any. It is either patient talent or groups come out from town. I missed church on Sunday for the first time, last Sunday.

All my love, Darling,
Daddy

Upon Papa's arrival at the narcotic farm, he was photographed, issued a number, and strip-searched, much like a criminal. Criminals and destitute addicts comprised most of the narcotic farms' population. Papa recognized that "So many of the patients here have a heck of a situation 'Outside'. Nothing to look forward to but more of the same." Through his own initiative, my grandfather received a gift in the form of a last, best chance to pull himself together. A careful reading of the letters, particularly those from Nana, revealed that there had been prior failed attempts to manage the "sickness" that was his addiction.

I've learned through my work that hitting rock bottom often involves family members and close friends either abandoning an addict or staging an intervention. Either way, external forces come together to propel an addict into treatment. One such external force is a criminal conviction, where drug treatment/rehabilitation is a condition of the sentence. Papa was surrounded by addicted convicts who were compelled to be there, without any sort of support network on the outside.

For a short time in my career, I worked directly with probation officers tasked with supervising the compliance of felons who were court-ordered to treatment. Time and time again, they appeared in court, having been picked up on a warrant for noncompliance. I grew impatient with those probationers. Why couldn't they get it together? How could it be that the looming threat of incarceration was not sufficient to motivate them to stay clean and do the program?

As time passed and I gained a greater understanding of the psychology of addiction, my perception of an addict shifted. For some, deeply engrained behavior patterns—brought on by neglect or abuse as a child—contributed to a need for something to dull a debilitating emotional pain. For others, such as those addicted to heroin, for example, the need for the drug was not a craving inasmuch as it was as essential to survival as food and water to keep the debilitating effects of withdrawal at bay.

I can see how the extensive research occurring at narcotics farms was of immense interest to my highly curious grandfather. He had the ability to accept the hardships that he chose to undergo in his quest to understand his situation as well as that of his fellow inmates/patients. Unlike the others, however, he had a safety net and a loving, supportive family in San Diego.

I pulled out the first letter Dad wrote to Papa when he learned of Papa's decision to enter a narcotic farm. He wrote, "Above all Dad, remember you are the most important person in my life and I love you with all the heart and soul that's in me."

Deep in his heart, Dad has always possessed a staggering capacity to love. As a child and young adult, I took it for granted. Now, reading his letters, I see where that love came from. It was a love he took with him when he married Mum and started our family. In its own way, each of the letters in the file folder transported me into a family very different from my own. It was the family Dad grew up in, where everyone felt loved, safe, and supported. The absence of cynicism is striking and almost shocking to my senses. It forces me to acknowledge that, despite Dad's efforts, Mum's behavior made it challenging for us to gel as a unit during the tough times. Quite the opposite, in fact. For as long as I can remember, I was planning my escape.

Papa left behind a very challenging situation when he checked into rehab, and that's putting it diplomatically. While he was able to take his first thirty days in a narcotics farm in stride, Nana also required thirty days "to get myself in hand." What that meant for her, I'll never know, but I saw nothing in the letters to indicate that it involved histrionics or blaming.

This past week was a brutal reminder that after more than fifty years, our family of four continues to paddle in different directions. As the family member who dredged up Dad's criminal activity from out of the vault, I feel significant pressure to balance my desire to understand what happened with the need to minimize the shame that Mum is piling on the situation.

My therapy assignment is to figure out a way to talk to Dad alone. It's time to come up with a strategy.

CHAPTER 19

Now: April 2017

As it turns out, I am brilliant. And manipulative. And a risk-taker. Jennifer gave me the assignment of figuring out how to get some time alone with Dad. Coincidently, Mum's birthday was coming up, and I had not yet thought of a gift. Then, as if the universe was responding to my desperation, I spotted an advertisement in the newspaper for an orchestra concert that I just knew Mum would love—and I've had half a century to become finely attuned to what she loves. The concert was scheduled for the very next week. All I had to do was buy a ticket, take the day off from work, offer to drive her to the concert, drop her off, go back to their place, and spend two glorious hours with Dad.

Brilliant!

Now, the risk; she could easily decline. She was completely unpredictable, after all. But with the ticket already purchased, the odds of that decreased significantly.

As it turned out, the gift was a smashing success. She was overwhelmed by my thoughtfulness and had no clue about any underlying motive on my part. My entire presentation was on-point.

That's the manipulative part. I've had many years to perfect my craft, after learning the methods to make and keep her happy. I suspect that may have been her primary expectation of me from the very beginning.

At last, the day has arrived. I'm so excited I can barely contain myself as I stride through the door, ready to drive Mum to the orchestra.

Her level of panic takes me aback.

"I can't figure out which shoes to wear!" she exclaims, shakily. Near tears, she stands on the steps leading up to their old bedroom, holding a pair in each hand.

"This pair," she lifts one pair up, "looks so much better, but they hurt my feet."

In the moment, I am talking to a plaintive child—something I've never been very good at.

"These days, I find that I have to choose comfort over style." I respond, trying to remain cheerful. Far be it for me to make any recommendations as to which shoes she should wear.

She is having none of it.

"Let me just say hello to Dad, and we can be on our way." I have this overwhelming urge to get away from her, if only for a few seconds.

I make my way to the bedroom/family room where Dad is established in his recliner, eyes closed. As I enter the room, he immediately opens them and smiles broadly at me.

"You're here!" he exclaims, heartily. I rejoice. It's one of his good days!

"You bet I'm here! I'm just going to zip Mum to the orchestra, and I'll be right back!"

"I'll be right here!" Given his circumstances, his ability to radiate cheer never ceases to amaze me.

I stop in the kitchen to open a bottle of root beer. At last week's hospice meeting, Dad had the audacity to tell the team that he missed having root beer. I watched as Mum glared at him. The hospice nurse was remarkably kind. And knowledgeable.

"You know, you can add the 'thick-it' powder to root beer. You just need to let it flatten before you do that."

Mum rolled her eyes while I made a mental note to *pick up a six-pack of root beer.*

I figure there'll be enough time for it to flatten so that Dad can have it with his lunch. Leaving the open bottle on the kitchen counter, I return to the foyer to collect Mum, who is now struggling with her purse.

"I wanted to take this purse instead of my usual one, but I just can't get everything in—"

It is stuffed to the gills. For a moment, I feel immense sadness at how her anxiety will likely ruin this whole experience for her. But right now, my mission is my top priority, and the first step is to get her out the door and to the concert. As we make our way to the car, she continues, her speech rushed, explaining how she had struggled to find the right purse to hold all her important items.

"I need to have my insurance card so if we're in an accident, they'll know where to take me."

"Are you planning for us to be in an accident?" I roll my eyes behind my sunglasses.

"Well, you never know . . . or if something happens at the concert, someone will need this information."

"Mum. What do you think is going to happen at the concert?" I concentrate on tamping down any sign of exasperation, as she is remarkably good at picking up on that kind of thing. "You have your cell phone, right? I'm the only one you need to worry about contacting."

"I don't think I have your number."

"It's programmed in the phone. Remember how I showed you how you can just push the button to call me or Scott?"

"I know you did, but I need the number." Her agitation is ramping up.

Before we even get out of the driveway of their complex, I stop the car, pull out a slip of paper, write my cell phone number on it, and give it to her. The small gesture pleases her immensely, and she stuffs the paper in her bulging purse. Unfortunately, this relief is short-lived. As we ease onto the freeway, her fears intensify exponentially, matching the car's acceleration into traffic. She gasps several times as I change lanes and the cars whiz by. Apparently, the accident she's predicted is coming around the next bend. My heart starts to race as she babbles non-stop. Within a few minutes, her mania has shifted from fear to a sort of giddiness. I imagine this is how children act when they're going to the zoo or a water park or something.

"You know," she brags, "I told everyone I talked to this week about how wonderful my daughter was to do this for me."

A good daughter is a reflection of a good mother.

She goes on to reveal that she spoke with both her own sister and Dad's sister, Auntie Ann, about this. Unsurprisingly, she found Auntie Ann's response entirely inadequate.

"She barely gave me any room."

I have no idea what that means.

Mum then beams as she describes her own sister's reaction. "She just gushed and gushed and gushed. Whether it was sincere or not, I didn't care!"

There it is in a nutshell. Who cares if you're sincere? As long as you act upbeat and enthusiastic, that's all that really matters. This was a message I received loud and clear from the time I was a young child. I'd watch how Mum and Gamma would belittle other family members yet put on a show of great affection when face-to-face with them. We all were required to perform, and this requirement would ultimately shape my relationship with my own mother into one that felt entirely superficial. Every good deed I attempted was an effort to conceal a gaping hollowness on the inside, one that a mother's love was supposed to fill.

Mum's mood continues to improve as our destination comes into view. My heartrate slows as I watch her hurry into the concert hall. Hopefully, she will have no need for her insurance card or my cellphone number.

Back at my parents' townhouse, I can barely contain my excitement as I reach for Dad's box of memorabilia in the back seat of my car. I am grateful I didn't get a speeding ticket in my rush to get back. Always prepared, I've compiled an agenda for our time together today. But first, I need to share with Dad what I have been going through. Then, I want to go through the photos and letters I have brought with me and have him fill in the gaps. It feels selfish, but my hope is that it will be a welcome respite for him after enduring countless conversations about his physical limitations and the inadequacies of the hospice team.

"There's M'Gil!"

Dad opens his eyes and grins as I walk in. "M'Gil" has always equaled "my girl." It was one of several pet names Dad has had for me since I was small; it always felt like warm, cozy mittens for cold hands.

"Everything go alright with your mother?" he asks.

"Well, you know, there was the usual—" I trail off, not needing to say any more. He knows.

"I brought your box of memorabilia."

He snaps to attention, expectantly.

"First, though, I need to tell you that I have been seeing a therapist to help me deal with Mum. I just need help so that I don't keep getting into these fights. I like to think of the therapist as my assistant."

He nods. "That's probably a good thing."

And just like that, we are right back into our old conversational habits from thirty-plus years ago, when I still spent time at home. Dad always had an uncanny ability to convey complete understanding without saying much. I didn't appreciate it growing up, but as I matured, I was able to pick up on it more easily. Ultimately, I realized that I could count on Dad to balance all the emotional unease I felt around Mum.

This balance is slipping away.

But I can't tell him that. The last time I admitted that I was struggling, he took responsibility, like he's always done for everything. Unlike Mum, who preferred to ignore it or make it all about her. So instead of going on about my feeble efforts in therapy, I choose to report the story of the car ride to the concert and how Mum clearly preferred the histrionics of her own family to the emotional restraint demonstrated by Dad's family. Her distain couldn't have been more evident.

"I really like Auntie Ann." I blurt out suddenly, surprising myself.

"What's not to like?"

"That's just it, Dad. Why does Mum dislike her so much?"

"I wish I knew, M'Gil."

With Dad, what you see is what you get. There are never extra layers to sort through, no ulterior motives, no deep-seated resentment about anything. Mum is the opposite. With her, everyone and everything exists to be judged against an impossible standard she has created in her own head. Exhausting.

I certainly don't want to spend more of our precious time together on this topic. I must first wrap up the details of the drug-smuggling incident. I show Dad the photocopy of the pardon I had received from the pardon attorney. He takes it from me eagerly.

"Oh, yes, Herb Brownell." Dad points to the scrawled signature sandwiched between the lines "By direction of the president" and "attorney general."

The familiarity in his voice astonishes me. "You knew him?"

"He was a lawyer in town."

A lawyer in town. Later, a Wikipedia check would reveal that while Herbert Brownell grew up in Nebraska, he never practiced law there. In time, I would learn that Uncle Lee managed Dwight Eisenhower's presidential campaign in Nebraska and was rewarded with an appointment as assistant attorney general in 1953 when Eisenhower took office. Herb was attorney general and Uncle Lee was his assistant. Uncle Lee had been the one to procure Dad's presidential pardon.

Dad makes it sound like no big thing.

"I can't believe you were able to get this," he remarks, looking over the photocopied document. Dad was always curious about technology, which could be maddening, as I did not have the capacity or interest to have a conversation with him about how my phone could take pictures or how the internet worked. But today, I want to make sure that I am not pushing *my* agenda to the point where I deny him the opportunity to talk about what *he* wants to talk about. Mum has been doing that forever.

Today is, quite possibly, our one and only chance to have a conversation that she can't hijack.

"I just sent an email to the United States Pardon Attorney and got this by reply email," I respond merrily.

"Remarkable!" He is quite impressed.

Our time together is already flying by, and it is time for lunch. I'm excited for Dad to try the root beer concoction.

"Not too bad." He smacks his lips. I can't tell if it is a resounding endorsement.

"I've left the other bottles here, so hopefully Mum will make more for you." *Why is stuff like this so hard for her?*

I keep an eye on the clock. It won't be long before I have to go retrieve her, bringing an end to this very special day.

I show Dad the file folder of narcotic farm letters and remove the rubber band. I start by handing him the ID card/badge issued to his father upon his admission in December 1951. He takes it from me, remarking with wonder:

"I don't know if I've ever seen this."

"I've been researching the facility where your dad stayed. It was really quite the place."

I then show him the book I've been reading about the narcotic farm. He is riveted. Dad has always been interested in stuff like this. I read him a few passages and show him some of the incredible photos. I explain what my research has uncovered, as Dad listens with rapt attention.

Then, I read his first, loving letter to his own father, my throat catching.

Dad looks off, his eyes misty.

"My father and I were always very close."

However, when I ask him what he knew about Papa's intentions when he stopped in Fort Worth and abruptly decided not to return home to San Diego, Dad merely shakes his head. After all, it came as a surprise to everyone. Although he is short on details, he can remember feelings and emotions. I don't want to linger in the heaviness of this, so I pull out one of my favorite letters of his and read aloud:

March 20, 1952

Dearest Dad:

I hope this reaches you in time for your birthday for it is meant as a birthday greeting. I wanted to send you the programs from the shows that I saw when I was in New York but I was afraid that the mail regulations there might not allow them to be sent to you. Anyway, let me tell you all about my trip.

I left Boston last Friday afternoon and arrived in New York about dinner time. I drove down with my ex-girlfriend Selma. She was going to visit her parents in Penn. We had dinner that night at Forano's a place that specializes in Spanish dishes. (I hadn't realized before what a difference there is between Spanish and Mexican cooking.) The food was very good but it seemed to lack the zest that Mexican food has.

After eating I checked in with Phil and Carol Simpson, a couple I knew in San Diego and who had invited me to stay with them. Bill Kraft came over later that evening and we discussed income tax. Everyone was in a last minute rush to finish theirs but I who had sent mine in in January. The next morning which was Saturday I got up early and made the rounds of the ticket offices, I guess I was lucky for I wound with a ticket to every show that I wanted to see. (and could afford) They were "Pal Joey," Mrs. McThing," "The Shrike" and "Stalag 17."

I remember the first time I visited New York City and how exhilarating I found it to be. I was close to Dad's age, too. His adventurous spirit shines through in this letter.

After obtaining the tickets I called Mr. Hammerstein's office to see about an appointment. His secretary said that he definitely wanted to see me but I would have to call back Monday to find out when he could take the time. I made a note of this and proceeded to attend the Sat. matinee performance of "Pal Joey." It was very enjoyable all the way through but there was something about the way that it ended that I didn't feel was quite right. After dining at a very nice Chinese restaurant, I made a few phone calls to a few Calif. friends I found out were in New York, and then on to see "Mrs. McThing." This was an utterly charming show. (I imagine you saw the "Life" article about it. So ended a wonderful day. Sunday after sleeping quite late I visited with Bill Byers an old friend of mine who is in New York writing music for the Sid Caesar "Show of Shows" a TV program.

That evening after a delicious waffle supper at the Simpsons, I spent the rest of the evening with some friends I knew from Boston who were trying to break into TV or Theatre in New York. It is just as hard to break into as everyone says maybe more so. In fact if you don't have some contacts to begin with you might as well not try. The next day was St. Patrick's Day and naturally I had to see the parade. The stripe that separates traffic on 5th Ave. was painted green for the occasion. The parade was interesting but I like the ones in Calif. better. More pretty girls.

I called Mr. Hammerstein's office as directed and was told to meet him at 10 E 63rd St. at six the next evening. I said fine and began to wonder just what I would talk to him about. That evening I had a ticket to "The Shrike" a new play with Jose Ferrer. I was a little let-down by the performances of the leads but found the play itself very interesting. By this time the increased tempo of life in New York caught up with me and I found myself sleeping nearly all day Tuesday.

I smile at the phrase "increased tempo of life in New York." Can't imagine what that meant . . .

I got up about four in the afternoon and had a shower and got all spruced up for my visit with Mr. Hammerstein. At about five-thirty Fred Blumberg, the other scholarship student, came by and we took off for 10 E. 63rd St. which turned out to be Mr. Hammerstein's home. We were admitted and were told that Mr. H was expected any moment. We waited in his luxurious living room and I was reminded of the time I had visited Ginger Rogers home with Dick Entringer.

Well in a few minutes the man arrived. We introduced ourselves and he invited us to his study where he thought we would be more comfortable. He asked us about B.U. we told him what we were doing and what our ambitions were. He was so warm and friendly in fact it is hard to describe all that went on at that meeting other than the aspects of theater which we discussed. I think the thing that impressed me the most about Oscar Hammerstein was that he didn't once discourage us or even intimate any of the old trite expressions like "well you've got a long way to go." At all times he spoke in very optimistic terms concerning theatre and when we finally left him after about an hour of very stimulating discussion Fred and I were simply walking on air.

We celebrated by having a big dinner and then we went to the top of Rockefeller Center and where we felt we were really on top of the world. I had forgotten that I had a ticket to "Stalag 17" but it didn't matter, I was too elated to care. The next morning I met Mr. Lannom, a teacher in the School of Music of B.U., and I drove back to Boston with him. Thus ended a visit to New York which I will long remember.

Have a very Happy Birthday Dad.

With all my love,

Ralph Jr.

Dad smiles broadly. These events he remembers as if they had happened last week. His capacity to recall names has always been outstanding. He helps me fill in the gap between his high school graduation, the unfortunate detour to Mexico, and his subsequent relocation to Los Angeles where he found the direction that he had thus far been lacking in life.

"I was in LA working odd jobs. One of them was for the children's theatre. Through the children's theatre, I met this woman named Mavis. Mavis was affiliated with Dr. Harold Case, who was the head of a Methodist church in Pasadena. Then, in 1951, Dr. Case was asked to become the president of Boston University."

"Wait, Dad, how does that just happen?" I am a bit incredulous about this chain of events, but Dad can't provide an explanation.

"All I know is that Dr. Case agreed to take the position if he could bring Mavis with him, as well as his choir director and his organist, Max Miller."

I knew Mr. Miller's name from Christmas cards. He and Dad remained friends for decades. So, apparently, Dad had "in" with the incoming president of Boston University and was able to enroll as a junior. Were strings pulled somewhere? Perhaps, but who cares? It is such a neat story! I've learned from my father how to take advantage of any opportunity that's offered me. Life's way more interesting if you do.

Dad remains focused on the letters and how I had gotten them. I try to explain how I had discovered them in his box.

"What's obvious to me is that your father wanted them preserved. He writes throughout that he wants the letters saved. Why do you think that was?"

Dad is silent.

I press on. "Do you think this situation caused shame or embarrassment to the family?"

He is unable to answer this question but offers, "I do wonder if there was some sort of coincidence between this and what I went through with that indictment business."

At almost eighty-nine years old, so much of Dad's past has simply been sloughed away. Probably for the best. For a moment, I wonder if it was a good idea to dredge all this back up. But at this point, it's a little late to try to put the toothpaste back in the tube.

There was one more question I know I must ask, though.

"Do you think he relapsed after he got home?"

"I really don't know. I don't think so. At least, I never saw anything that would make me think he had." Dad continued. "I remember learning that he had ended up in the hospital. I dropped everything to go to him. When I got to his room, he was sitting on the end of the bed, clutching something. I don't remember what it was. I stayed with him for a bit, and then I had to go. I told him I'd be back soon. But he died before I could see him again."

I immediately regret going down this road. I squeeze Dad's hand, struggling to hold back tears. Regardless of the outcome of Papa's life and addiction, the letters bore testament to a deep and enduring love.

Thus far this afternoon, Dad and I covered topics that had been buried in his box of memorabilia for forty years. Now, together, we endeavor to understand how and why some people—namely Mum—decided that certain subjects were off-limits. As Dad and I speak philosophically about all this, I regret not initiating this kind of conversation sooner. Apparently, I've already forgotten all about the barriers Mum threw up time after time.

We compare notes about what it was like to be a twenty-something. It's a self-centered time of life. When I was in my twenties and thirties, I was not focused on my family history beyond the interesting tidbits I'd included in school assignments. I couldn't be bothered with the stories of my ancestors, regardless of their significance. I hadn't been thinking about my identity, my lineage. I was self-centered, but not self-aware. Similarly, Dad was in his twenties when his own father battled stress and addiction. It's quite possible that Dad simply did not have the capacity to pay close attention until it was too late.

Time to lighten up.

To conclude this special encounter on a happy note, I pivot to the little memory book and read aloud some of Dad's passages about his childhood in Sutherland. He brightens considerably. "Those were quite the days." He sighs.

They sure were.

As I pack up Dad's box at the end of our time together, it occurs to me that Papa had an indefatigable spirit that he had passed along to Dad. Whether it was through things they did together when Dad was a little boy or Papa's willingness to share his experience at the narcotics farm, the bond between father and son was substantial. This spirit would subsequently manifest itself in Dad throughout his life. It was a bond repeated between Dad and his children.

When he went to see the great Oscar Hammerstein as a twenty-three-year-old college student, Dad envisioned a career in the theatre for himself. Obviously, that never panned out. But for the rest of his life, he would continue to reinvent himself as a husband, a father, a teacher, and trainer. He never gave up the hustle. Even now, homebound, with a wife who, by all appearances, despises everything about him, he still manages to project a cheerfulness that I can hardly imagine anyone capable of.

The very least I can do for him—and to honor the memory of my grandfather—is pull myself together.

CHAPTER 20

Now: May 2017

CLINIC NOTE: The patient discussed a conversation that she was able to have with her father regarding their relationship, questions about family history, as well as how they felt about each other. She indicated that she had sent her mother to the orchestra in order to get this alone time with her father. She reported that the conversation with her father was wonderful.

Although she indicated that the conversation with her father had gone well, she still desired to have more alone time with him. However, due to her mother, she found this nearly impossible without a fight. The patient was visibly distressed over this and was torn between wanting to tell her mother how she felt about her and keeping peace in the house due to her dad's illness. Processed the patient's feelings and role-played different ways that she could talk to her mother.

◆ ◆ ◆

"Keeping peace in the house." That, unfortunately, has never been my strong suit. I've frequently wondered why that is. It's not like I yell and scream the way Mum does. It's more a refusal to placate. My brother has observed the differences in the ways we each communicate with Mum and recently admitted that he generally just says whatever will keep her calm and stable. I have the ability to do that, but the internal stress that comes along with that type of repression is unbearable at times. While my fighting spirit has served me well in my many years as a prosecutor, there isn't much use for that particular trait within my current family situation.

Maybe that is why I find the letters so soothing. They reveal a different way of dealing with a crisis. A way that, up until now, was unfamiliar to me.

Every so often, Nana would acknowledge at least some amount of stress:

This is very jumbly – that seems to be the way my mind works these days – I will be so glad when all is back to normal again for us all – my work is very pleasant and good for me, and not too much at all. I am happy to do it and love doing it. As far as the love and kisses you know they are between each word and line and you know it. We think you are wonderful to do what you're doing – only we miss you so – but we want you well and all the rest will take care of itself.

My great-grandmother wrote, "We are so happy that you are feeling better and also happy it won't be long before they find out what causes the asthma."

This made me wonder what she actually knew about my grandfather's situation. Did she think he was at the narcotics farm to be cured of asthma? He did allude to that when he made his initial decision to stay at the Fort Worth facility rather than go on to Lexington. He had referred to the "asthmatic background" at Fort Worth as one of the primary factors in his decision.

I still believed that his ultimate goal during his four-month stay was to find out how to manage his dagger point without resorting to narcotics. In researching asthma, I learned that stress is often a huge factor. A WebMD article stated, "Stress may cause [one's] asthma symptoms to worsen and cause [one] to feel frightened. When stress levels start to creep upward—whether it's over bills, work, or a kid's jam-packed calendar— asthma symptoms can kick into overdrive . . . a vicious circle can begin where anxiety worsens asthma, and asthma worsens anxiety."

Demerol, as well as other narcotics, had become my grandfather's remedy of choice to break this vicious circle. At the narcotic farm, he was learning to manage his anxiety in a different way to reduce his chances of an asthma attack. In essence, he *was* learning about what caused his asthma.

But, as he had previously written, "I had another conference with Dr. Osberg. He is not going to be able to give me as much time as I had hoped for. I am a very complex personality and to find out what makes me tick in an asthmatic way would be like taking a complex watch apart. Maybe I should have been an Ingersoll or an alarm clock which are easier to fix".

Complexity can produce conflict. Conflict can produce stress. Stress can produce any assortment of unpleasant side effects. People in my profession, just like physicians, often resort to substances to "take the edge off." The internal conflict that has been building over the past year has created stress that I, too, must learn to manage without the use of substances and without checking into a locked hospital.

Papa acknowledged that he was not going to get as much time with the psychiatrist as he had hoped. And it's *how* he acknowledged it that I find inspiring. He didn't feel sorry for himself. He didn't complain about the program not being what he thought it would be. He simply carried on, doing what he was told to do, living where he was directed to live, and taking each day as it came.

I will need to do this all on my own. I just hope I can summon up some of Papa's fortitude.

PART FIVE

"If you're going through hell, keep going."

Winston Churchill

CHAPTER 21

Then: February 1952

Febr. 24, 1952

Dearest, and All –

The last couple days have been cool cloudy and humid. The result has been a little heaviness in the chest and just a wee bit of wheeze – not all the time – just at night. And that cannot be much because I am only awake about once. A few puffs and I go back to sleep. I take a little nap at noon nearly every day. Today, what do you suppose wakened me? A sparrow was scolding me from the window sill. I had neglected to put some crumbs out and I was being told. One patient, a round headed roly-poly individual with red hair and a red sweater, feeds the cats outside. There are seven or eight of them. They come running when they see him. A flock of pigeons live in the various cupulas. They take a notion to exercise every so often, like our neighbor's pigeons.

Papa's asthma seemed to be improving, or at least that's what he conveyed. I'm guessing he didn't do much napping when he was working full time. As I read his observations about the birds, I realize that I inherited my love of nature from him, through Dad.

My wind-breaker jacket came. I am not able to use it because of regulations, but a solid color wool sweater will be alright so I am looking for the arrival. I believe that this one will pass. At this time of year, the weather is changeable so it will be a comfort.

Dr. Osberg was very nice to let me finish the insurance blank reports in his office. Every patient that comes in here is assigned to a psychiatrist. I guess I told you that I was assigned to him. Dr. Fagen is handling the asthma, but all business goes through the psychiatrist. I hope the answers to the questions were all in order.

Now to answer your letter. I believe you can send me the clippings about Buddy (Censor, please cross this out if she cannot). I am glad that our children want to go on to school. The ignorance of so many of the people is appalling, even my spelling. Many would not be here today if they had an education. Many of them had the chance but did not take it.

Oh! Yes! Do send me Ann's poetic effort. I am her collaborator you know. More particulars about Bruce's golf trophy, the one he is after, I mean.

Love to all. I hope we hear from Buddy soon. You may want to send this on to him??

All my love. Daddy

By "learning new ways" to manage his asthma, which would presumably alleviate the need for narcotics, Papa's optimism was well founded. His self-awareness likely helped him progress in a way that many of his fellow patients could not. A little over sixty days in, with the jagged havoc of withdrawal behind him, Papa had the time and space to just breathe. And watch the birds.

When I was seven, we moved out of town to a large house built to Mum's specifications and located, aptly, on the corner of Paradise and Scenic Drives. It was colonial gray, with red shutters and a white rail fence, set up on a hill, and tucked into a heavily wooded, one-and-a-quarter-acre parcel. Mum busied herself with decorating, and Dad hung birdhouses and whistled a cardinal's whistle as he cut wood with a chain saw. An old snowmobile trail ran through the vacant lot to the south. My brother and I followed it out of the woods and found ourselves on forty acres of rolling pastureland we dubbed "the meadow." So much room to roam!

The meadow was actually a pasture for horses that were boarded farther down the meandering road. Scott and I spent hours riding our bikes on the trails created by the horses and playing all sorts of make-believe games with the neighbor boy, Stephen, who just happened to be Scott's age. Coincidentally, to my great joy, there was also a friend for me. Carol, a girl my age, was technically our next-door neighbor, even though their house was on the other side of their forty-acre property. Carol's family owned the land on which the boarding stable sat, and they rented it to the people who ran the stable.

Scott and I were often away from home for the entire day. Fortunately, Dad developed a powerful whistle that seemed to carry to the farthest boundaries of where we were allowed to stray. Nine times out of ten, we'd hear that whistle and then yell at the top of our lungs, "Coming!" before hightailing it back. It was an efficient system, except when we didn't hear it, lost track of time and faced rather punitive consequences.

The elementary school was five minutes away, and Dad drove us to school on his way to work. From a very early age, I was a voracious reader. In first or second grade, I was selected to read *The Adventures of Pippi Longstocking* to the class. In doing so, I became convinced that hers was the life for me. I wanted nothing more than to live in a house with a monkey and a horse and do everything by and for myself. I made my own horses out of cardboard boxes and galloped them around the yard.

My first experience riding an actual horse was on the back of Stormy, a handsome Appaloosa gelding owned by Stephen's teenage sister, Julie. Exhilaration surged through me as Julie urged Stormy into a canter and I gripped the back of the Western saddle. A few years later, Carol received a horse for her birthday. I did not. However, it didn't matter, as I was allowed to ride one of the boarder horses with her on those rolling meadow trails.

Although I would never get my own real horse, we did add a cockapoo puppy to the family when I was nine. The first day Muffin came home, she was relegated to a pen in the basement, much to her—and my—dismay. After a few minutes of enduring her plaintive whimpers, I joined her, sitting on a chair with her asleep in my lap. My arm fell asleep in the process. Once she was dependably housebroken, she moved upstairs and into my bedroom at night. She became my confidant as well as the recipient of any maternal instincts I might have possessed.

College transformed me from a country girl into an urban dweller, but I always sought opportunities to escape the noise and lights of the big city and go out to the exurbs and the rolling farmland beyond. There, inevitably, a calm would settle over me, and I would return to the hustle and bustle of city life feeling refreshed and reinvigorated.

After I graduated from law school and decided that I would set down my own roots in Minneapolis, I bought a cozy little bungalow in a charming neighborhood where the houses stood just forty feet from one another. The backyard was not much larger than the tennis court at Carol's house. People generally buy houses to raise families. I bought mine for its location on a bus line to work and for the backyard, where I set about recreating the Pippi Longstocking lifestyle.

I was thirty-one when I closed on the bungalow.

Dad was thirty-one when Papa died.

When I moved in, Dad prepared a little list of all the things I would need to know about homeownership. While Mum expressed skepticism at the notion of her daughter purchasing and living alone in a house, Dad countered it with enthusiasm. I consulted with him regularly about house and yard maintenance.

My first "child" was a golden retriever puppy named Molly, and she quickly moved into the space in my heart that had been left gaping after Muffin died. I don't recall if Pippi considered herself a parent as much as a pal to her housemates. I've always viewed my role as a parent of sorts (sometimes described as a "pack leader") to all the dogs with whom I've had the honor to share my life. In eighteen years, there have been five. All of them came to live with me as puppies. I would like to say that as each new one came through the door, I improved slightly as a dog owner/parent/trainer. Still, I never came close to desiring any human children, or even human roommates, for that matter.

Now, as another summer advances, I seek respite from the conflict within my human family in my modest backyard with the three dogs that make up my current pack. Several years ago, the giant box elder tree, the anchor of my plot and prized canopy during hot summer days, blew over in a storm. In the blink of an eye, my cherished patio and garden were transformed from a cool, shady refuge to a blazing, unprotected, and vulnerable space. The garden, ablaze with colorful blooms, was swiftly destroyed as the removal crew trampled through my yard, clearing away the wreckage. Surveying the damage, I fought off a feeling of devastation. After all, people all over the world rise from far bigger catastrophes than a lost tree.

"You could put a screened porch back here."

Those eight words, spoken by my dear neighbor friend, were all that was needed to fire up my imagination. I jumped on the idea, hired a contractor, and within a couple of months, added the room that would end up being the most-used space in my house between the months of April and October. The addition of the porch completely transformed my beloved backyard, rendering it better than ever.

While Mum expressed surprise that I would choose to spend my money on this kind of space—demonstrating yet again how little she actually knew me—Dad celebrated this decision and made his thoughts plain to me during one of our rare times together when Mum wasn't around. This occasion, a couple years back, had not been planned. The three of us were supposed to attend a midmorning orchestra concert, but several days prior, Dad had a bad spell and collapsed. Mum did not feel comfortable bringing him along, but she was desperate to go to the concert, so I offered to return two of the tickets and hang out with Dad at my house for a couple of hours while she attended the concert. Mum eagerly accepted this arrangement.

"It seems I could just sleep all day." Dad looked out the car window as we approached my street.

"You're eighty-seven, Dad. You've earned the right to sleep all day if you want. I brought work home, and I can do that while you rest, if that's what you want."

I helped him into the house. It was a gorgeous spring morning, and I'd opened the windows, allowing the persistent merry chirping of the neighborhood birds to be heard inside.

"Where do you want to hang out?" I asked.

"Can we go out on the porch?"

"Of course, we can!"

I helped him down the narrow steps and out my back door to the porch. Once we'd gotten ourselves situated, though, he didn't want to sleep. He wanted to visit with me about anything and everything. He was so pleased to be out there. We talked about what a great investment the screened porch had been. We talked about the work that I had put into my house and how it would hopefully pay off when it was time to sell it. We went through pictures of my gardens over the years. We talked about baseball. We talked about running wire through the house to hook up speakers on the back porch. I told him that I was pretty sure I got my MacGyver skills from him.

At one point, he said, "It's hard to be old."

Returning to the present moment, I force back tears.

He'll likely never be here again.

To turn my mind and heart away from my troubles, I watch the birds, just as Papa did. They're an amazing and effective distraction. A cardinal couple recently moved in, and I'm obsessed. Mr. and Mrs. Cardinal are a handsome pair who spend lots of time on the fence bordering the north side of my yard. They've been searching for the perfect spot to build their nest, and to my delight, they've settled on a sprawling barberry bush in perfect viewing distance from the porch. As I listen to them sing, it occurs to me that this was the very song Dad would whistle during the summer at our house in the woods. Some days, I can hear it and feel joy. Other days, I cannot control the tears.

Anticipatory grief.

Over the course of a few weeks, I've gained a front-row seat to the care and raising of baby cardinals. Through storms and other challenges, Mr. and Mrs. C. tend to their fledglings until the two clumsy adolescents can make their ways into the big wide world. Bird parents are incredibly efficient. Mr. and Mrs. C. remind me of Nana and Papa, whose exchanges revealed a steady, supportive approach to parenting. Papa's absence seemed not to have impeded the forward progress of his fledglings. Dad inherited that approach, always encouraging my latest plan or idea and providing much needed relief from Mum's histrionics.

As I reflect on how much I fretted about the fledglings while they were growing up, it dawns on me just how desperate I am to control outcomes. When they escaped the nest, and lolled about in places I deemed unsafe, I kept returning them to their home. Except it wasn't their home anymore.

This is exactly how I'm trying to control Dad's last chapter. Perhaps I should take a page out of the cardinal playbook, focus on the things I can control, and let go of those things I cannot control.

CHAPTER 22

Now: July 2017

CLINIC NOTE: The patient stated that things in her life had been going well and that she continued to feel more supported by her brother. She indicated that he was engaging with the family more often and now understood how difficult it had been for the patient to deal with her mother alone.

The patient appeared healthy and in a happy place in her life. She no longer expressed as much anger toward her mother's behavior and displayed empathy and compassion for her family. She was able to process her continued fears over her father's ailing health and quality of life but also recognized that she could not control the situation and could only be there as a support for him.

◆ ◆ ◆

Appearances can be deceiving. I'm simply getting better at pretending that everything is fine.

I've decided to space out my therapy appointments to every couple of months. I just don't see the point in going more often. I really don't need to spend an hour rehashing my struggles with Mum. Nor do I want to talk about how I wake up every day thinking this will be the day Dad takes his last breath. Without guidance, or at least a plan forward, it's turned into a huge waste of time.

I opted not to tell Jennifer about the day back in April when I was unexpectedly and involuntarily transferred to a new position in my office's civil division. Sitting across the table from the deputy county attorney, tears rolling down my cheeks, this easily was the worst day of my professional life. How does a tough-as-nails violent crimes prosecutor cry in front of the boss?

Assuming the transfer was due to some shortcoming in my performance, I pressed for an explanation. It turned out that it had very little to do with me. Another lawyer with a year's seniority wanted my job, so they gave it to her. And then, the powers that be figured I could do hers, despite my knowing absolutely nothing about the subject matter. We were all indistinguishable cogs in a large public office system, where two decades of honest, dependable work failed to guarantee me any sort of consideration.

By June, it felt like as good a time as any to try an antidepressant. The incessant weeping, which I'd thought was in the past, was now back with a vengeance and needed to be curbed, ASAP. Just like therapy, pharmaceuticals turned out to be a crapshoot. As I sat in my new office, chatting with an old friend and colleague, I wondered if he could see the sweat pouring down my face. Was it a hot flash or merely one of the possible side effects of the medication? I soldiered on until dry mouth and bowel changes showed up to the party, at which point, I raised the white flag and quit cold turkey.

Despite this internal unraveling, I somehow managed to stick to my own life plan of adding a puppy to my Pippi Longstocking household. It was time. Or at least I'd convinced myself it was time. I learned early on with Molly that dogs are pack animals, and some really hate spending an entire workday alone. Since then, my proclivity for family planning has maintained itself through almost two decades. For a short time, I might have three before the eldest passes and I'm back down to two. Casey, my eldest, turned eleven in the spring. I'm painfully aware that none of my dogs have lived past eleven.

The newest addition to my household is a cute yellow lab puppy whom I've named Watson. In my experience, nothing beats a puppy to banish sadness. Watson chases the other two dogs around my too-small backyard and enjoys our daily morning walks through the neighborhood. In between Casey and Watson in age is an exuberant five-year-old flat-coated retriever named Jet. He loves Watson and is teaching him how to be a very good boy.

Now, a couple months after my unplanned transfer, I've discovered an unexpected benefit of my new job—absolutely fantastic colleagues. One even offered her car for me to run home to let Watson out at lunchtime. I try to practice gratitude. Puppies are useful in that regard. Their simple joys are contagious. Still, I have reached the point where my dogs, my cramped backyard, and the resident birds are the only things keeping me sane.

Dad asks about Watson all the time, so I muster the courage to ask to bring him over. Mum is less than enthusiastic, but Dad and I persist. Predictably, Watson is adorable. And luckily, he's still small enough to not ruin any of Mum's vast array of knickknacks. I snap some photos and try desperately to bottle this moment when all is well with the world. Puppies are also a great diversion from family conflict and disfunction.

I continue to dutifully show up at my parents' place once a week to be helpful and because it's expected of me. The problem is, just like the cardinals in the backyard, Mum doesn't want to let me be helpful. Or at least, not in the way I think I should be helpful. On one occasion, she wanted to change a light bulb and asked me to get the ladder for her.

"Mum, can't I just do it for you?" I asked.

"Oh, no! I just need help getting the ladder up from downstairs."

I stood by as she grunted, wrenched her neck, and struggled with the lightbulb. I felt the familiar rage boiling up and gritted my teeth as I tamped it back down. Or was it fear? Was this how I was supposed to relinquish control? In my head, I reviewed all the things I would love to say to her. It provided marginal relief.

For as long as I can remember, we've been on a regimented

Saturday-morning phone call schedule. We talk every Saturday at nine in the morning. Originally, I was expected to initiate the call. One time, I forgot.

"We wondered if something had happened to you," Mum said when we finally connected.

Once we made it past the enormity of my transgression, we decided that, going forward, they would initiate the call. Over the past year, as it took longer and longer for Dad to get going in the morning, the call time shifted to 9:30. If I missed the call for some reason, Mum would leave a plaintive message, successfully heaping on the guilt. As a result, I quickly learned to be proactive and let them know if I was going to be unavailable on Saturday morning. It was all so tedious.

◆ ◆ ◆

The Saturday-morning phone call right before Father's Day starts innocuously enough, with Mum going on about how she had mistakenly picked up a box of frozen pancakes instead of frozen waffles at the store. As if the manic, rambling presentation weren't excruciating enough, Mum takes what feels like an eternity to tell this story. I feign interest. After all, it's meaningful and important to *her.*

Then, the conversation shifts to the very unfortunate cancellation of their visit from Dad's weekly shower aide. "We're just going to muddle through on our own today." Her voice is in that register of false cheerfulness I have grown to both fear and loathe.

"Wait a minute. Did you not call the program and request a substitute?" I ask.

"Well, you know, there are so many vacations at this time of year, and they're always so short-staffed."

Mum always makes assumptions, most of which are not based in reality. This kind of misstatement, announced with all the conviction in the world, drives me crazy. I bite my tongue, though, reminding myself that it is not my job to convince her otherwise.

Then, the conversation really goes sideways.

"It's been a very bad week." Her voice is ominous. "It seems Dad may be taking a turn."

Taking a turn? What the hell does that even mean? Dad's on the line. I wonder if he's going to speak for himself anytime soon.

"Did you contact hospice about this?" I ask, struggling to remain calm.

"I needed to talk to you about it." She's ramping up. "How would you feel if he took his last breath before you got to see him?"

I'm stunned. "You know I'm coming over there tomorrow for Father's Day, right?"

As Mum responds with more incoherence, my head spins. I'm vaguely aware that I cannot do anything about Dad's condition. The problem is that I have absolutely no idea how to properly navigate this conversation, despite having spent what seems like an excessive amount of time in therapy.

What am I even doing in therapy?

I decide to feebly try to establish a boundary. I think that's something Jennifer may have mentioned in one of our sessions. "I'm sorry," I say, "but you're going to need to have this discussion with the hospice people or Scott or Auntie Jan or someone else. I'm just not able to have these conversations with you."

That statement lands with a thud which makes Mum huffy. Without words, she convinces me, once again, that I am the worst daughter ever for shirking my primary responsibility of being the ear for her complaints.

Mustering more courage, I press on. "Mum, I'm in therapy because of these kinds of situations. I just can't take in this kind of information anymore."

If this registers at all, she betrays no sign of it.

I take another deep breath. "Mum, you need to call hospice."

"I'll call them Monday."

Monday?

"If you don't, I will."

As she begins to escalate, we're cut off. I'm not certain if she hung up on me, but at this point, it really doesn't matter.

I wait five minutes and then call the after-hours hospice nurse line. I explain that my mother is describing what sounds like a rather dire situation, but she is unwilling to contact them herself and so I am doing it on behalf of my father. They promise to have a nurse call her within fifteen minutes. Later that afternoon, I take a chance and call Scott. Wonder of wonders, he answers his phone. I'm wracked with guilt and momentarily forget that he really doesn't have the bandwidth for my feelings about anything.

"Do you think I should stop over this afternoon?"

"Nope."

The apathy in his voice punches me in the gut as I try mightily not to resent the comfortable cushion that physical distance provides him. As we review my conversation with Mum, we both marvel at how she could, in one breath, talk about frozen pancakes and giving Dad a shower and in the next, paint the direst picture of a man close to death. It is absurd and not fair to me. Scott's boundaries with Mum are firmly intact.

Maybe I could learn something from him.

On Father's Day, I show up laden with dinner, homemade cheesecake, and a cheerful disposition. Astoundingly, it is as though the previous day's conversation never happened. The only tell is Mum alluding to the fact that someone came over to give Dad a shower. "You must have called hospice," she says dryly. That's the extent of it.

Am I hoping for a little gratitude? A little acknowledgment that I did the right thing? If so, it's not happening. Instead, Mum launches into her complaints, with the cringe-inducing degree of detail I've come to detest, about how they only offered two time slots, neither of which was really convenient. About each and every inadequate characteristic of the person who showed up. About how the hospice program really doesn't seem to be that well run . . .

I endeavor to let it all simply wash over me by concentrating on maintaining a cheerful demeanor and mixing a bourbon Manhattan for Mum. It's something Dad did for her all those years.

I've also come prepared with lots of things to talk about besides Dad's relentlessly deteriorating condition. When he asks about my new position, I launch into that topic, capitalizing on my skills as a storyteller. As Dad and I talk about appraisals and real estate as it relates to condemnation law, Mum fidgets restlessly. I then shift to the backyard cardinal drama. It's a good little yarn, and I have the skill to tell it with sufficient flare.

As she sips her Manhattan, Mum softens. We talk about the old days in the house on the corner of Paradise and Scenic. Mum and Dad vacated that house almost two decades ago, much to my dismay. Even though it was Mum's choice to leave it at the time, she frequently would express regret over that decision in the ensuing years. Depending on her mood, it was not always wise to initiate a conversation about the old house.

Fortunately, it turns out that remembering the occasional cardinal at the old house is a memory we can all enjoy at this moment. As I describe my experiences birdwatching from my screened porch, I reference the one Dad built at our old house.

"How did you manage that all by yourself?" I ask, hungry for this information.

"I used the concept of theater scenery flats for the screens." Dad beams.

Of course he did.

My mind sneaks away for the briefest of moments to a childhood memory of that screened porch. I'm reading a book—*The Black Stallion*, perhaps? Muffin is on my lap, and a cardinal is chirping merrily from one of the nearby ironwood trees.

Peace settles over me, if only for a moment.

CHAPTER 23

Then: March 1952

I recall Papa's words, "Do send me Ann's poetic effort. I am her collaborator you know." When I first read them, my mind went instantly to Dad. He was always my collaborator, and now, I could see that it was a skill he inherited from Papa. As I return to these letters, I find myself wanting to know more about the father-daughter bond between Papa and Auntie Ann.

As if on cue, the next letter in the stack fulfills that desire. It's addressed to "Precescious," not "Precious." It was a special nickname Papa had for Dad's younger sister, Auntie Ann.

March 5, 1952

Precescious:

Papa was only allowed to write two letters a week, and up until March 1952, the bulk of his correspondence was with Nana, with a few scattered letters to Dad in Boston. I smile as I come upon the first letter with this salutation.

I saw your picture in the Saturday Evening Post and it made me want to get right on a plane and head for home. Your pose on the first page was scandalous. Now how do you suppose that I knew that girl in the lower bunk was you in that ungainly position?? I had fun showing some of my friends here the item and explaining it to them.

Some would not believe it. Said that they saw no mention of anyone by the name of Russell in the article. There are so many tall stories going around here that I do not expect everyone to believe anything they hear. But I know who it was and as far as that is concerned that is the main thing. You were lucky to be in the foreground and to be chosen for the pillow fight picture. Maybe it was the mole on the back of your leg that identified you.

I smile at Papa's gentle teasing.

Friday there are to be two operations at which I will be present, I do not know in what capacity as yet. One is on one of our few woman patients and is to fix up a broken collar bone. It will be an operation similar to the one I did on Aunt Molly many years ago. She (Aunt Molly) that is, had fallen down the steps that went up into the third floor of our hospital. What an exciting time we had. I fixed up an old bicycle inner tube to make a figure eight around her shoulders, then we either pumped it up with a bicycle pump or went to a filling station and filled it up with free air. When we went to the show, she would let all the air out so that it would be more comfortable.

The more I read Papa's writings, the more I believe creativity is something that's inherited. Dad wrote all about some of Papa's inventions when they lived in Sutherland. As a kid, I loved making things and doing experiments. One such experiment involved deep frying doughnuts and not realizing that hot oil would break a glass container.

I tried to finish this little thing that I am making

you, yesterday. But I was called back to the hospital and will have to work on it another day. The Occupational Therapy Department is where hobbies are developed. Right now there is a representative from a plastic manufacturing plant here to teach us how to make things out of plastic. Dr. Lewis and several of the personal doctors are taking advantage of the opportunity to learn the work.

I just know that you and Bruce are just as busy as can be, but mother is not telling me everything so either you will have to write or Bruce will have to write. Mother is so busy, so just once in a while you might just give me a little news. Tell me about the girls that I know, how is the girl you correspond with, what is her name??

"Tell me about the girls that I know." Even though Papa had been working four hours away from home for three years, he still knew some of his daughter's friends.

One thing I definitely want is the poem that you have written in school. That will mean more to me than the picture because it will not be just a "happenchance."

You all have gotten so used to me being on the desert that I should think that this absence would not be missed so much. Just pretend that I am an explorer of olden times. One of those individuals who would sail away to unknown lands, for not months, but for years. Two months more and I'll set my sails for the west coast of the U.S.A. and will try to find that nice harbor that they call San Diego. I will not be confused like some of the old timers were and try to get into Mission Bay.

Lots and lots of love,
Daddy

"You all have gotten so used to me being on the desert." In many ways, this family reminds me of a military family whose loved one is on an extended deployment. As I consider this, I start to see how, perhaps, Papa's decision in December 1951 was not as jarring as I first presumed. After all, families everywhere were still rebounding from separations and losses brought on by World War II.

Auntie Ann's response is on stationary half the size of the official narcotic farm stationary that Papa wrote on. Unlike Nana's, which has her name and address printed at the top and is a periwinkle blue color, Auntie Ann's stationery is parchment colored. She wrote out her own name and address in careful cursive writing:

Monday, March 10, 1952

Dear Daddy,

I'm terribly sorry I have not written you but I have been very busy with school and all. I'm very glad that you recognized my picture in the Post. I guess by deduction you could figure out that I was the one in the yellow pajamas, almost upside down (and hind side too.) Remember I told you that I helped the photographer put up the flash bulb things? Well evidently it turned out alright.

I'll see that Bruce gets busy on your snapshot idea. And one will be included of Dulcie (all combed and brushed.)

That wallet you made was beautiful!!! How did you do it? The other one (which I am using) is nice also. Although I like the ivy much better.

You asked about the girl I correspond with. Well, her name is Jackie Johnson and she lives in Georgia. I have written a few times but she hasn't answered.

About my "poem." I am still undecided about the last part. Mr. Storm (remember him?) has his idea and I have mine. Maybe you can help me decide. Here it is, anyway:

Glorious Music

Music
Soft music
Music with soothing quietness
Music to let you love and dream
And think of your past and future.

Music
Sad music
Music with droning tones
Music that swells and swells in your heart
And makes the whole world look dim

Music
Bold music
Music with brilliant dignity
Music to make you stand up and breathe
And look at the world before you

Music
Bright music
Music with lilting gayety
Music to set you dancing and laughing
And living a happy full life

Now this is the one I'm not sure about: The first is the original, the second is my changing, and the third is Mr. Storm's changing.

Music
My music
Music rich with inspiring beauty
Music with laughter, love and tears
That makes you strive on forever

(my changing:)
Music
Glorious music
Music I love
Music with laughter, tears and confidence
That makes you strive on

(now Mr. Storm thinks):
Music
Glorious music
Music I love
Music with laughter and tears, cuddling
That makes you strive on.

He says warmth, comfort, expectation, anticipation, courage, contentment equals cuddling

He thinks that you can just see laughter and see tears. But you can't see love and all of the others. He says that hope and courage and love are used so much in poems that they hardly mean as much as they used to. He thinks cuddling is a very beautiful word and so do I. What do you think?

Well right now I am here alone and mother and Gran and Auntie Dear are over at the Thiels, (howeveryouspellit) and Bruce has gone to Boidens to school. We have been having some more wet weather here. As a result, some terrible traffic jams. The other day they had to close part of Pacific Hwy. because of the flooding in the underpasses. It took Mr. DuPaul, Helen's father, something like 45 minutes to go from De Falcos food market to Tennyson St. That was because of the jams there where you turn off to go down Harbor Drive, and way down here at Lyton by Leo Voltz's I hear it raining outside now. It will probably take mother (and co.) a little longer to get home.

Well, it's getting late and must go to bed now. So, "goo bye" for now.

Lots and lots and lots and lots and lots and lots and lots of love to "yawl,"

Precescious

By all accounts, Auntie Ann was living the life of a normal, active teenager. When I think back to my own teenage years, *self-absorbed* is the best way I can describe myself. My school and social life took all my time and attention, to the point where I was able to effectively shut out Mum and ignore her histrionics. But Dad was always there, my understated guiding light.

Papa devoting a few of his precious letters to his youngest child shows his deep and abiding connection with his children, which seemed to be weathering the lengthy separation. That close, wholly nonjudgmental connection is much like the one I share with Dad.

March 16, 1952

Dear Precescious:

My! What a nice long letter. It must have just taken you ages to write so much and do not think that I do not appreciate it because I do. What with all the schoolwork you have to do, etc. etc. The grades were satisfactory as usual and it makes me mighty proud. The grades in that school do not run too high, I believe. Buddy said that he would spend his vacation in New York and maybe see Mr. Hammerstein. Won't that be something?? What do you think of your biggest brother anyway?? We will both be home again in May. Only six weeks more for me.

Now about your poem. I think that it is very nice. One can see that you love and understand music. That last verse still is not right. Now Mr. Storm may associate music with cuddling, but I never did. Ask mother if she ever did. He was probably a young man when a popular song came out which was entitled "Cuddle Closer." We all associate certain music compositions with certain events in our lives. So maybe that explains it. Another verse might be given to "Religious music" as some of the fine stirring music is metered to stately beat of spiritual inspiration. The clash and crash of some of the music we get over the radio would probably not come into the scope of your poem.

I love Papa's efforts to coach Auntie Ann on her poem!

If you do have to make out more book reviews or reports, I hope some of Joseph Conrad is on the list because he is one of the most descriptive authors that we have. Owen Bryon Davis is another that is a master at description and one who makes you feel that you are right there. I went to the library today and took out two books. The Young Lions and a mystery – Robbery of the Sun.

I also inherited my love of books from Papa, someone I never actually knew. This continues to amaze me.

I do much less walking now that I have transferred to this ward. Most of the walking is around the ward seeing the patients. We had a very interesting operation on the collar bone that I believed I mentioned before it happened. Well Dr. Levy found the ends of the bone which were pulled apart and took a piece of bone from the top of this woman's hip and placed it with wire so that it bridged over the gap. Then in addition he put a wire in from outside the shoulder and threaded the collar bone on to the wire thus –

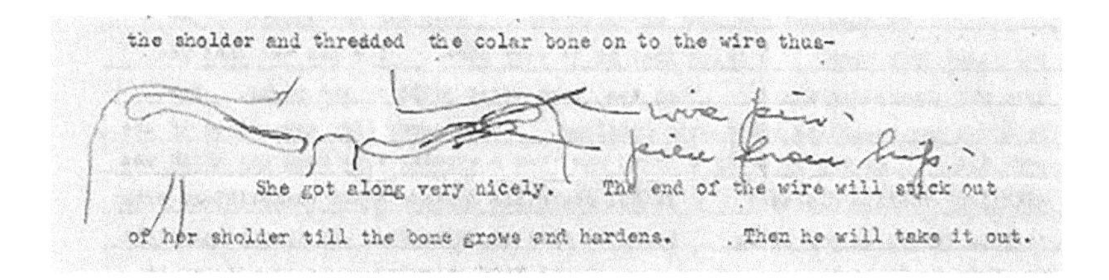
the sholder and thredded the colar bone on to the wire thus-

She got along very nicely. The end of the wire will stick out of her sholder till the bone grows and hardens. . Then he will take it out.

Another operation I assisted with was a sort of a plastic on a man's forehead to take out a malignant growth. Tell mother that I will try to finish up the Mexican papers tomorrow and get them back to her.

Lots and lots of love, from your Daddy

While these letters are illuminating, I still want to know how Papa's condition and frequent absences over the years affected Auntie Ann. I already knew that Dad, as the eldest, shared a very strong bond with Papa. Now, I need to know more about the bond between Papa and Auntie Ann, because I can't imagine managing without Dad during my teenage years. I need to understand how Auntie Ann did it.

I flip back through the folder and realize that I missed a letter from Auntie Ann, which she wrote much earlier, in January of 1952:

January 20, 1952

Dear Daddy,

Well, I hope you are more rested than I am right now. Last night and the night before I have gone to formal dances. One Friday at Gladys Bowens, and one last night at a new Masonic Temple in Ocean Beach. The occasion was an Installation and dance afterwards of Jobs Daughters. Grandmother bought a lovely pink formal for me for Christmas, so I was all set. Also, mother got me a gorgeous red velvet ¾ length evening coat. The coat is made and the style is so that I can wear it all through High School and College.

Next week I have semester tests to take. On the 29th grades come out and I will send my report card to you soon after. Do you remember my English teacher Mr. Storms? Well, I'm not so sure of my grade in there because I haven't gotten any books read for book reports. A few weeks ago I talked to him after school about it. But the other day he called me a "dope." So I don't know what to think.

Last Thursday I was the mistress of ceremonies at the election assembly at school. I introduced all of the candidates to the students and then the candidates said their speeches. It was quite an experience.

It seems that Buddy at sometime had bought a tape recorder. Probably when he was developing his voice for radio etc. Anyway, Bruce and I have had some fun with it. On the nights that he worked from 6-8 I would record, from the Magnavox, "Beanie." Remember "Beanie" the puppet show? Anyway, he would come home and listen to it then. Once when I was alone I recorded myself playing piano and singing. One thing I like about the recorder. That is, you can erase. After I played back what I had sung, I promptly erased it. Very convenient. Mother sent it on to Buddy before we could record a conversation. But I did dedicate and record one of my pieces he had asked me to learn some time ago.

Mother is working today from 1:00-8:30. Grandmother is downstairs watching television and Bruce is doing the yard. He played a tennis match this morning after we all went to church. And he is still top man on the ladder.

Well it's getting late and I still have some homework to do so I will close for now.

Lots and lots and lots of love,
Precescious

P.S. I will send you my report card later on. Ann Russell

Well. No big deal that Papa was in rehab. At least, not that I can tell from reading this letter from Auntie Ann. I stop to ponder why I skipped it in the first place. Perhaps my shock and outrage at Papa for not consulting his family before making the decision to stay in Fort Worth two weeks prior to Christmas had something to do with it. Plus, how much of my own experience influenced how I first reacted to this situation? I undoubtedly injected drama where, perhaps, no drama existed.

When I talk to Dad about this time, his memories are blurred to an extent by the fact that he was in college, away from home. Auntie Ann was still at home, yet by all accounts, Papa's extended absence was causing her little, if any, discomfort.

I'm dying to talk to her about this. But will she want to talk to me about it?

CHAPTER 24

Now: July 2017

The Russell family secrets are now percolating in the open. I need to share a couple of these letters with Auntie Ann. For some reason, though, I'm conflicted about it. Jim didn't have the slightest inkling of their existence when I first told him about them. How will Auntie Ann respond? The last thing I want to do is cause her any pain. On the other hand, my desire for information easily overwhelms any impulse to "keep it in the vault," as Mum has urged me to do.

I decide to scan the ones Papa wrote directly to her, as well as the two she wrote to him, and the first introductory ones.

Holding my breath, I press *Send*.

Two days later, Auntie Ann responds:

Dear Debbie,

Thank you so much for scanning and sending these letters to me. They represent a very difficult time in our family's life that, until now, has been nearly impossible for me to relate. In those days, a family addiction just was not discussed or shared. Because of the letters, I have the opportunity to look back at that time and realize how we managed to get through it all and it's now much easier to talk about. Bruce went to church with us today and came back to the house for brunch. He and I went over the letters and we had a great conversation about all this.

All for now. Thank you again for the letters!

Ann

Auntie Ann has now confirmed what I previously struggled to believe based on my own family dynamics; while their family may have been taken by surprise when Papa decided to stay in Fort Worth, everyone just picked up and carried on. No fuss, no screaming, no sobbing. This familial support system contributed to Dr. Russell being one of the exceptional candidates for rehabilitation at the Narcotic Farm.

Even in the years before Papa entered treatment, when he was working in Blythe, his connection with his family remained strong. I press Auntie Ann for more information on that period, and she graciously obliges:

During a couple of summers, I spent 2-3 weeks with him in the desert at Parker Dam. In addition to taking care of the families there and at the three pumping stations up the line, he kept busy learning ceramics. He created his own potter's wheel out of a table Singer sewing machine. The foot treadle moved the wheel. I had fun learning that, and of course he was a great teacher . . .

I basically knew that Dad was addicted and that he was at a special hospital to get special treatment. I did not blame him because I knew how he suffered with asthma and whatever he was taking made him feel better. For a number of years, he and I would go see the Oscar winning movie that year. I was always embarrassed by how loud his wheezing was and that he had to use his "puffer" when the music got loud enough to cover the sound. When he couldn't sleep at night, he would sit on the edge of his bed with his elbows on his knees just to breathe. I heard it from my bedroom and it made me nervous. But he would eventually improve from these spells. So, when he found something that made him feel better, I closed my eyes and felt relieved. Plus, we never really talked much about addiction in those days--certainly not like today.

According to an employee of the narcotic farm in Lexington, interviewed for the book I read on the subject, "[T]he people in the narcotics hospital were from every walk of life, but they weren't a random sample. Rarely did they have stable marriages with children. They were different from 'Ozzie and Harriet' kind of Americans."* Papa was the exception to this rule. He *did* have a stable marriage and children who adored him. The optimism he expressed early in his stay—while likely in the throes of withdrawal—was genuine and grounded in a quiet confidence that his home base would be there when he came out the other side.

In another email, Auntie Ann writes:

Bringing up these memories is very painful. Much easier to remember him as the loving, accomplished, and inventive father he was to me, the family, and his patients. He made some of the instruments he used in surgery, he built various items for our backyard on Goldsmith, and he did medical research with several dozen guinea pigs backyard. His creative bent was inspirational and has been helpful in my own life. When I went on hospital rounds with him and worked summers in his offices, I realized how well he knew his patients. It has been rewarding to learn that the hospital/home he built in Sutherland has been renovated and reconfigured into a medical clinic today. He was my greatest encourager and booster. In spite of his shortcomings, I loved and admired him greatly.

My heart skips a beat as I read those last two sentences. They are sentences I could have written myself.

She closes her email with, "My only regret was not being able to tell him goodbye, but I have gotten over that. I was in San Francisco when Buddy called and told me the news."

With Dad now entering his nineth month in hospice, I'm starting to think that Auntie Ann's experience of losing Papa may have been a whole lot easier than what I'm presently going through. And what Dad is going through.

---

* Campbell, Olsen, Waldon: *The Narcotic Farm* p.86.

CHAPTER 25

Now: August 2017

CLINIC NOTE: The patient stated that she believed that she might have a pain disorder. She reported lower back pain and shoulder pain. She indicated that she had been to a lot of different doctors and even has a surgical consult set up for September 19th. After reading a book that her friend had given her on pain disorders, she started to wonder if the pain was due to emotional stress, rather than physical. Additionally, she reported that her medications don't work to help the pain, so she opened up to the idea that it might be an emotional issue she is not dealing with at this time. She discussed how she always had to walk on eggshells with her mother and brother, and that she was so busy always taking care of other people, that she often forgot that nobody worried about taking care of her.

◆ ◆ ◆

Have I reached my own dagger point?

Dad turned eighty-nine a month ago. He'd had a rough day, so he stayed confined to his chair rather than walking the fifteen steps into the living room where we typically held our family celebrations.

He struggled to open the cards. I made a mental note not to seal them anymore.

He struggled to read my handwriting, so I read aloud to him.

"I am who I am because of you."

Scott sent him a CD he'd made, comprised of special jazz pieces that the two of them had listened to on Sunday afternoons at the house on Paradise and Scenic. I gave cash; it's what Mum preferred. Dinner was good, and Dad loved the key lime pie I brought.

During a visit several weeks later, I entered Dad's room and immediately noticed the three large Band-Aids placed parallel to each other at an angle on his forehead over his right eye. Although Dad had been prone to scrapes and cuts for many years, this sight unsettled me.

As I complimented him on his haircut, I tried to make a joke. "Did Mum jab you with the scissors or something?"

"Well, here's the thing. I fell out of bed."

"You *what*?"

Mum then jumped in with, "Now, don't get all worked up over this. Didn't Scott tell you?"

"Um, *no*, he did not." I steadied myself for what was to come.

"Well, the only reason I told him was because you were coming over today, and I figured he'd tell you."

On cue, my head started to throb. I chose my words carefully. "And otherwise?"

"Well, we weren't going to tell anyone about this," she responded conspiratorially, as if that were the most normal thing in the world.

She then explained how she woke up at 4:35 on Friday morning to the sound of Dad calling out, "I've fallen out of bed."

Friday morning. Two days ago.

"So, I turned the light on, went over to the other side of your dad's bed, and found him lying on his back. Somehow, we managed to get him up. That's when I noticed the blood."

I struggled to maintain my composure. "You didn't think it necessary to call hospice?"

"Oh, no. You see, I got it all cleaned up, and we had these nice bandages that Daniel the nurse had given us for his bottom," she exclaimed brightly, proud of her resourcefulness. "They worked out so nicely! But then, I peeked yesterday and saw that I should probably change them."

"Well, it seems as though a hospital bed might have prevented this," I responded evenly. As the words came out of my mouth, it dawned on me why she had wanted to keep it a secret.

"And that's exactly what we don't want," she said, confirming my suspicions.

Mum then launched into a lengthy dissertation about how a hospital bed was just not feasible. It wouldn't fit, and most importantly, it wouldn't look good aesthetically. Always with the aesthetics.

I concentrated on my breathing.

"I'm guessing you and I aren't going to see eye-to-eye on this," she concluded.

"No, we sure aren't, so I think it would be best if we changed the subject."

A week or so after that scene, desperate for a nice day, I decided to take my oldest dog, Casey, out for a mommy-and-me adventure that would include a stop at a native plant shop and hiking around the St. Croix River.

As I lifted the dog ramp for the car, I threw out my back. I cried out as the searing pain tore through my body. Casey, not yet in the car, looked at me quizzically.

My neighbors drove by in the alley. Slowing to a stop, they asked how I was. Shakily, I explained that I thought I had just thrown out my back. I couldn't even stand up straight. As they expressed their condolences and drove on, I realized that their inquiry had been rhetorical, which did nothing for my morale. How many times do we inquire into how someone's doing with the sincere hope that the response doesn't require additional output on our part? Thanks to my mother's training, I've always been extra empathetic which, it appears, has come at great cost to my own well-being. Maybe it's time to rethink some of that.

It wasn't even nine in the morning, and I was already at a crossroads; either I give up on the day or grit it out. I refused to give up my plans. Sunny summer days with low humidity are a rarity in August. Somehow, I mustered up the strength to take some ibuprofen, finish packing up the car, and depart the house. Anything else was simply not an option.

While in the car, trying to ignore the stabbing pain in my back, I managed to engage in the regularly scheduled Saturday morning phone call with Mum and Dad. Today's topic was the necessity of another POLST for the hospice program. Mum still couldn't wrap her head around the fact that Dad wanted to die peacefully at home. Instead, she went on and on about how she couldn't live with herself if she didn't do everything she could, which I interpreted as, ship him to the nearest hospital to be placed on life support. At least he'd be out of the house.

"And for what purpose?" I asked.

She didn't answer.

"Is this what you would want for yourself?"

"Oh, noooooooo."

"So then what makes it right for somebody else?"

She couldn't answer and deflected by telling me how she made it clear to the hospice staff that she did not agree with what Dad was choosing for himself.

"But these are Dad's choices." I waited for Dad to chime in, but there was only silence. He regularly faded out during her monologues. Whether it was like at the restaurant, where he was literally unconscious, or he was actively choosing not to participate, I couldn't tell. In either event, I hated talking about him as if he weren't there.

Mum continued without responding to my point. "The chaplain visited this week so we could start working on funeral arrangements."

I wondered if the sudden spasm in my back was in response to this statement. I fervently hoped that Dad had fallen asleep and wasn't hearing any of it.

"She asked your father what he thought happened when he died. His response was, 'There's a funeral?'"

Always the jokester, my dad. Years ago, I'd arrived at my own conclusions regarding death, and none of them included any sort of afterlife. It made everything so much simpler. This is all we have; make the best of it.

Finally, I was able to hang up with Mum, and as if on cue, my back pain eased up slightly. I wondered what it was like for Dad to participate in a conversation about his own funeral. Once again, I wished I could be his collaborator, just as he had so often been mine. But that role was solely within my mother's purview. As the hospice social worker had informed me almost ten months ago, this was *their* journey.

The back pain did not subside in any meaningful way in the coming days. An MRI showed bulging discs, stenosis, all things I'd had for years. Why had the pain ramped up now, in this way, and how was I going to manage it?

The latest email from the doctor's office was terse. "I sent over a Medrol dose pack (prednisone). Do you want narcotics?"

Did I want narcotics?

That didn't work out so well for Papa, so I should probably take a pass.

My grandfather recognized the mistake he had made and set out to correct it. As he detoxified his body as well as his mind, Papa knew he could rely on the support of his family. Historically, when I had a problem or didn't know what to do, I could always rely on Dad. Not anymore, though. As his body and spirit are giving in to the ravages of old age, my own body and spirit are doing the exact same thing, perhaps in unconscious solidarity.

But I am not eighty-nine. I have only just crossed fifty-one. I am pretty sure I still have a fair amount of living to do.

In fairness to us both, I've got to find a way to live without him.

PART SIX

"In the midst of winter I found there was within me an invincible summer."

Albert Camus

CHAPTER 26

Then: March 1952

March 12, 1952

Dearest Dad,

I have read and reread your letter with much enjoyment. I am glad you like "Lord Jim" so much but the Asthmatic incident was purely accidental I assure you. (or coincidental I should say)

This passage in a letter from Dad to Papa catches my attention. I never read *Lord Jim* myself, so I need to jump online to find the "Asthmatic incident." It's dreadful and the direct cause of death of one of the characters. Moving past that, though, I delight in focusing on father and son sharing a book review. That love of reading passed down through the generations warms my heart yet again.

Are you being wishfully optimistic when you said that you might be discharged the first part of May, or were you giving an accurate prognosis? I hope it's the latter as I will be through school for this year around May 20th and then like MacArthur we can make our triumphant return together.

At the time he wrote this, Dad was almost five years past his federal drug indictment, but still four years away from the presidential pardon that would help fully restore his reputation. Yet he'd already managed to change course in a significant and remarkable way.

Reading these letters convinces me that Papa had likely guided him through those years, even if Dad can no longer recall the specifics.

Auntie Ann may have shed some light on that, as she shared the following in an email to me:

I remember when Uncle Buddy was older, I'm guessing early 20s, I was quite jealous that he and Dad would go into Buddy's room and talk for hours at a time with the door closed. I asked Buddy about this when we visited in October of 2016, and, to my surprise, he said he did not remember this.

I'm putting together a puzzle, and sometimes the pieces come from unexpected places. I'd asked Auntie Ann when/how she learned about Dad's federal indictment, and she responded that she was ten years old at the time and only knew that Dad couldn't join the military because he had "something on his record." Makes me think she was shielded from this information, but that Papa was closely involved in trying to get Dad back on track.

I just received a letter from Mother today, and I realize that I have fallen down somewhat on my correspondence. I have just finished playing a part in the first production of the semester. It was called "Dr. Knock," by Jules Romains, a French playwright. I played the part of a small-town general practitioner. I was pretty convincing if I do say so myself. The play was a satire on medical practice and as such wasn't too well understood by the audience. This was due for the most part, to a rather poor conception on Mr. Warfield's part, he was the director. We had a slight discussion on the matter but I had to give way to "20 years theatre experience."

There was a time in my late twenties when I contemplated leaving the county attorney's office to hang out my own shingle. I sincerely believed that I was the next F. Lee Bailey and could bring in millions defending rich criminals. Fortunately, my more sensible side prevailed, and I opted instead for a government job with a guaranteed pension. Life is a series of tradeoffs. Papa, Dad, and I all experienced that in our own ways.

I am really counting the days until I can leave for home and thaw out somewhat. I am planning to run down to New York during our spring vacation which starts the end of this week. I am also hoping to see Mr. Hammerstein if he isn't too busy. I saw a very wonderful play here last Friday night called "Flight into Egypt." It opens in New York this week I think, and I'm anxious to see what the critics think of it, as I thought it was really quite wonderful.

Well Pop, as things look now, I think I will be able to combat the "end of the year slump" in good order. If I can only keep up the rather high standards I set last semester, I will be alright. Must close for now, but I'll try to drop you a line from New York and let you know what I'm doing. With all my love and prayers, I am,

Your faithful son,
Ralph Jr.

How different this letter reads from that first one written just three months prior, when Dad was ready to jump on a plane and travel halfway across the country to see Papa. Through these letters I see a remarkable rebound in the Russell family morale. Perhaps that was because it was a strong enough entity to not fall too far off the track in the first place?

March 13, 1952

Dearest and All:

Your March 11th letter arrived today. When I come back, I hope that we can do some entertaining and not need to say anything about a return or anything like that. You would be surprised about some of the things I have heard about some San Diego doctors.

What sorts of things? I'm dying to know. Gossip among professionals can be some of the worst of its kind.

I have moved my quarters again. Yesterday that is. I am now quartered in the hospital ward. I have a little room to myself in a suite of four rooms, one of which is a bath. The other rooms are at present occupied by Dr. Lewis and Miss Ryner, the nursing supervisor of one shift. She unfortunately turned her ankle and being a rather heavy girl, she is temporarily incapacitated. It is very nice of them to want me to be over here. On the other hand, it is nice to be here because I do not like the walking around that I had to do. I do miss my friends on 3B2. There was one Dr. there that was really getting friendly. You see we talked the same fishing language. Another Dr. and I talked the same obstetrical language and compared cases and methods. I did not especially like the cafeteria on account of the waiting in line and the delay afterward. I will say that it was an interesting place to study character or the lack of it as the case might be. We have been having more cool, damp dusty weather. If you can imagine that kind of weather all at the same time.

I keep marveling that Papa was unlike the other few voluntary patients. I've located an article published in the *New York Times* in October 1951 and written about a doctor who had lost his license due to writing fraudulent prescriptions for morphine. This doctor, like Papa, had admitted himself to the Fort Worth program voluntarily. Unlike Papa, though, he did not complete the program. In the article, he claimed that he never received any psychotherapy and asserted that, had he stayed longer, it would have been "destructive" because of his exposure to "a population which was predominantly a criminal element."*

I take issue with his assertions as well as his attitude. Unlike Papa, who appeared determined to make the most out of whatever his circumstances were, this guy seemed bound and determined to place blame elsewhere. It's much harder to dig inside ourselves and try to figure out how we contribute to our own problems. It's my current struggle. Every. Single. Day.

`In talking about the weather, I did not mention how I felt. Well along with the dust and moving to a new place I did have a touch of wheeze but not bad. I've gained weight again, up to 166 again, so that makes me short winded, also, maybe.`

`Well, enough of this and off to bed.`
`Lots and lots of love, to all`
`"Ralph"`
`(well...you always sign – "Ruth")`
`Daddy`

So many factors could have pushed Papa to give up during his time in Fort Worth, just like that one doctor before him did. Instead, he leaned into all aspects of the experience. He described his cell as

* 'Doctor Recalls His Treatment as Addict' *The New York Times*, October 24, 1951, p. 26

"cheerful." He studied "character, or the lack thereof" in his fellow patients while waiting in line at the cafeteria. He accepted whatever quarters were assigned to him without complaint. He possessed within himself, that "character" that would allow him to hang in there and stay put until the professionals at the facility deemed him ready to be released.

With this letter in my hand, it hits me. *I have this character.* I inherited it. It is a part of me.

I must shake off the despondency that has consumed me for the better part of a year now. I am better than how I have been responding to what has befallen me. I didn't get to be a successful trial lawyer, homeowner, and dog parent/trainer/competitor by chance. I got there through perseverance and optimism. I cannot let these traits that I inherited from Dad and Papa evaporate just because the going feels rougher than it's ever been. I must make the best of it, just like Papa did when he was fifty-one.

CHAPTER 27

Now: September 2017

CLINIC NOTE: The patient reported that her chronic back and leg pain were feeling much better. She continues to open up emotionally during each session in a way that she has not previously demonstrated. Therefore, her progress is moving along, and she is starting to deal with the tough feelings that she has pushed down for years and kept to herself. Initiated a discussion with her about addressing her own needs more often, and different coping styles. She is moving forward in therapy and her prognosis is good.

◆ ◆ ◆

In my very first session, Jennifer asked if I could list three good things about my life. I reacted emphatically. "*Of course!*"

Despite that strong response, though, the events of the ensuing months demonstrated a failure on my part to shake my feelings of dread, sadness, and total abandonment. And then, the *coup de grace*—I was completely wiped out by debilitating back pain.

When I texted one of my best friends to tell her that I had scheduled a surgical consult, her reply was terse and insistent. "We need to have lunch. I have something for you."

Kristi arrived at the restaurant's sun-dappled patio after me and plopped a gift bag onto the table. While we waited for our server, I opened it and pulled out two books, both by Dr. John Sarno. I was drawn to the title of the first book, *The Mindbody Prescription: Healing the Body, Healing the Pain*. Kristi had been a dear friend for over a decade and had weathered plenty of family drama of her own. When we were first getting to know and confide in each other, our friendship blossomed through the trust inspired by shared experiences.

There's something about middle age that brings with it a veil of guardedness. We all want to look like we're in complete control of our lives. When we're able to find people with whom we can be vulnerable, those friendships gently pull our veils aside. If we're really lucky and put the time and effort into nurturing those relationships, we form bonds with these people, creating new families of choice.

Kristi is one of my sisters of choice. When she shared that she had been estranged from her own mother for much of her adult life, I began to realize that I was not the only adult woman out there struggling with a difficult relationship with her mother. It's not something that either of us would want to shout from the rooftops, but upon sharing the pain of growing up with a mother that couldn't or wouldn't bond, we could take steps together to heal those wounds.

"I went through what you're going through right now," Kristi confided across the table. "These books changed my life."

Sarno's theory is that as we age, we all develop degenerative conditions, such as arthritis and stenosis. But not all of us develop *pain* from these conditions. According to Sarno, the pain (referred to as tension myositis syndrome, or TMS) is actually unconscious anger and not at all related to the actual physical condition. Some might consider this idea wacko.

Talking through it with Kristi, though, it made total sense to me. Almost twenty years ago, when my parents first relocated to Minneapolis, my back went out for the first time, which I attributed to doing Army sit-ups. Looking back, I can see the connection between that pain and my newly acquired stress of feeling responsible for my parents' happiness. After all, who else did they have besides me? When Mum repeatedly expressed dissatisfaction with the area and their first condo, it hit me right in my lower back.

The "mother wound," as it's called, is a real thing. One previously unknown benefit of breaking down in front of people I trust was that I learned it's far more common than I ever imagined. One such collapse occurred in the middle of a private obedience lesson with then-six-month-old Watson. I'd aspired to big competition goals for him in agility, obedience, and field. But he'd been a challenging puppy right from the start. He was fearful and manifested this fear by growling and barking at people. It completely threw me for a loop, and I spent most of my time with him just trying to acclimate him to other people, places and experiences.

Adding insult to injury, I hadn't been able to keep up with his formal performance training over the summer because I couldn't focus or even summon the patience needed to work with him on the foundation exercises. Then there was the back episode. Once the pain was tolerable, I rushed back for a lesson only to dissolve into tears, frustrated at how poorly we were performing. Luckily, my trainer is also a friend. Fifteen years older than me, she is smart, funny, assertive, and an amazing dog trainer. Most importantly, though, she gets me. Or at least the *me* that I presented to her while she helped me train my dogs.

That day, my unexpected tears pushed aside another veil. She invited me to dinner, and over drinks and perfectly grilled steaks we exchanged stories of mothers whose expectations motivated us to become super-human, Type A, overachieving freaks. I stared at her, mouth agape, as she shared her story that felt remarkably familiar. I never would have guessed that she struggled with so much of the same debilitating sludge. That dinner showed me how the way we function on the outside can heavily mask what's happening on the inside. As we age, we cling even more tightly to whatever confidence we can still muster, like it's a badge of honor.

When I first took the TMS information to Jennifer, I asked her, point-blank, whether my repressed anger at Mum for the abysmal way she was handling Dad's demise might be a source of my pain. What I didn't ask was whether some more unconscious anger could be attributed to my belief that she—a professional with whom I'd entrusted the treatment of my mental health—was doing absolutely *nothing* to help me. After all, I'd been skating along in therapy, talking about what I wanted to talk about, with little-to-no pushback from Jennifer. I controlled the sessions. And because she let me, I was making little-to-no progress.

Control. It is a tool of the anxious. If I can control my environment, control outcomes, I can relieve my anxiety. But I cannot control something that is unconscious. If I have unconscious anger, how do I control it? *Can* I even control it? Sarno says that we should not seek to control that anger, but rather to acknowledge and release it. I devoured both of his books and then purchased a thirty-day workbook, intent on either proving or disproving this theory.

More significantly, though, this physical breakdown on my part seemed to jump-start Jennifer, transforming her from an enthralled listener to an active participant in my sessions.

"You're finally ready!" she exclaimed happily.

Finally ready? I'm so annoyed at this point. But she's the expert. Now, she's giving me homework assignments and informs me that we will increase the frequency of my sessions back to once per week, at least for a while. She wants me to keep a journal and meditate, among other things. I've purchased books about meditation in the past. I even bought a CD with the sound of a rain shower to assist in the process. But I never seemed to develop the habit. With a professional now directing me to meditate (translation, I am now being held accountable), I will have to take it more seriously.

It turns out there's an app for that called Headspace. I decide to give it a go. There are all sorts of topics and guided meditations to choose from, and they range from a single episode to five-, ten-, and twenty-day "packs." I select a five-day pack entitled "Change."

Listening to the soothing, British-accented voice of Andy

Puddicombe, I quite suddenly—and to my great surprise—start to sob. His words wash over me. "Whether we like it or not, change is inevitable. Everything is changing, all the time. Whether it's externally—the things around us, the places, the people—or whether it's internally—our emotions, physical sensations, thoughts—everything is continually changing, shifting, moving. But we tend to have this idea of change only as a concept, as an idea in the mind. Very rarely does it filter through into our sense of being. So, there's always this sort of conflict between how we feel we should deal with change and how we actually do deal with change."

My breath heaving, I cry for what seems like forever.

I have not been dealing with change. Instead, I've been fighting change. When I look into the future, all I can do is panic. When Dad is gone, I will be an orphan, even though my mother will still be alive. This feeling of dread, accompanied by a gaping emptiness, penetrates my heart and soul, threatening to completely consume me.

It's time to stop fighting change and, instead, start filling that future emptiness with my very own dreams.

Dad would want it no other way.

CHAPTER 28

Then: March 1952

Throughout the month of March, Papa's letters showed steady improvement. On March 18, he wrote:

We have been having some tough asthma weather. I did not realize that Texas was such a dusty state. It can rain one day and the next will have a cold dust storm. And of course, the cold and the dust is what I do not like.

I am getting a little fidgety to get to doing something on my own and incidentally getting paid for it and maybe getting my wife off the payroll. I had such a nice letter from Bruce. I'll get around to answering it soon. I was very proud of his typing and the thoughts conveyed. His typing, I believe has a little edge over Buddy's.

Do you know that it will only be less than 6 weeks till I'll be on my way??? I can hardly wait. It's harder sometimes when it is self-imposed than when mandatory.

Five days later, even better:

Dearest and All:

This has been a lovely day after three days of dust and wind. This was the laziest day yet. My trouble most of the time is to be able to sleep. Well, this morning I got up, ate breakfast, cleaned up my room, looked around for something along my line to do, found very little and went back to my little room and went to sleep. Slept for about an hour. Read awhile and then dozed off some more. A little before dinner I made rounds with Drs. Kozy and Lewis. Sugar and smoked ham for dinner with yams and a Jello dessert.

So you can see from all this that my nerves have calmed down a lot. Some people wonder why they think it is necessary to stay so long to get helped. Well that is just another reason. To get the nerves tuned down. Do you remember how restless I was, well it is so much better.

I'm not sure my nerves have ever been "tuned down." Tuned out, maybe.

Papa was a patient man. So is Dad. Remarkably so, in fact, just the opposite of Mum. My brother and I are a combination of our parents' personalities in differing percentages. In my opinion, neither of us inherited a sufficient quantity of patience and we both bear the burden of excessive irritability. These less-than-desirable traits come straight from our mother. As I muddle along in my fifty-second year on this earth, I'm constantly craving the quick fix. But, as they say, Rome wasn't built in a day.

Papa turned fifty-two on March 22. Nana sent him birthday greetings on March 19:

Dearest -

I am awfully busy – trying to tend to all I have to besides the yard and house care – marketing and my social life, which doesn't amount to too much but yet I love to keep up my activities here and there. Yesterday was Guild and tomorrow, Mother and I are guests of Grace Wallace at the fashion show of a club she belongs to. I work today from 4:30-8:30.

We will be thinking of you on the 22nd and are looking forward to May of course, but want all to be well with you for sure this time – as we can't go through this again.

We all send love and kisses and birthday hugs and will celebrate this summer – you betcha!

All my love – Ruth

By mid-March, the tone of Nana's letters had turned quite cheerful, to the point where she could describe for Papa her resumption of the social activities associated with the family's position in San Diego society. But tucked into a sentence late in the recitation of all those activities was a thinly veiled admonition:

"We can't go through this again."

Knowing what I know about the cycle of addiction, I wonder how many prior times Papa may have tried to overcome his dependence on narcotics. This latest attempt forced him to celebrate his fifty-second birthday in a locked facility far from home. The stakes were the highest they'd ever been. Soon after, he wrote:

March 27, 1952

Dearest, Mother, Bruce and Precescious:

I guess that gets everybody. I'm getting so far behind in my individual correspondence that I am going to have to "fudge" a little and make it all in one.

I have had a very interesting day. Or I should say 24 hours. It took me back to intern days to be able to see two autopsies. They were very instructive. There is always something new to learn, no matter how much you think you know. Well this morning, I was able to be in on a conference with a Neurologist to discuss several very interesting cases. The basis of the discussion was x-ray studies of the cases. I believe that if Cornelia had taken sick in these times, that a great deal more could have been done about here.

After this conference, Dr. Fagen met me in the hall and invited me to hear a talk by Dr. Isabel from the USPHSH in Lexington Ky, where I had originally heard from. I told Dr. Fagen that it was primarily through Dr. Isabel that I was here, although Dr. Isabel did not know anything about it. Just the Drs. of the hospital and the top personnel were there. He gave a very elucidating talk about the founding of these hospitals. He said that drug addiction was much worse in the 1920s than it is now, but there is much more publicity about it right now. He explained the various groups of drugs which are commonly used and how they have been tested. How new drugs are being tested before they are put on the market so that medicines like Demerol are not available without prescription like it used to be. He told about animal experimentation. Then he showed motion pictures of the actual effect of various drugs and the use of the medicines to counteract the effects of withdrawing the narcotics. I missed my dinner but it was worth it.

Wow. Just wow. Papa could not have asked for a better opportunity.

On April 3rd, an extensive skin graft is scheduled, which will be very interesting. It will involve skin flaps, which I have not seen used.

Bruce: You are doing the right thing at Boyden's if you think that it helps you learn to study. Learning how to study is one of the most important things to have in order to get an education. The ability to memorize and the ability to correlate (you may have to look that one up, and if you do you will probably see that I have misspelled it) is very important. Any memory aids help. Then correlation is sort of good old common sense. About college – It will not hurt you to stay in San Diego for a couple years more for school. I believe that it is important for your future to keep on with your friends there. There is plenty time for your "higher education." Older students in medicine do better as a rule. I'll be home soon now and we will be able to go into the details of future plans at that time.

Well, this is all for now, God
bless you and I love you all,
Daddy

Oh, how I wish I could have known this intelligent, curious and caring man! I also long for a "do over" with Dad, in which we have more time for him to share his memories of Papa with me. Whatever grief Dad felt over Papa's premature death, he never revealed to us. What I know now is that Dad parented us the way his father parented him and his siblings: with a steady hand, open to all possibilities the future might hold. That steady hand steered me through all the storms and tumult that Mum created. If I didn't realize it in real time, I completely get it now.

CHAPTER 29

Now: October 2017

CLINIC NOTE: The patient arrived on time to session. She talked about how she can sometimes keep people at arm's length. She also discussed The Wisdom of Insecurity and how she was not responsible for her mother's happiness. The patient is showing good progress and invests a lot of time outside of therapy to work on herself. About halfway through the session the patient terminated due to feeling uncomfortable with her therapist's state of mind.

◆ ◆ ◆

On my way to therapy, I try to call Scott. He turns fifty today. The mid-century mark. The milestone. The gateway to a mid-life crisis.

Last weekend when I visited Mum and Dad, we reminisced about Dad's fiftieth birthday and looked at faded pictures in a photo album. It was 1978 and I was coming up on thirteen years old. Jim, Auntie Ann, and the rest of the family were visiting from San Diego. We cousins were meeting for the first time since our family departed California when I was just three. We'd just finished Dad's birthday dinner and were all still sitting around the dining room table when Mum presented Dad with a small package. One of the photos in the album captured Scott giving a backward glance to Mum. It was a look of concern, maybe even fear.

The package contained a ring—a "tiger's eye" ruby. As I stared at the photo, the memory of Dad's response crashed into my mind:

"We can't afford this."

I remember feeling mortified. The photo captured that exact moment with remarkable clarity. Our family resided in a world of mixed messages. One day would be marked by Mum's hysterical sobbing about our family's bleak financial picture. Another would be marked by the purchase of a ring for Dad—one he didn't need—to look good in front of his family. After Auntie Ann, Jim, and their family returned to San Diego, the ring was quietly returned to the store.

Almost forty years later, Auntie Ann discovered, and sent to me, a letter Dad wrote to her the year after their visit:

June 29, 1979

Dear Babes:

This is a real belated birthday note. I had really planned to call you on your birthday, but as you probably guessed, the good intentions got lost somewhere. I have been thinking about you a lot lately. I don't know where the time goes, but I do know that it seems to me to be going by much too fast. I guess also that once you have passed the 50 mark, you begin to look at time a little differently. Anyway, I did want you to know that I was thinking about you and how I wanted to tell you what a great sister-wife-mother-lady-person I think you are. I also wanted to put it in writing . . . now.

I must admit I am very apprehensive about the future and I don't mean for this letter to sound gloomy, but I feel a great compulsion to share some of my feelings with someone whom I feel would understand these feelings without getting upset, jumping to wrong conclusions or otherwise thinking that I am going off the deep end.

Hmmmmm . . . can't possibly imagine to whom Dad might be referring.

It is difficult for me to write this because as your older brother, I guess I still feel I should be the model person, the one to be looked up to, the successful one etc. etc. The fact is, that for the first time in my life, I am really scared. Ever since I was denied my tenure at the University, I have felt my life has been in a tailspin. At least financially. The real estate business has just not produced the income I had expected and as a result, I have gotten us deeper and deeper in debt. I have been job hunting for over a year now. I have tried to follow every lead. Registered with employment agencies etc. etc. Joanne is aware that things are tight, but I am sure that if she knew the whole story it would have a devastating effect on the family. I have not been willing to risk this.

That familiar rage surged as I read these words. In 1979, we lived in a big, beautiful house and took trips to Disney World. And yet, behind the scenes, Dad was silently panicking over his inability to afford the lifestyle Mum demanded. What would the "devastating effect" be? I don't have many memories of that time, except for the feeling that just existing in the same house as Mum was devastating enough on some days.

I keep hoping that any day now things will turn around and we can gradually recover. But it just doesn't happen. I have been getting some psychological help for my periods of depression. There is nothing you can do. (except maybe pray for me.)

I am sorry to have had to unload this on you,

goodness knows you have problems of your own without me adding to them, but you are the only one I feel close enough to. To tell you the truth, I feel a little better already just getting this down on paper. Maybe I won't even mail this. If I do though, this is strictly between you and me. O.K.

In the meantime, my love to you and your dear family. We feel so fortunate to have been able to get to know Bryan, Carolyn and Jimmy. I had high hopes of taking my family out to California sometime, but right now I sadly wonder if I will ever see California again.

Your loving brother,

R.

"You are the only one I feel close enough to." My father, about to turn fifty-one himself, was living in a loneliness that, as a kid, I never comprehended. Unclenching my jaw, I focused on the benefits of reading this letter thirty-eight years after the fact. For one thing, Dad landed a steady, well-paying job and we *did* go to California, a mere four years later. Another thing, despite his internal suffering, Dad collaborated with me to break a gender barrier. I tried out for—and won—the role of Ebenezer Scrooge in my seventh-grade production of *A Christmas Carol*. Dad had played the role at Boston University. Inspired by my success, he pulled out the newspaper clipping about his performance from his box of things. Night after night, he helped me perfect my delivery, which, ultimately, was a smashing success, even receiving a write-up in our hometown paper, just as Dad's had twenty-five years prior.

Unbeknownst to me, that high point in my life coincided with a very low point in my father's. I also realize that I never knew he went to therapy—except for one time during a meltdown when Mum alluded to him spending money on a psychologist. Like it was a terrible thing in the long list of terrible things Dad had done over the years. Looking back, my heart bursts with gratitude for the strength he summoned to be my collaborator at a time when he didn't know how he was going to keep the family afloat financially.

Now my younger brother is turning fifty. I dial Scott's number on my way to therapy and it goes to voicemail. Why would today be any different? I haven't spoken to him in over two months, as every call I've initiated has gone to voicemail. We aren't fighting, at least as far as I can tell, yet he has ducked out of our relationship once again. I wonder why. I sing the entire "Happy Birthday" song into the phone, suppressing my disappointment at not actually being able to converse with him. As I pull into the clinic parking lot, I concentrate on letting go of yet another thing I cannot control—the crappy relationship with my only blood sibling.

I step into Jennifer's lovely space and immediately notice that she is slurring her words. She grabs a bunch of papers, some with paper clips that she attempts to remove, and they spill out of her hands to the floor.

"I know you're wondering about a plan, and I have a lot of stuff for you," she says, in one long, blended blob of syllables. I pretend not to notice.

She wants to talk about codependency. I tell her about a new book I just got by Alan Watts called *The Wisdom of Insecurity*. She eagerly writes down the title.

As the session continues, I grow more and more uneasy. Jennifer's eyes are glassy. She continually tries to rest a foot on the coffee table as she crosses her legs, but it keeps slipping off. Her sentences drift off. She searches for words. This is getting tough. We aren't even close to being on the same page. After about a half hour, I've had enough.

"I need to say something."

She leans forward in an exaggerated motion, resting her chin somewhat unsteadily on her hand.

"Tell me," she says sort of conspiratorially, eyes wide.

"I'm feeling a bit uncomfortable. You seem to be under the influence of something."

Jennifer sits back, astonished, as am I for saying these words out loud. I choose them carefully, as I have no idea what is going on except that she looks like she consumed at least half a bottle of Chardonnay. Given that it's 4:30 in the afternoon, I find that idea hard to believe, unless she'd been partying at lunch.

There's a pause. Then, she confesses, "I've really had a tough day."

Before I can respond, she breathlessly launches into a story about some "very difficult" sessions with several couples. I'm horrified. *Should she be telling me this?*

"Okay."

She finally switches gears. "Now, I want to talk about these—" She fumbles again with the handouts. There are two copies, but she's lost track of which ones she gave me.

I finally need to end the charade. "I think I should go. You seem impaired."

"Impaired! Yes, I want to talk to you about the *impaired* boundaries between you and your mother."

What the hell does that even mean? Ironically, this is starting to feel like a conversation with Mum, complete with me feeling like I'm losing my mind. Pounding in my head is also interfering with my ability to comprehend what Jennifer is trying to say.

"I really need to go," I say for the third time, standing up for emphasis.

Her eyes fill with tears. "I'm just so sad," she slurs.

"About what?"

"About you, and your dad."

Now I just want to slap her.

"Well, for today at least, you're sadder than I am."

I collect the worksheets, my coat, and my purse and leave her office, heart racing. As I approach the reception desk, I know I have to say something to somebody. The receptionist is still there, as is a youngish man, casually dressed, who is on the phone. There's also a woman waiting in the lobby. I wonder if she is Jennifer's next appointment.

"Is there someone I could talk to for a minute about Jennifer?" I whisper to the receptionist.

Her face totally gives her away. *She knows something is up.* She nods toward the guy on the phone and whispers back, "He'll talk to you."

I don't want to speak in front of the woman waiting in the lobby and don't know where we could go. The guy gestures towards the door. As we step out into the marbled atrium, I start to explain what happened in my appointment. Just like the receptionist, his face immediately betrays him.

"I'm the husband of one of the founding therapists," he responds, after I've given him a brief account of my experience. "I do IT work for the clinic. Jennifer suffered a family loss a couple of weeks ago."

Shocked, I try mightily to focus on what he is saying. He goes on to tell me that Jennifer had been on medication (what kind or what for, he doesn't spell out), but apparently, the dosage was recently modified. Or perhaps she was taking it at work when she shouldn't have? Or something else? It's all becoming jumbled in my mind, even as he speaks. Am I having an out-of-body experience? It sure feels that way. I hear the phrase, "little white pill," and it's at that point I decide that I cannot remain in this building a minute longer.

I cut him off. "I lent her a book, and I hope I can get it back."

"Oh, we want to have you back. We have other therapists you could see," he replies eagerly.

He's got to be kidding. Is this really the way therapy works?

After taking the big plunge into it, I landed with someone worse off than myself, someone who needs to medicate herself to the point where she appears drunk on the job? And now, they're just going to pass me off to someone else? Why had they not cancelled her appointments if they knew she was not fit to see patients? Smiling through my fury, I make my way out to the parking lot, fumbling to unlock the car door.

In 1951, M.L. Pescor described the effects of morphine, using this description as an example of all depressant narcotics. "Within a few seconds after an injection of morphine there is a flushing of the skin accompanied by a mild itching and tingling. The pupils of the eyes constrict, and the mouth feels dry. As the drug takes hold the individual passes into a comfortable drowsy state called 'being on the nod.' There is a feeling of warmth, general well-being, freedom of pain or discomfort, and relief of tension. Imagination is given free play in pleasant reveries. Worries are forgotten. This is the bliss which the addict seeks, a state of intoxication without being drunk."*

This fit my impression of Jennifer to a "T."

Driving home, I vacillate between rage and pity. I have no idea what will happen to her. Why should I even care? Something about what the guy said made me think that this was not the first time such a thing had occurred. My mind darts to Papa, another professional, whose emotional condition resulted in an "all too frequent use" of a narcotic. He'd needed psychological help to kick his addiction, despite all the knowledge and experience he possessed.

I also thought of Dad when he was fifty and his attempt at therapy. Did it help him?

Does therapy ever help? Or does help really only come from within?

---

* Pescor, *supra.* at *475*

CHAPTER 30

Then: 1988

I have my own boxes of memorabilia. I've now lived for over a half century, so it would be sort of odd if I didn't. When Mum and Dad moved out of the house on the corner of Paradise and Scenic, they packed whatever was left in my childhood bedroom into a couple of boxes and turned them over to me. I, in turn, shuffled them down to the basement with all the other boxes belonging to my ancestors.

Occasionally, I comb through them, mostly when I'm looking for something specific. One consequence of this effort would be the discovery of something unexpected that would unearth memories I had not accommodated in decades. One such surprise item was a folder overflowing with newspaper and magazine articles about horse racing and jockeys. An envelope addressed to me from *The Registry Office of The Jockey Club in New York City* jumped out. It contained a pamphlet entitled "Information for Apprentice Riders." At age thirteen, I was completely consumed with the idea of being a jockey. Then, I looked at the postmark on the envelope; June 29, 1979, the same date Dad wrote that desperate, lonely letter to Auntie Ann.

When I outgrew my first planned career as a jockey, I decided to become a veterinarian. I watched our vet perform surgery on Muffin when she developed mammary tumors. I was puffed up with pride in my ability to, 1) not get sick, and 2) not break down emotionally, as Mum did in the waiting room. I began my college career in the pre-vet program at a state university campus in a small farming community three hours from home. It was perfect.

I eagerly jumped into all that college life had to offer. I had not, however, anticipated struggling with the heavy science curriculum. By the end of my first semester the writing was on the wall. I would never get accepted into vet school. Just like that, I had blown it.

Luckily, one of the perks that came with the good job that Dad had landed when I was in high school was a toll-free number. In 1985, when calling long-distance cost money, it was the best thing ever. I confided my defeat, and together, we started formulating Plan B. I settled on international affairs because it sounded interesting. I buckled down, increased my course load, and brought my grades up. Then, as if out of the blue, it dawned on me that a degree from a state university located in a small farming community in the Midwest would have little value when I applied to be a diplomat, my new career choice.

I decided to finish up my bachelor's degree in Washington and, after reviewing the transfer policies, applied to George Washington University. I was ecstatic when I, along with every credit except for bowling, was accepted. Dad, too, was thrilled. Of course, Mum perseverated on how I couldn't pay for it. I tuned her out. I'd won a substantial scholarship in high school, which had completely covered my first two years at the state university. I'd also been working since I was fifteen years old and had amassed considerable savings. This was going to work; I just knew it. So did Dad. Or at least that was the message he conveyed.

Late in the summer of 1986, Mum and Dad drove me and my stuff across the country in a rented cargo van. The only memory I have of that trip is of being in the backseat with earbuds in, listening to my Walkman. I also recall Mum's horror at the coed living situation in my assigned dorm. Again, I tuned her out. With no family subsidy coming in, I worked twenty hours a week in a large law firm and graduated a semester early, thus saving myself a substantial amount of money.

Living in Washington was amazing. To be going to college mere blocks from the White House was unlike anything I'd ever dreamed of. One of the partners in the firm where I worked, Joseph Califano, had served as secretary of Health, Education, and Welfare under President Jimmy Carter. One of my tasks as a mail room clerk was to wrap Christmas presents for his family members.

One day, while walking to class, I saw a recruitment poster for the CIA. I signed up for the initial test and, based on my score, was invited to a top-secret, weekend-long, head-shrinking event. Despite my feelings of insecurity and pessimism, I not only survived but was offered a position as an operative, i.e., spy. The arrangement required that I spend the summer between junior and senior year in an undisclosed location and subsequently commit to a ten-year tour of duty. In exchange, the federal government would pay for my last year of college. At the time, I had just started dating my first serious boyfriend and decided that I did not want to spend my last summer of college holed up in a random Xerox plant somewhere in middle Virginia. I would much prefer hanging out in DC, drinking beer, and dancing to the Violent Femmes.

While I was soaking up the DC experience, Dad, now fifty-nine, changed jobs once again. He would later sum up his exit from the previous job as a mutual parting of the ways. "I told him I quit just as he told me I was fired." That terse recounting of the event made me uneasy, but I didn't dwell on it. Fortunately, Dad quickly landed a new job as a training specialist for a large bank, a position he really liked. For some reason, though, the powers that be required him to shave his goatee. There would ultimately be other chafing aspects of this position, but Dad managed to successfully ride them out until he retired.

Meanwhile, my initial aspiration of becoming a diplomat had fizzled shortly after my arrival in DC. Who could have imagined such a career would require political connections? With the end of my college days in sight and having turned down an opportunity with the CIA, I was increasingly unsettled about the prospect of finding a job. In my final semester, I again shifted my focus, this time toward public relations. The hit show *Thirtysomething*, about a couple of friends in advertising, captured my imagination much more than the drudgery of foreign service.

Despite sending out lots of applications and expending what seemed like all the effort I had, the day arrived when I had to move out of the dorm, pack up everything I owned, and return home to my old bedroom in the house on the corner of Paradise and Scenic. After a year and a half of flying high through all that college in Washington had to offer, and imagining all sorts of exciting futures for myself, the crash hit hard and fast.

Because I'd graduated at the end of the fall semester, I arrived home in time for another glittery Christmas, and for a short time my personal misery was pushed aside as I focused on helping Mum make it a smashing success. After the family gift exchange concluded, Dad left the room for a minute. He returned and shyly handed me a clumsily wrapped package. It was a book entitled *Creative Careers: Real Jobs in Glamour Fields*. The tag read, *"To My Dearest Gill (Girl) May all your dreams come true, From your Dad with Xmas Love XXXOOO"*

He, more than anyone, knew my soul and was rooting for me.

I kept this book over the years, despite landing in a distinctly uncreative career. One day, I pulled it out of one of the built-in bookcases in my cozy bungalow. I wanted to make sure to show it to Dad on one of my next visits. As I paged through it, I spotted two pages of yellow legal pad tucked inside the back cover. My heart skipped a beat as I stared at the topmost line. "Muffin: On the Death of a Friend." Beneath that was written: If only I had gone back for an extra semester, I would have been far away from the sadness that has filled the house in the last weeks. It was a situation I had always hoped for with all the hope of a coward.

She gave me the best years of my life. She shared in my victories, and in defeat, when I cried, she was there – pushing a cold nose into a tear-stained face. Why, then, is it that now I must cry alone? Why did she have to leave me with a fading childhood and an uncertain future? Why can't dogs live people years – decades of them?

It was my handwriting, and yet, I had no memory of writing it. And just like that, a scab was scraped off, and the blood flowed freely.

Muffin had died just a few short weeks after Christmas. She'd been in rough shape when I had returned, and her breathing was often loud and labored. With all the selfishness of a struggling twenty-two-year-old, I banished her from my room to my parents' room one night when it was time go to bed. Within minutes, she had crawled under Mum's bed and breathed her last. The three of us—Mum, Dad, and I—huddled in a frantic, sobbing mass of grief. The next day, Dad called Scott and asked him to come over and help him take her body to the vet.

I worked through my grief by writing this essay, which ended on a hopeful note:

Pushing my tears aside, I see the once beautiful Christmas tree and remember the magic and joy of this past Christmas. And I slowly realize that, as real as the holiday snapshots of Muffin are, so is her spirit which will never leave us, as long as we remember. And the famous phrase "time heals all wounds" is with me as I think of Muffin . . . and know that soon I will not cry, but smile.

In contrast, Mum's sorrow seemed to only increase as time went by. She excoriated herself for multiple transgressions, including not taking Muffin to the vet sooner. It grew wearisome. I avoided her as much as I could, focusing my attention on my job search, writing passionate letters to my boyfriend, and trying to imagine a future that looked anything but bleak. After scoring an interview for a flight attendant job with Pan Am and being rejected because of my weight, I threw myself into a diet and exercise program.

Eventually, I could no longer tolerate this state of limbo. I consulted with my friends and colleagues back in Washington and decided that my best chance of success was back where I knew people and had connections, rather than in my small hometown, where I had not lived for any extended period since high school. Once I figured out a place to stay, I announced my intentions. As per usual, Dad was supportive and Mum was devastated, expressing tearful outbursts and fearful predictions. But I remained steadfast in my plan, and in the early spring of 1988, I moved back to DC.

I hadn't been back in Washington a week when a package arrived from Wisconsin. Inside was a cassette tape and a couple of other items. Dad had sent me a verbal letter, just like we used to do with Nana when I was a child.

Now, as I reflect on this time in my own life, a sense of urgency comes over me. I need to find that tape. It isn't in any of the boxes in the basement. Fighting off a sense of panic, I wrack my brain, trying to think of where I would have put it. I open a drawer in which I have stored old cassette tapes. Success!

It is simply marked *Deb's tape.* I still have a dual cassette deck, a relic from the 1980s. Trembling slightly, I insert the cassette. In an instant, Dad's voice, strong and cheerful, emerges from the speaker. He greets me with the same nickname he used for his beloved sister Ann:

Well, hi there, Babes!

I just thought I'd do a little tape to you today. It's Sunday, of course. And I know that you won't be able to record back right away because that means you'll have to get your setup—your stereo setup—put together and all, but I thought at least you could play this on your Walkman and you could hear this little letter on its way. So, that's why I'm doing it.

Also, I just happened to find a thirtyminute cassette that was just banging around and had nothing on it. So, I thought this was one that we can use to go back and forth to you there in Washington.

I'm looking at your face right now. I'm looking across over the top of the sofa here over by the electric clock there, you know, and I see your smiling face. So, it's just going to be hard to get along without you for a while, but we'll do the best we can.

So, yesterday, I got home about five, and so I had a little visit with Mom, and of course, she was all in tears, and so on and so forth, and Scott and Debbie, and Debbie and Scott, and what's going to happen, and how are we going to do this, and on and on. Anyway, I tried to get her kind of shaped up and everything.

Whether I recognized it at the time, I'll never know, but I see it now—Dad's role in keeping Mum "shaped up."

So, we had—we had our nice Saturday evening doings, and I—I brought home a couple small little steaks and cooked them up on the charcoal out on the back porch.

And so, I thought, let's get this going while it's on my mind, and I can get it done, and get it back to you so that you'll have it there, and it'll be all ready to go for you to report back to us all of the exciting things that are happening to you, which are going to happen. And there's no doubt about it in my mind. I just—I don't know. I have great feelings of—of course, I've had them all my life, but they even seem to be stronger now some way. I think this is going to be a real good year for all of us.

Through the letters from 1951-52, I have proof of my father's wonderful, optimistic attitude. Hearing him acknowledge this is a gift I will always cherish.

I'm very optimistic about this coming year, about the future. I feel very good about my job and my situation, and I feel that at least having a steady income gives me a base. I'm still keeping my eyes open, and if some kind of an enterprise presents itself that has very little or no risk connected to it, and I can make a little extra money, I want to do that. I'll be able to take off on a Saturday or maybe a Sunday, and do just a one-day seminar in something or other, either dealing with real estate or selling or something like that, because I have all of this background and all these materials now that I could probably do it.

And it's just a question of finding what—what sources or what people need to have that done, and connecting up with them, because that's—you know, I could augment my income, and that will make things better for everybody.

I think that's going to work out well for me. I'm not sure about Mom. As far as Mom is concerned, why, you know, that's kind of status quo. We're just going to have to hang in there and keep her—stop thinking about how bad everything has been and how awful things are going to be in the future, because the things were bad in the past, and they'll continue, and all that. So, I have to keep working on her to keep forgetting about all that.

The kindness in Dad's voice chokes me up. While I only knew how to avoid Mum's histrionics, he leaned in and made it his mission to care for her. That said, I now can see, whether he intended to or not, in 1988 he promoted me to family copilot. After all, he had been thrust into a similar position when Papa stepped away from his position as captain of the family ship. While I spent my twenties running away from this role, it ultimately caught up with me when my parents moved to Minnesota. Now I wonder if this is a responsibility that I must forever accept.

I think you have a very bright future ahead of you. I—every time I think about the resume and those letters of reference and your positive attitude, I think you've inherited at least some of that from me. And I think you're so right to get back there and retain these connections that you have with these various people.

And there's no question about it. The opportunities, I think, for what you want to do are at least started there in Washington. And through other contacts, and so forth, we should be able to—you should be able to connect up with other possibilities or opportunities in maybe New York or Boston. I don't know. New York is—I would put that last on my list, because the living in New York, I—and speaking from experience here—is really . . . well, it's not the best.

As I listen to Dad's take on my big move, I'm reminded of how Papa was able to get behind his eldest son's theatrical aspirations. Had he hoped Dad would have followed him into medicine? If so, his letters never betrayed it.

But I was just thinking the other day about contacting Uncle Lee. And—maybe I'll do that. I'm even thinking about doing that today—to contact Uncle Lee and Auntie Dear. They're out in Los Gatos right now, and I should ask Uncle Lee the name of that law firm that he—after he retired, they asked him to come to this Washington law firm to, you know, do a couple of cases or take over for somebody who it—was either sick or they had—were on some kind of sabbatical or leave of absence or something.

That was—and you know Uncle Lee, he would be—he would only be with the top law firms. But he might have some connections yet around Washington. I might give him a call today, and if I do, I'll send the name and address right along in the envelope of whoever it is that he thinks you might contact there in Washington.

Dad knew the value of connections. For himself and for me.

So I guess the theme of this tape today is optimism and bright future. These are just kind of some of my thoughts as I was sitting here and looking out, and I see the sunshine, and I think this time of year is one that is very conducive to optimism because you've just come through the winter months when the sun is at its lowest ebb, and the days are the shortest, and now we're gradually seeing the days getting a little bit longer, and the sun seems a little brighter and warmer because the angle is getting better, and that sort of stuff.

I think I can see why people were sun worshippers in ancient times because, you know, with their lack of education and knowledge and everything, why, they—I guess they figured that every year, why, this might be the last time they'd ever see the sun. It starts disappearing there, you know, in the short days of December, and then along about this time of the year, they can really see that the sun has—is becoming more and more prominent, and their days are getting longer, and the days are getting warmer, and it just gives you a lot of hope, I think. At least, that's my—that's my impression. That's my idea.

But I'm looking forward to a real good year. And I think I'm going to have a good year. I think you're going to have a good year. Mom will have a good year if she decides to have a good year or if I can talk her into it. And Scott, I think, is going to have a good year if I can just keep him on the even keel, or if I can encourage him to keep himself on the even keel.

Dad seemed to have the parenting thing down. Guiding his offspring without controlling us.

You know how it is when you set goals. It—first of all, you got to set the goal to begin with, and then, you got to try to participate or activate those things that are going to get you to where you want to go. So, I've got to keep my eyes open and keep my feelers out for additional income opportunities to make that trip to Florida a real possibility, a real eventuality.

Well, what do you know? I think I'm almost to the end of the tape.

But I'm kind of running out of gas as far as whatever to talk to you about anyway, because as you can tell, it was just sort of a stream-of-consciousness rambling along here with . . . I try to have a theme. Now, the theme was optimism, and you know, there's a general theme there. But kind of a little too much digression for a real—a real organized presentation here, I understand.

So, I'm going to be winding things up here and wishing you the very best and all our love and so forth and so on. And we'll hope that each day brings a little more—you a little more closer to what you want to do and so forth and so on.

And so that's about all for now, folks. So, we're going to say "byebye" and love to my dear sweet Gi'l, and "byebye" for now.

As I listen to this tape, a warmth settles over me, like when the sun comes out after a storm. Even though he had no idea how the future would unfold for any of us, Dad chose an attitude of optimism. He understood each of us so well. He was so much more than a breadwinner. He responded to the emotional needs of his wife and children in a way I may not have appreciated until now. As I wrote in his birthday card, everything I attained in my life, I owed to him.

His words echo in my mind long after I finish listening to the tape. "And your positive attitude, I think you've inherited at least some of that from me," he'd said. Indeed. I need Dad to hear this. He's nearing the finish line. Mum has already consigned him to a last chapter that has been defined, as all the others before, by a failure to meet her expectations. Unlike ancestors who accomplished big and important things, Dad spent much of his adult life simply loving and caring for his family as best he could. He'd learned that from his father, my grandfather. And that very love propelled me to a life of my own that has been nothing short of spectacular. It was, as William Wordsworth said, "the best portion of a good man's life: his little, nameless unremembered acts of kindness and love."

The next time I visit Mum and Dad, I bring the recording, which I've now had converted to a CD. Unsurprisingly, Mum has no interest in listening to it. "I want to live in the present," she spits out, before stomping off. Within minutes, we hear the roar of the vacuum. It's just as well. She has no idea what the present means for Dad.

I hit *Play*.

When Dad's voice signs off at the end of the recording, I take his hand in mine. "Thank you for everything," I say, gently. "I know how much you've cared for Mum—for all of us—all these years."

He smiles. "It was like second nature."

PART SEVEN

"You cannot swim for new horizons until you have courage to lose sight of the shore."

William Faulkner

CHAPTER 31

Then: March 1952

By the end of March 1952, Papa was in the home stretch of his program and eager to share what he had learned with his eldest son:

March 30, 1952

Dear Ralph:

I just came from seeing the Eddy Cantor show on the Hospital T.V. set. The institution has a number of these machines scattered around at suitable places. They are so useful to take up the evening time. Perhaps you did not know it but there are shell shocked patients here and others of a similar nature. It is hard to keep them occupied and also entertained. The Hospital ward where I am now stationed for work and lodged for board and room has a T.V. that is on nearly every night. Other sets are shared etc.

"Shell shocked." The phrase brings me up short. I realize suddenly that Papa was at the narcotic farm during the Korean War. World War II had ended just seven years earlier. He likely encountered veterans of both wars who had succumbed to narcotics as a means of self-medicating their PTSD. Here we are, seventy years later and not much progress has been made on this front.

Your letter about your trip to New York was very interesting. I am glad that you are able to see Mr. Hammerstein once in a while. Knowing so little about him I want to know more. What little I have heard sounds like he is a good and remarkable man. I have cut the lyrics that he has written out of the Cosmopolitan Magazine. Of course, they are not all the lyrics that he has written but a group of his better ones. I will have them at home when you come, if you would be interested in having them.

Papa was not like most doctors I've encountered. I don't know if it's a generational thing, but many medical professionals heavily self-promote, even as they attend to my health concerns. My orthopedic surgeon preferred to tout his own success rate rather than respond directly to my questions and concerns. Maybe it was to hide insecurity. Papa, on the other hand, seemed quite secure in acknowledging what he didn't know. He craved knowledge—interested and curious—especially about things beyond his own expertise, like Oscar Hammerstein's lyrics.

A consistent feature of my conversations with Dad is his interest in and curiosity about *me*—what I'm doing; how my dogs are; how my iPhone works. Although he's been that way my entire life, I can see now why he'd much rather talk about anything besides himself and his worsening health.

I will precede you by a few days. I am not stating any certain date of arrival but it will be close to the first of May. This is quite definite because things are shaping up nicely. I am getting my feet under me in good shape. I am changing the address on my Post Subscription so that it will send the May issues to San Diego.

"I am getting my feet under me in good shape." Papa, always patient, was also hopeful and proactive.

This past week has been especially interesting and informative to me. A Dr. Isbell from the USPHSH at Lexington Ky. was here on a visit of inspection and instruction. I was allowed to attend several of the sessions that he conducted. This made me feel as if I was still in the medical profession. Although I have come to know a good deal about this drug problem, he was able to unify and crystalize these ideas so that they will be better remembered. He was the one to whom I wrote a way back in August. I had read an article by him in one of these pocket medical journals. It so impressed me that I began to worry about my problem and whether I was not overlooking a very serious situation. I wrote to him and explained it to him. He did not answer me directly but turned it over to someone else to tell me that such problems could not be taken care of on the outside and be supervised by the Public Health Service. Also was enclosed an application for admission as the answer to my question as to what should be done.

This was the second time Papa had shared his insights about his own condition, his reasons for contacting Dr. Isbell, and ultimately admitting himself to the narcotic farm in Fort Worth. He'd first shared them with Nana and the rest of the family, but he now took the time to repeat them for Dad's benefit. Not all of us can look inward, identify a problem, and follow signs from the universe to fix that problem. I'm good at identifying problems; it's the looking inward part and surrendering to the universe that I struggle with.

I thought that I could straighten myself up by the first of November when I was re-entering practice in San Diego. When November First came, I was no better off. In fact, I was worse off. I struggled through November and even made a good record. When December started, I knew that I did not want to continue that way. I have never regretted coming here. There have been rough times. Adaptation for an old man like me is a problem. On top of it all is the sickness, which Dr. Isbell so aptly reviewed for us. Some of my sickness was already gone or underway to go before I came here.

"Rough times." A rather vague description and I'm dying to know more. But Papa's "adaptation" was the very thing the doctor from the *New York Times* article was unable to accomplish. Even though he claimed to get through the detox/withdrawal aspect, he could not, for some reason, get beyond the fact that he was being housed with criminals—men very different in upbringing and personality from himself. As a result, he up and quit. Papa, on the other hand, hung in there and embraced the experience as an opportunity to learn.

Being in Scripps Hosp. for the four days under the same type of treatment as is carried on here did help, but the sickness is a lasting thing with "D" and hangs on and hangs on. It was just about 60 days before I could say that I felt normal again. Sleeplessness, asthma, aching (not bad, but a nag), what appeared to be a sinus infection but probably was part of the "getting it over with." This is a letter that I want to have for my files because I have tried to describe a few things, so keep it or send it home for later filing.

Bravo, Papa, for recognizing just how dire things had become! And bravo, Dad, and Nana and everyone else, for gathering these letters previously scattered across the country and placing them carefully in the file folder. They could never have imagined what a wonderful guide they would provide for the next generation of Russells.

Week after next, Dr. Lewis, the surgeon in charge will be back "on the ball" and there are a number of cases coming up for surgery. This will mean a busy and interesting time, although the cases are not too major. There may be some chest surgery and brain surgery with outside help scheduled and done before I leave.

I hope that this finds you well and that you will be able to finish_up your work with no unfinished business. You probably have been too busy to keep up the notebook that I am always talking about.

Lots of love and I think so much
of you and about you,
Daddy

In his 1953 article, M.J. Pescor opined that "since most addicts have some sort of personality disorder, it follows that the basic attack on the problem of addiction is to prevent the development of such disorders. It is the current belief that most of these result from frustrated drives for security, recognition, and affection, particularly during childhood."*

The dearth of photos and writings about Papa as a child leave me with the impression that he may not have received sufficient security, recognition, and affection, specifically from his own father, Calvin. That notwithstanding, he excelled in school, went on to receive his medical degree, worked as a staff surgeon at the Mayo Clinic, opened his own hospital in Sutherland, Nebraska, and continued his work as a physician in San Diego and Blythe, California.

In other words, he was an overachiever.

---

* Pescor, *supra*. at 471.

I can totally relate.

Somewhere along the line, though, stress made his asthma worse, and he found something to relieve both.

Pescor further explained:

> There is one group of addicts who rationalize their addiction on the basis of seeking relief for physical discomfort which may range from extreme pain to a state of fatigue. On the face of it this seems to be a substantial excuse. Nevertheless, there are very few individuals who have a painful disease necessitating the continuous administration of narcotic drugs, outside of terminal cases of cancer. The majority of medically addicted individuals find the drug supplies something that has been missing from their lives, so that even when the original physical cause for addiction has been removed and the patients withdrawn from drugs, they relapse in order to "feel normal."*

As it turned out, the spring of 1952 would be pivotal for Papa, Nana, and the rest of the family. They would come to attempt a "new" normal, one that did not include Papa self-medicating with Demerol and morphine.

As Dad noted in his 1988 cassette letter to me, spring is the time for hope and optimism. He wrote back to Papa almost immediately, despite being very busy with his three pursuits:

April 4, 1952

Dearest Dad:

Well, here it is a wonderful spring day in Boston and made more wonderful still by your letter. I am doubly

---

* Id at 479

appreciative when I hear from you because I realize the limitations of your letter writing.

I am about to embark on a weekend of term paper writing. I am beginning it by writing to you in hopes that I can loosen up a little in my writing style and also try to achieve some efficiency in my typing.

Since I wrote you last, I have been engaged in several pursuits: some academic, some which would be classified as "practical experience," and some I guess I would call pleasureful recreation. In the academic field I have been doing a good deal of research into the field of "Problems and Techniques Involved in Teaching Acting." This is the title of my research paper for my Advanced Theatre seminar course. It is proving to be most enlightening and I am getting a lot of satisfaction out of clarifying my own philosophy and thinking on the subject.

A sort of shame creeps in as I consider my own college career, especially when I was at George Washington. Aside from a passing interest in international law and an all-too-late expressed desire to go into advertising, I barely thought about what I was studying beyond what I needed to do to get a good grade. I never took a philosophy class and would be hard-pressed to even understand the philosophy of what I was studying. College was a means to an end that, as it turns out, had not been well-defined from the start.

In the line of "practical theatre experience," we did a performance of "Raggedy Ann and Andy" at the local Childrens' Hospital. It was quite a rewarding experience, in spite of all the obstacles we had to surmount. I am also looking forward to the 27the of this month at which time I will be doing a bit part in the Metropolitan Opera Company's production of "La boheme" when it comes to Boston. Of course, our own school production of Romeo and Juliet is now in rehearsal and we have been notified that on the 7th of May, Mr. Hammerstein and other dignitaries will attend the performance. I am given to understand that there will be "great expectations" in store for all if things go well.

I am forwarding your letter on with a letter that I am writing Mother. I can't wait 'til we will all be home together again. 'Til then I send all my love.

Ralph Jr.

On the back, Dad also scrawled in pencil:

P.S. I have found in my research on acting, that performers are never usually very prolificate writers. Perhaps this accounts for my laxness in keeping up with my "notebook." However, I think when I write my memoirs, my vivid memory will serve me as it did my remarkable Grandad.

RSR Jr.

Dad never wrote his memoir. Instead, he devoted most of his adult life to caring for an unstable wife and two precocious and creative children. It was not the life of his grandfather, Calvin Parker Russell, nor was it the life of his great-uncle Howard Hyde Russell. Nonetheless, it was a life well-lived.

Now, as I watch it slip away, I'm overwhelmed by a need to preserve its legacy. But the further I've gotten in this endeavor, the more I see how, in the process of capturing Dad's life, I've also shone a light on my own.

CHAPTER 32

Now: October 2017

"What does retirement look like to you?" inquires Steve, my recently retained financial advisor.

I smile broadly as I sit in the small conference room with a large window on one wall and an equally substantial TV screen depicting charts and graphs on another. It hasn't even been two weeks since the debacle in Jennifer's office left me unmoored once again, yet I've managed to pick myself up and resume paddling. As time marches on, I can only march along with it, even if some days, it's more like a belly crawl.

I once described my life to Jennifer as being like a pie chart, with each piece depicting some aspect of my existence. This metaphorical pie is divided among my friends, work, my dogs, the care and maintenance of my bungalow, and the game of Whack-a-Mole relating to family crises. Now that I've crossed fifty-two, the family piece is threatening to become the entire pie. Not French silk pie, either. More like mincemeat. Repressed anger, built up from clinging to unrealistic ideas about how life and family dynamics should be, has revealed itself as debilitating back pain.

Midlife arrives in multiple ways, but it always seems to bring with it a moment of reckoning. Papa's moment arrived at age fifty-one when he admitted he needed to jettison an unrealistic notion that he could manage his dependence on Demerol without professional help. Now, as I step back from the tragedy that I've built up in my mind, I'm focusing on the off-ramps popping up. I'm also pivoting toward the people who can propel me forward, rather than hold me back.

I once read a book by Richard Wiseman called *The Luck Factor* and learned that "lucky" people simply recognize opportunities and possess the courage to take advantage of them. Dad understood the "luck factor" and presented it to me in the 1988 cassette when I was twenty-two and had no idea what lay before me. "I'm very optimistic about this coming year, about the future," he'd said in that long-ago talking letter. "I'm still keeping my eyes open, and if some kind of an enterprise presents itself that has very little or no risk connected to it, and I can make a little extra money, I want to do that."

Four months into my new position as a real estate/condemnation lawyer for the county, I was presented with an opportunity to attend a conference, which happened to be held at a resort on a lake a mere two-hour drive away. Attending would require that I board all three dogs. Fortunately, another trainer and good friend owned a boarding kennel, and it was right on the way to the conference.

Walking through the door on my return to pick them up, I ran into a vaguely familiar face. Steve was a friend of a friend, and I'd met him once or twice over the past decade. He also happened to be a financial planner. Several years earlier, while on a dog training trip, my friend had encouraged me to reach out to him. She'd been retired for a while, and Steve had mapped it all out for her. Plus, he was a fellow dog owner/trainer, so he would totally understand my lifestyle choices. It's hard to imagine that a lot of planners would. It's a bit out of the ordinary.

Despite my friend's urging, I still hadn't put forth the effort to track him down and find out what he could do for me. But for over twenty years, I'd been stashing close to half my earned income into a retirement account. As a government employee, I could access that account when I took early retirement at fifty-five to supplement the greatly reduced pension I'd be getting. So far as I could tell, my investment strategy was on the right track. I checked out some sort of retirement calculator when I was forty, and I seemed to be close to my target. Now, fate had plunked Steve right in my path.

"Steve?" I asked, a bit tentatively. It had been ten years or so since I last saw him. Thankfully, my memory was correct, and he turned toward me at the sound of his name. "You probably don't remember me. I'm Debbie, a friend of Marie's."

"Oh yes!" He smiled. I couldn't tell whether he actually remembered me or was simply being polite.

"Marie's been encouraging me to get ahold of you. I'm pretty close to retirement, and I think it's time to bring in a professional. She wasn't sure if you were taking on new clients."

"Oh, she has, has she?" He grinned. "I'll tell you what—" He trailed off as he fumbled around in his wallet for a business card. "None of this is current except the email address. Shoot me an email and let me know what you're planning to do and when you're planning to do it. I may be able to take a look at your situation."

Score! The next day, I sent him an email, basically asking him to look at my investments and tell me if I could retire in three years. It seemed like a straightforward request.

His response surprised me:

If you want a comprehensive look at your scenario, I can provide that service. If you are wanting investment advice only, then, as much as I'd like to work with you, I'm afraid I'm going to have to refer you elsewhere because I don't look at investments without coordinating it with your other financial areas.

Huh. Apparently, there was a bit more to it than just getting the rubber-stamp of approval I was hoping for.

I wrote back that, *yes*, I wanted it all!

His next response was even more daunting:

Hi Debbie,
To proceed, I will have my associate work with you via email to get an initial meeting scheduled. We will discuss the process and get clarification of your financial dreams and goals. In order to make the best use of our time together, I will ask you to bring the following to the meeting.
2015 and 2016 Tax returns
Copy of last two paystubs
Company benefits statement for current benefits and retiree benefits
Most recent statements for your investments
Copy of your Social Security statement detailing expected benefits
Copy of your PERA statement detailing expected benefits
Copy of MN Deferred comp current balance and payouts
Value of house
Mortgage statement
Balances of any liabilities and the terms (e.g., car loan at 2% interest, payment of $200/m, payoff date July 2017)
Copy of Estate documents if you have them (Will, Power of Attorney, Health Care Directive, Trusts, etc.)
I will also have a budget work sheet sent to you. Please complete this using your expected expenses in retirement.
Steve

Good grief.

For a second, I hesitated. It was all very overwhelming. Maybe this could wait until I'd regained my sea legs. After all, the one-year anniversary of Dad's initial hospice meeting was coming up at the end of the month. I was still weary from being buffeted between joy and sorrow, calm and chaos. As I mulled this all over, Dad's words from 1988 popped into my head: *"First of all, you've got to set the goal to begin with, and then you've got to try to participate or activate those things that are going to get you to where you want to go."*

Steve was ready to help me with my financial dreams and goals *now*. I owed it to myself to participate in the process on the schedule that was presented. I dutifully gathered all the requested information and filled out the budget worksheet.

It's all getting real.

Now, as I face him across the table at our initial appointment, I'm more than prepared for his inquiry, "What does retirement look like to you?"

At long last, I get to say out loud the dream I've had for almost fifteen years. "After I'm retired, I want to move out to the country. If I can find a place about an hour out of the cities, that would be ideal."

His eyes twinkle. "I think you should consider selling and moving now."

That's a hard no. I'm adamant.

"I could never do the commute."

"It's only for a couple of years. The market is hot right now. We don't know how long that will last."

We don't know how long that will last. Isn't that true with everything?

Papa never got a retirement, having succumbed at fifty-nine to asthma, exacerbated by working too hard. Dad's retirement was controlled entirely by Mum. When they first moved to Minneapolis, he was eager to join a barbershop chorus. Dad adored barbershop music, a very specific type of vocal a cappella close harmony. His favorite part of our trips to Disney World was hearing the Main Street "Dapper Dans" barbershop quartet belt out old-timey tunes from the '30s and '40s. Mum wouldn't let him, claiming they didn't have the money. Or, at least, not the money for *that.*

On the way home from my meeting with Steve, my mind starts racing as I contemplate how I might pull this off. My future is coming into view.

Time to own it.

CHAPTER 33

Then: April 1952

April 4, 1952

Dearest and All:

A Friday and a Monday letter to answer since my second letter last week went to Buddy and probably has not got to you via Boston. He will probably send it on to you. Now to answer some of the questions in the letters.

I have been promised some suntan treatments as my time gets short so that I will not look so ghastly ghostly. Weight up to 173. Several here have been commenting on it and say that 180 is the limit.

I will see Dr. Osberg tomorrow and for the three successive Fridays for an hour each time. He knows the most about my intimate affairs and will be the one to help me the most until I get home. Then he has suggested a psychiatrist be contacted there. Don't let this alarm you. I asked him if he would suggest anyone that might help me to visit with to help reestablish myself in practice and in society. I thought that I might want an attorney friend or a minister. Dr. Osberg, being a psychiatrist, would suggest one, I guess. I have forgotten the name of the Dr. in La Jolla who saw me only once and agreed that I should come this way. Dr. Warner had his crack at me and said that I knew as much as he did, so he sort of passed me over at a time when something might have helped me. Maybe he felt too close to me to act as a supervisor.

These snippets hint that there was more to the story:

"I have forgotten the name of the Dr. in La Jolla who saw me only once and agreed that I should come this way." When did Papa see this doctor? What was discussed? Ultimately, it doesn't matter. Papa's feelings about his condition were validated by another professional and propelled him forward. Similarly, as I move forward with my plans, instead of allowing my mind to be filled with doubt and discouragement, I must honor this legacy of hope and optimism from my grandfather.

I am so glad that you are feeling good. I wish that when the telephone man was there, he had put in a switch that we can turn at night and cut off calls. When I get back, I am going to be very selfish and make my life revolve around my home instead of the practice. I am going to suggest a few things to Dr. Osberg about a schedule of work for me, when I return, that is.

Taking responsibility for his own life, Papa spelled out in writing the changes he wanted to make. He could finally see how his commitment to his work had interfered with the rest of his life and, most importantly, his health. I linger over his choice of the word "selfish." For much of my adult life, my mother embedded in me the notion that unless my world revolves around her, I am selfish. Despite blazing my own trails, making my own friends and serving crime victims in my professional life, the nagging feeling of guilt—the idea that I'm not doing enough—is always with me. Papa was the same. His practice and his patients took priority and compromised his health—physically, mentally and emotionally.

I appreciate that you are willing to have me stay longer, however I feel that when the minimum time is up that I will have received the benefit that I have needed.

And that further time will make my "rehabilitation" only more complex. I would rather come home and start in more slowly with office hours and hospital rounds to fill in the time when you will not be home. After my next Friday hour with Dr. Osberg, I may be able to tell you what he thinks I should do about beginning.

I am beginning to count the days.

All my love to my little family,
Daddy

For four months, Papa was forced to unlearn a routine he had spent years building and shaping. It was a routine that depended strongly on narcotics. He would never be cured of his asthma, but he now had tools with which to manage it. If he were to be successful back home, he would need to adhere to all that he had learned in the narcotic farm.

As Jennifer observed before we had to part ways, I'd always put my parents and brother ahead of myself. The hero cape became increasingly heavier with time, but it was a weight I had placed on myself. My need to micromanage was my version of Demerol. It made me feel worthy of being loved by my mother, which was the high I was always chasing. In the end, just like Papa's, it was unsustainable.

Perhaps, as I start focusing more on myself and my life, I can leave the hero cape in the closet, where it belongs.

CHAPTER 34

Now: November 2017

CLINIC NOTE: Debbie reports feeling "stuck." She used to feel strong and confident and now she feels "vulnerable." She shared how she met with her financial planner who gave her the green light to retire in three and a half years. Debbie was wondering about whether to tell her parents this news.

◆ ◆ ◆

That's right; I'm back in therapy. Despite my very best efforts, my life is still too heavy for me to lift on my own. This time, I roll the dice in search of someone who specializes in grief. Grief seems to be the one thing I cannot manage, despite all the exciting things happening. My oldest dog Casey—the one who started me down the road of advanced dog training, the one who opened my world to countless wonderful friends and mentors, the one who we dog owners and lovers refer to as the "heart dog"—has developed yet another cancerous tumor in her lung. She's eleven, and I won't put her through a second lung lobectomy and chemotherapy. It wouldn't be fair to her.

It's now been a year since Dad entered the hospice program. At the conclusion of yet another excruciating meeting where I focus on not saying the wrong thing, I use the excuse of a work meeting to leave immediately, walking out with the staff.

"We've never had a hospice patient in the program this long," Andrea remarks as we make our way out to our cars.

"I think he's hanging on for my mom." I don't think it; I know it.

I spend the next several weeks pinballing. The highs of envisioning and planning an exciting, yet also distant and fuzzy future crash hard against the lows of a much more immediate future. This future feels dismal at best, devastating at worst.

The relentless return of the holidays, coupled with the recognition that I'm barely treading water, is the final impetus that propels me into therapist number two's office. While Thanksgiving came and went with no bigger dilemma than whether Dad was going to have enough strength to leave his recliner and eat dinner at the dining room table, the familiar feeling of holiday distress still punched me in the face. Hard.

Dad struggled with his food. I stuck to topics that wouldn't stress anyone out, carefully avoiding any mention of my little property visit the previous day. Using Realtor.com, I'd found what appeared to be the perfect little house sitting on ten acres, with lake access. Realtor.com is a lot like Match.com, in that appearances can be deceiving. I learned this the hard way after driving two hours round-trip to see the property. Despite it being a bust, the adventure itself exhilarated me. Over Thanksgiving dinner, though, I kept it to myself. Instead, I babbled on about Watson and my job. I couldn't bear to talk about Casey's condition, either.

Now, I shake off the feeling of being a big failure as I climb the stairs to Colleen's office. It's located on the second floor of a dated building with worn carpeting and a musty odor in the lobby. Thankfully, she immediately feels like a better fit than Jennifer. Maybe it's because she appears to be around my age. She wears a fuzzy sweater with a festive scarf. Our rapport is instantaneous. She feels authentic. Or maybe I'm just craving authenticity.

After a couple of sessions, she imparts some devastatingly practical information as we explore my relationship with Mum:

"Assuming your mom has BPD, her emotional maturity is that of a toddler. You're never going to get what you need from her, as she simply doesn't have the capacity to provide it."

What was that quote about the definition of insanity, again?

Looking back at the past year, I'm able to see that nothing much has changed—except we're all one year closer to death. And in Dad's case, its imminence has worn me down more than I've cared to admit. If I look at my life as separate from that of my parents, I see how change is coming at me like a tidal wave. I've reached the point where I either must jump on for the ride or risk being sucked under.

At our post-Thanksgiving therapy session, I share my conundrum. "I've started looking at land where I might build a house," I confess. "I'm afraid to tell my parents about this."

Afraid to tell my parents. How pathetic. But I know that Mum will view any effort on my part to forge my own path as an abandonment. I'm preemptively feeling guilty. And selfish.

Colleen doesn't hesitate. "I think you should tell them. How your mother reacts is not your concern."

So simply put, yet her response has a profound impact on me. Living my own life is not an abandonment of anybody, even if those others happen to be my own parents. I'm now fifty-two years old, damn it. It's way past time for me to muster up a bit more pluck in this regard.

The next time I'm at their place, I shyly pull out some photos I printed out.

"So . . . I've started looking at land."

Mum gasps. The shock on her face is undeniable.

I take another breath and plunge in, starting with financial adviser Steve's recommendation that I sell my city house while the market is hot. "If I'm going to sell it, I need to have somewhere to go, so I'm trying to figure out what kind of property would work. I really want to be out in the country. Right now, it may be cheaper to buy land and build."

"Boy, I always thought you were a city girl," Mum exclaims.

The voice in my head responds with what I dare not speak aloud. *No, Mum, you're the city girl. You insisted on moving from Paradise and Scenic because you wanted the excitement and stimulation of city living. I only live in the city so I can be close to work. And I've had enough. I've longed to return to the peace, quiet, and wonderment of the country for a very long time now.*

Dad's eyes widen with interest. "Maybe I could go with you when you're looking," he says.

I'm incredulous. He hasn't left the house in over six months.

"Is he delusional?" I ask Colleen at our next session.

"More like optimistic."

A jolt runs through me at her choice of words. There's that Russell optimism again. Time to grab on and let it take the wheel.

CHAPTER 35

Then: April 1952

April 15, 1952

Precescious and All:

Your nice Easter card came and cheered me up like everything. And the pictures were so thoughtful. Do you know where I put the little one?? Well, I wanted to carry it with me, but I did not want to lose it, so I put it into the little cellophane envelope that my picture pass is held in. Now whenever I go outside, I show the security man my picture and my daughter's at the same time. They say that she is a good-looking child. Or rather – girl. Today I flashed the pass several times because after receiving mother's letter with the checks, I was allowed to buy an air mail envelope to send the checks back and the censor kindly said that I might include this letter.

Papa never allowed his ego to impede his ability to tolerate his surroundings, tough as they may be. As I read his letter, I can't help but continue to contrast his experience with that of the New York doctor who simply could not accept being treated like an inmate. Papa's resilience, evident as early as when he was undergoing detox, was even more obvious now that he was in the home stretch.

He portrayed the censor and the security guard in a manner likely to make it easier for Auntie Ann to read about such things. He minimized any details that might highlight the prison-type atmosphere he inhabited. Whether he did that for his own state of mind or to protect his daughter from a grim experience, it served them both well. Auntie Ann verified for me that she never worried about Papa. His letters, always cheerful and to the point, didn't allow for those reading them to worry.

I then had to go two blocks to the canteen then to the occupational physiotherapy. Miss Sims wanted me to get a little cloth for a little project that she wants me to finish before I leave. Then I came back two blocks through the sunshine to deliver the envelope then back again to begin the project. I hope that you will like it.

I have been real busy today. I had four dressings to do before surgery at nine. Dr. Lewis did a gallbladder operation and I helped him. This took until noon. I was late for dinner, but the kitchen chief saved me a tray. I laid down for a short while and then took care of the checks. Came back to the ward and did a few more dressings. This evening I played chess with a chap that beat me last night. I finished him off in great style tonight.

It looks like May is a good month for me to start back to practice. With Dr. Person gone in June and Dr. Martin gone in July and maybe Dr. Batterton gone sometime or other.

I am going to make a point of outdoor exercise in the sunshine. I have reduced the ACTH and the KI but it is a little hard to do. We shall see. I hope to go downtown tomorrow and purchase a suitcase to bring all my accumulated junk home.

I've been trying to do a little sketching so that I can show you a little about this place. It's pretty crude. You should see my little room. A white bedside table with a black hard rubber top, a drawer, little cupboard and a towel rack on each end. My dandy little radio, (gets all kinds of programs) sits on the table with a nice table lamp which has an octagonal dark green base and a five-sided red shade. A high hospital bed with a hard mattress. In the window are several library books. Then I have an over-bed stand that holds my chess set and board, three heavy surgical books and a couple Posts. Oh yes and a wooden hall tree on which is a blue jacket and my nice brown wool sweater. So you see it is quite cheerful. A top light and a head of the bed light also. The floors are tarries and a nice bathroom is across the hall. I take a shower almost every morning.

Now that everything is working smoothly, it's time to go home.

Lots and lots of love, Daddy

"So you see it is quite cheerful." Papa's describing a prison cell. Or maybe a dorm room. If this isn't resilience, I'm not sure what is. I've discovered another wonderful quality that Papa shared with Dad, the ability to be content—even happy—in conditions others might find completely intolerable. His serenity soared off the page, especially with his closing line, "Now that everything is working smoothly, it's time to go home." I wonder if the prospect of returning caused Papa any stress. If so, he wasn't letting on.

Dr. R. S. Russell April 18, 1952

Dearest -

Your good letter received yesterday - it sounds to me as though you are gradually finishing up there and thinking of a definite day of return. We are all agog of course wondering when you will be able to come - it will be so wonderful so let us know.

I wanted to write Dr. Osberg – but guess you've told him about the family and how we want to help in any way. Let us know the big day.

Loads and loads of love – R.
Mrs. R.S. Russell

Repeatedly, Nana expressed unwavering support for her husband. I can now understand why I initially read these letters with such skepticism. I'd never experienced it—at least on a consistent basis. Where was the anger? The resentment? I'd grown up with a mother whose primary reactions to everything came from a place of anger and resentment. When Dad was struggling financially, he unburdened himself to his younger sister, not his wife of twenty years, writing, "I am sure if she knew the whole story it would have a devastating effect on the family."

My therapy sessions with Colleen enable me to see how Dad understood and accepted Mum's deficiencies in a way we kids could not. In his role as her caretaker, he couldn't burden her with "the whole story." As a casualty of this family system, I learned at a very early age to be my own source of support as I watched Dad wither in the face of Mum's rage. But somehow, his inherited resilience carried him—and me—through the tough times. As I grew up, he showed me how to summon that resilience. I wouldn't be where I am today if not for him.

I'm guessing that's been the source of my panic all along—the notion that without him, I won't be able to function. Since I can't stop time, I need to learn how to summon this resilience all by myself.

CHAPTER 36

Now: Christmas 2017

A year to the day after I first walked into therapy, I'm preparing to say goodbye to my beloved bungalow. The tidal wave of change that began with my first visit to Steve in October had swept through and dropped my dream home into my life. This dream came into better focus each time I pulled into a vacant parcel with a For Sale sign on it. I'd get out of the car, let the dogs run around, breathe deeply, and stare up at the sky, imagining life far away from the chaos of the city. At some point, I learned that manufactured homes were cheaper than stick built. I emailed a builder to get a quote. I still had no idea how much my dream was going to cost, but I kept my imagination fluid.

Dad eagerly lapped up stories of my adventures. Mum reluctantly engaged when I asked them about their purchase of the land on Paradise and Scenic. This was a topic that we could all talk about without Mum getting upset. Thinking back to that property on a hill in the middle of a forest, I realize that it couldn't have been the easiest project for an architect.

I was aided in my own land search by a young coworker, Matt. Standing well over six feet tall and built like a linebacker, he was quick-witted, hardworking, and, most fortuitously, possessed a real estate license. He'd recently turned thirty, and one day, out of the blue, it occurred to me that he could be my son had I decided to take on actual human motherhood. When, over lunch one day, I mused aloud about looking at properties, he eagerly offered his help.

My price range significantly limited my options. Some of the properties we looked at with houses may well have been previously used as criminal hideaways. There was nothing typical about them, and they all involved a lot of driving. Matt brought his wife along for one of the showings, and afterward, we had lunch together in a dive bar in the small town where the oddly configured home/workshop was located.

"This could be your future!" he joked.

"Couldn't be any more different from the present, eh?" I laughed, trying to subdue any doubts I had about what I was doing.

A third meeting with Steve, who advised against buying property that abutted a county road unless it had a fence (dogs could get hit by cars), convinced me that acting sooner would be better than delaying. I reached out to another friend in the mortgage industry to see if I could pull any cash out of the bungalow to pay for a second property. I'd done a great job of paying down the mortgage, even with taking out money to build the screened porch, and the little bungalow's value had skyrocketed over the past few years.

The problem was, I wasn't finding anything. With Christmas coming in a couple of weeks, it seemed wise to temporarily suspend my search. After all, I had the benefit of time. I was still over two years away from retirement, and I'd been pushing myself unnecessarily. Perhaps it was simply an effort to distract myself from the permeating sense of sadness that lurked in times of inactivity. While admittedly better than narcotics, this madcap driving around and furiously researching building and financing options was getting out of hand.

Matt, for better or for worse, embraced the madcap wholeheartedly. Each day, he had a new idea. One day, he suggested that if I found a manufactured home for sale, I could buy it and move it to a parcel of land. That felt complicated, but the idea intrigued me enough that when I got home from my meeting with Steve, I jumped online and changed the search criteria in my property dating app.

As if by magic, my dream appeared right there on the computer screen in the form of a listing complete with a drone video providing a virtual tour of the property. The video had been created in the fall, showing off the vivid colors of the blazing red maples that were at their peak. It captured the experience of driving through the property along a gently winding gravel road, bordered by a swath of birch and other hardwoods. At the final turn, the woods opened to a bright clearing where the "house" came into view.

And by house, I mean a double-wide manufactured home.

Mesmerized, I watched as the video brought me up to the house and then inside, where sunlight poured through skylights and windows. I saw three bedrooms, two bathrooms, and, unlike most double-wides, a full, partially finished basement downstairs. After the virtual tour was complete, the drone ascended and flew over the house, revealing a chain-linked enclosure in the back, more trees, a creek running through the woods, and, best of all, not another house in sight.

Sitting at my computer, I felt dizzy. But a good kind of dizzy.

The property was under contingency. Heart pounding, I sent the link to Matt. *Look at this one!*

His response was terse: "You changed your criteria again."

Damn straight, I did. Make this happen!

The next day, we drove out to look at it. Even in winter, the land's beauty was undeniable. As we pulled up to the circular driveway that looped around several formidable red oaks, I could barely contain my excitement. I spotted a couple of Scottie dogs running around the back enclosure, barking their heads off. I didn't need to see anything else.

This is my home.

The interior was clean and sparsely furnished. A plate of cookies sat on the kitchen island next to a bouquet of fresh flowers and a scented candle. I took it all as a good sign; the owners wanted an offer from me! I didn't care that the toilet in the second bathroom wasn't bolted to the floor or that the master shower was water-stained. I stared out the windows at the beautiful birches nestled among giant pine trees and exhaled.

This is my home.

Departing down the driveway, over the creek, and through the swath of trees, I caught a glimpse of horses in the neighbors' corral. Tears sprang up, blurring my vision, as I left the driveway and turned onto the county road. My own Paradise and Scenic.

This is my home.

I made a cash offer. I knew only too well the dangers of becoming overly attached to a dream, but I strapped on blinders, focusing only on the things I could control while we waited for the other buyer to act on the contingency. I accelerated the refinancing of the bungalow, took out a personal loan, wrote out a check for the earnest money, and paced, attempting feebly to recite the serenity prayer.

And now, just two days before Christmas, Matt has emailed me the final executed purchase agreement. "*Congratulations and Merry Christmas!*" he writes.

I get up from the computer and walk into the living room, running my fingers along the beautiful old woodwork. I plug in the tabletop Christmas tree I purchased this year, having no desire to drag my full-sized tree up from the basement. My head throbs.

What have I just done?

I don't have the energy to share the news with Mum and Dad. Just getting through Christmas dinner takes everything I have. By the time we finish the meal Mum declared Dad could handle, he has filled two-thirds of a cereal bowl with phlegm, as he chokes on every piece of meat. It's an exercise in avoidance; Mum and me chattering on about whatever and Dad coughing up phlegm. My heart grows heavy as we clear the dishes and get Dad ready for bed. As I leave, he thanks me for my generosity. He may very well be the most selfless person I've ever known.

The next morning, I'm surprised by a call from Mum.

"Well, it's been a bit of a rough night," she begins with a false cheerfulness that soon dissolves into tears. Dad had coughed all night. At some point, Mum was able to get him into his chair, but now, there's no moving him.

"Have you called hospice?" I ask, steeling myself for her expected response.

"I just need you to help me get him to the bathroom. I had hoped it wouldn't be asking too much."

The acerbity in her voice has its desired effect and I arrive in the early afternoon. Dad struggles to articulate his words and muster the strength to stand. Mum's goal is just to get him to the bathroom, where she will change his undergarments.

I hate every second of this. About half an hour passes as Dad repeatedly tries and fails, even with our encouragement, to get himself out of his chair. Finally, Mum has made her decision. She lines up all her supplies and informs Dad that we are going to change him right here.

Donning my hero cape, I slip into cheerleader mode. "Alrighty, Dad, you can do this! We'll help you!"

After several attempts, Dad's finally able to stand. He grips his walker shakily as I cling to him, doing my best to support him. Mum peels away the numerous layers of adult diapers. As she arrives at the last layer, it's clear—Dad's had a bowel movement.

In the moment, shame creeps over me as I acknowledge that I don't have the stomach for this level of care. Perhaps that's why I was so desperate to foist hospice services on them a year ago. While I've recognized what Mum has been up against for the past year, I'd really not seen the extent of it. But before I let the guilt and shame render me helpless, I remind myself that this is her choice, not mine. And by her reaction, she seems quite used to it—chattering incessantly as I avert my eyes and try to mentally put myself out of the room.

"You would just not believe what I've had to go through with the staff and the ordering of these diapers. We were very clear that we needed the large, and wouldn't you know, there was the big carton of medium. So then, I had to make another call, and of course, they were so sorry about the mix-up and will send us another box, but now, I have this other box, and what am I going to do with it?" I don't respond.

"Are you with me?" she shouts at Dad to ascertain that he is still "with the program."

I hang onto Dad as he clings to the walker, willing him to stay upright.

And then, out of nowhere, he asks, "Is Watson still growing?" He's attempting small talk as he stands there, naked from the waist down.

"I think he might be close to all done," I reply with a smile.

CHAPTER 37

Now: January 2018

The package containing Casey's ashes is sitting on the front porch when I return from the closing on my new country estate. The drumbeat of my life continues, with every joyful event seemingly coupled with one equally painful. Right after Christmas, I broke the big news to Mum and Dad. The silence that followed seemed to last an eternity.

"Of course, we're happy for you."

The insincerity of her response was quickly revealed as Mum dissolved into tears. "I just feel so lost," she sobbed.

Dad gazed at her, his own eyes filling with tears. "I'll take care of you, Missus."

Thank goodness for Colleen. She'd given me two tasks to help me cope with this very moment—practice kindness and absolve myself of any responsibility for their feelings. Bracing myself, I showed them pictures and the awesome video, trying mightily to keep things upbeat. These efforts seemed fruitless.

"But instead of being twenty minutes away, you'll be an hour away." Dad's singular focus on the distance didn't help Mum's ability to cope with the news.

"We're in a very critical time," she said pointedly.

We? There was no *we*. There was just them and me. I wanted to scream, *"I'm in my own critical time. Can't you see that?"*

Casey's decline had been far quicker than Dad's. I came home early from work one afternoon to find her in the bathroom, panting on the cool tile. It was time. I called the in-home euthanasia vet and sat on the floor with her, memorizing the feel of her fur. As though she'd waited for me, she breathed her last before the vet arrived.

Meanwhile, email communication between Matt and the agent for the sellers of the country estate had been fast and furious. There was a well, a propane tank, a septic system, and all other sorts of things I knew nothing about. One day, the wife's email address was mistakenly left on a chain of communications. I busted through the professionals and contacted her directly.

With that, I made a new connection—one that lifted my spirits and carried me through Casey's death. The sellers invited me, Jet, and Watson to come out for a visit the Friday before closing. I decided not to tell Matt. No sense getting him all worked up over nothing.

As I got out of the car, I was temporarily blinded by the sun's glare on the massive expanse of snow. It was one of those spectacular winter days and not too cold. The sellers encouraged me to let the dogs run, and Jet and Watson bounded about, foretelling a perfect transition to country life. The husband guided me around the property's boundaries, showing me stakes that had been placed for future reference. Then, they invited me inside so he could discuss the mechanicals. They had put a fair amount of work fixing up the place, which they had acquired through foreclosure.

"If we were staying, I'd be putting a window in here," he said, gesturing to the wall against which they had set up their large flat-screen TV.

"You can do that?" I exclaimed, my ignorance on full display. I'm the furthest thing from a DIYer.

"Sure! Nothing to it!" With that, he pressed the housekeys into my hand. "We've pre-signed. We'll be out this weekend."

After our meeting, I was stuck on the idea of a large picture window that would look out onto the vast expanse of gorgeous land. I wasted no time in researching contractors and scheduled a meeting for an estimate on the day of closing. When Matt showed up to find me deep in conversation with the contractor, his eyes grew wide. "You don't own it yet!" he exclaimed.

I grinned, showed him the keys, and spilled the beans about coming out the week before. The color drained from his face as he hustled us out of there. Gleefully clutching the window estimate, I was not about to allow anything or anyone to interfere with my exuberance. It only got better as we breezed through the closing. I really needed uneventful after so much eventful.

Now, after basking in a celebratory dinner with Matt and his wife, I'm jerked back into sadness as I pick up the small package and unlock the front door to the home I'll soon be vacating. Watson and Jet greet me exuberantly.

They don't care that she's gone.

I trace the carved vines and flowers on Casey's box of ashes and remind myself of how lucky I was to share my life with her. I look around the bungalow at the two-decades-worth of memories I created within its hundred-year-old walls. Ahead of me is the monumental task of packing and deciding which parts of my past life will accompany me to the country. If nothing else, because I am the self-anointed family historian, it's a no-brainer that all those musty old boxes in the bungalow basement are coming along.

These are boxes I will transport myself, rather than entrust them to movers who are strangers to me. Several of these boxes are Mum's. Over the past year, I've primarily focused on Dad's boxes, because sooner rather than later, it will be all I have of him. This research project has uncovered far more than I ever would have expected, especially in terms of inspiration and motivation. Papa's carefully documented and preserved journey through drug treatment has illuminated for me the grace, courage, love, and resilience of my paternal lineage.

But I can't deny that I'm the product of two lineages. At some point, it will serve me to better understand how Mum developed from a child with a (presumably) clean slate, to a woman who loathed her husband and could not bond with her daughter. With this thought in mind, some days later I return to the basement and peek in one of these boxes. I open an envelope of clippings about my other grandfather Pompa's retirement at age sixty from a job he'd held since right out of high school. He'd worked for an insurance company, and I now have the Globe Wernicke bookcase that had been in his office. I never really knew him, as he succumbed to Alzheimer's at sixty-six. By the time we kids were old enough to interact with him, his speech had deteriorated to the point where Scott would ask, "Why is Pompa speaking Spanish?"

Gamma was sixty-three when Pompa died and only recently retired from her almost three-decade career as secretary to the superintendent of schools. She went to work when Mum was ten, leaving Mum in charge of Auntie Jan, who was six. Along with caring for her younger sister, Mum took piano lessons and learned how to iron men's dress shirts. After graduating high school, she enrolled at Rollins College, the "finishing school," as she called it, to "find and marry a rich man." Perhaps that was all that was expected of her and all she expected of herself. It was, after all, 1950s America.

Gamma's professional life, in contrast, seemed to have been quite fulfilling. After she retired, she then enjoyed an active life, filled with friends and trips all across the country. As a kid, I often envied her. She got to do whatever she wanted! When she turned seventy, she moved from Milwaukee up to our hometown. I don't remember whose idea that was. It seemed counterintuitive, given all the fights she and Mum had over the years.

Next, I pull out a scrapbook that I made for Gamma commemorating her seventieth birthday party. Mum hosted this gathering for her at our house. Each friend was invited to bring a photo or other memento of their friendship with Gamma. As I page through the scrapbook, I am struck by all the party pictures from over the years. Gamma enjoyed a robust social life.

Maybe Gamma's social life and job took time away from being a nurturing, supportive mother. For as long as I can remember, Mum chased after Gamma's affections. Their fights were epic, but I never really understood what they were about. Maybe this was because I'd already built my own fortress against all the volatility and inconsistency in my own mother's attention and affection. All I know is that as I got older, Mum's isolation increased.

Several years after Gamma died, when I bought the bungalow and started to put down my own roots, Mum decided that she and Dad needed to move near me. It was history repeating itself, just like when she and Dad moved from San Diego to Wisconsin to be near Gamma and Pompa. I felt trapped, but as long as Dad was able to hang in there and manage Mum's needs and moods, I could mostly ignore her and focus on building my own life and identity. But when Parkinson's made its stealthy entrance, everything changed. My identity became enmeshed with that of my parents.

Now, the off-ramp from that enmeshment is fully in focus. The idea that I have now rediscovered my authentic identity in a renovated manufactured home on ten acres of woods and prairie is both thrilling and gut-wrenching.

CHAPTER 38

Then: April 1952

April 21, 1952

Dearest and All:

Well, this is the big letter. Unless I let you know to the contrary, I'll be at the San Diego airport on Monday at about 3.15 P.M. It will be via Los Angeles. From here to L.A. on American and to S.D. via United. So I will wire you before I board the plan on Monday April 28th. I am to see Dr. Osberg tomorrow to get the wheels rolling.

I had a good hour with Dr. Osberg on Saturday evening. He wants me to choose a psychiatrist when I get out there. Some-one that does not know me too well. He does not feel that it is so necessary for present conditions but to ease the path that is before me. I will ask Dr Osberg if he wants to write to you. I do not know any reason for it. We certainly are not going to play hide and seek with drugs, nor is there any cops and robbers game to play. We are going to do more things together about the house, in the way of fixing things up ourselves. I am really looking forward to this.

The path of transition is always fraught with challenges, no matter the circumstances. I often lamented the lack of resources for juvenile delinquents who'd been sent to a group home or residential treatment center. Once released, they often returned to a chaotic home life. Papa clearly recognized that the structured, sheltered existence he would be leaving soon could not be replicated back home in San Diego. His reference to "any cops and robbers game to play" acknowledged that he would need to reestablish trust with Nana and the rest of the family. Once again, I'm struck by how much I'll never know about those years leading up to the Fort Worth experience.

To get back to my arrival in San Diego. I might have arrived on Sunday but from your letters, it looked to me like you might be on your job on Sunday PM and usually you write me that you and Bruce are doing some yard work on Monday and then going to work at 4.15. Now if it is hard to make arrangements to be there, do not worry about it and I will control my disappointment. If there is one thing that I have learned while being here is patience and not to be disappointed if things do not work out fast like you would like to have them. You may even think that I have become fat and lazy, and you will probably be right.

Oh, Papa, I too must learn patience and not to be disappointed when things do not work out the way I would like. The idea of sitting with uncomfortable feelings until they pass on their own comes to mind. It's a skill I'm learning through the study of stoicism. In hindsight, I believe Dad likely mastered it as a very young man. Or maybe he was born with it?

Oh yes, I did get downtown with Dr Lewis and purchased a light traveling case. It really is a woman's case part leather and part blue plaid fiberboard. It had to be this to accommodate our radio and the R.S.R. bag. Then after the shopping tour, I had a lovely dinner at the Lewis residence. It is right here on the hospital grounds.

Tomorrow we have two operations and two again Thursday. I have cut myself off of the ACTH. I do feel stuffy at times and have to use the vaporizer but the asthma is not bothersome if I remain serene. In reading the Cardinal, I have come to the conclusion that I have been doing what the priests call "retreat." Thanks to the friends that I have made, it has not been as rigorous as the religious retreats that the book tells about.

It takes amazing perspective to be able to think of a locked drug rehab facility as a "retreat." I am gob smacked. But maybe, compared to Papa's struggles with addiction, the facility served as a haven.

There will have to be a few things to save and tell later. This will be the last letter, I believe. Looking forward to a grand reunion and a steak. Loads of love till I get there,

Daddy

He did it!
My heart soars for him.

CHAPTER 39

Now: Mother's Day 2018

"You know, Auntie Jan asked if I had seen your new place, and I had to tell her I hadn't."

Mum's chiding, so typical for how she expresses herself, hits me like fingernails on a chalkboard. She doesn't necessarily want to see my place; she's not even asked about it much. Nope, she's sharing her dismay at the interaction she had with her sister over a simple inquiry.

I am not my mother's daughter.

Colleen has done a much better job than Jennifer ever did at helping me understand a mother who simply does not have the capacity to bond with her daughter. Objectively, it makes sense, regardless of how it might hurt. Our lack of connection is real, but contrary to Mum's assertions, it's not my fault. Never was.

My earliest memory of feeling inadequate was when Mum regaled relatives with a story of how I threw a tantrum in the airport when I was just two. Even as a child, I felt embarrassed as I pondered how I could have better controlled my two-year-old self. When I was in first grade, Mum set up an appointment with the school psychologist because she couldn't tolerate the fact that I didn't want to tell her all about my day when I got home from school. I always wondered what came out of that appointment, as I've only a vague memory of talking to a man who was not my teacher. I mentioned it to Jennifer when I started therapy and asked Mum to clarify what the results of the assessment were.

"Well, that's when we learned you were gifted." The sarcasm in her voice confused me. She continued. "We were told that we just needed to leave you alone, as you needed to have down time when you got home from school."

We. I'm pretty sure Dad was not part of that *we*. He would still have been at work when I got home from school.

Packing for the move was cathartic in many ways. While sifting through a box of trophies, I pulled out a small one from a civic oration contest I won when I was eleven. I threw out the rest, but this one made the move to the new place as a memento of my initiation into public speaking. Dad helped me write my speech and coached my delivery. Acting and public speaking gave me a self-assurance that ultimately would help disguise how I felt on the inside. I wonder if he knew that?

By the time I got to my forties, the internal/external split was complete. For two straight weeks in the spring of 2012, I was the most famous prosecutor in the state of Minnesota. Yet underneath the confident façade of a skilled litigator with nerves of steel, Mum's relentless reminders that there was something *off* about me lurked, threatening to knock me down at any moment. I've learned how mothers' opinions impact self-esteem in ways most other influences do not.

When I asked Colleen how it was that, aside from discreet episodes of horrific binge drinking, I never developed any addictions or dependencies—or even worse, contemplated suicide—her answer was enlightening, if unexpected. "Your dad was both mother and father to you."

Perhaps that's why I never recorded over the cassette Dad made for me in 1988.

After defying the predictions of the legal pundits and winning my big case, I attempted, unsuccessfully, to parlay my new-found fame by running for a vacant judgeship. Whatever internal inadequacies I felt in my personal life, they were largely outweighed by my confidence in my professional accomplishments. The campaign spanned the summer of 2012. I marched in parades, handed out flyers and chased endorsements. One day, in between campaign functions, I stopped by Mum and Dad's place for a brief visit while wearing my kelly-green *Russell For Judge* shirt that a friend had designed.

As I was leaving, Dad interrupted my internal preoccupations by asking, "Could I have a shirt?"

"What?" I was mildly annoyed. "The shirts are for volunteers."

"Oh. Well. I was just thinking I could wear it when I go to play pool or when we're at the grocery store. It would be a sort of advertisement."

That dear man. I chastised myself internally for being abrupt with him. "Of course! What a great idea!" I exclaimed.

Mum didn't request a shirt.

Colleen hit the nail on the head with her assessment. Mum simply wasn't capable of whatever nurturing was supposed to come with being a mother. She was preoccupied with her own fears and abandonment issues. Throughout my childhood, adolescence, and even my adult years, Dad's understated support shone through the darkness and chaos that Mum was always creating. His ability to see opportunity and positivity served him and our family well.

I moved to the country estate in March, just as spring was arriving. The increased daylight—just like what Dad had described in his cassette letter years ago—and the joy of living in the country quickly transformed me in ways I cannot fully describe. Every weekend, I would drive the hour each way back to the bungalow to get it ready to put on the market. Of course, I was determined to sell it myself. I didn't need an agent telling me that I had to paint it and stage it and pay him or her a commission to sell it. I knew it would sell as soon as I was ready.

On my way home, I would stop at Mum and Dad's. Immediately upon my arrival each week, Dad had questions.

"How's the job going?"

"Tell me about the train commute."

"How do the dogs like it out there?"

I showed them pictures and regaled them with stories about pollinator workshops and my quest to transform my property from a previously mowed plot to a more sustainable prairie garden.

And so, the afternoon Mum interjects with her comment about having to tell her sister that she hasn't seen my place yet, I'm ready with an answer: "Well, Mum, how about for Mother's Day, I come down, pick you up, and whisk you up there for a little tour? It won't take too long, and I can get you back down here before Dad has a chance to miss you!"

It's the perfect idea.

"I want to go, too," Dad says.

Uh oh. I didn't see that one coming. Mum and I lock eyes.

"Geez, Dad, you know how much I'd love that, but you can't even do your laps around the house anymore. You haven't gone up the stairs in almost a year."

"I can do it," Dad huffed.

"Now, don't be stubborn," Mum cuts him off. Even though she's exasperated with Dad, I can tell she's mulling over my initial suggestion of the trip just for her. "It sure would be nice to have a little outing."

"I can do it!"

Dad's not going to give in on this. I will need to break the stalemate.

"Alright, let's just calm down and think about this," I say before Mum jumps in again. "Dad, I think we need to check with the hospice staff and see if they think this is something you're capable of doing. We need to be realistic here. I know how much you'd like to go, but it's possible that Mum will just have to describe it all for you when she gets back."

"I'm going."

Ugh! My heart is racing. I can't tell if it's from excitement at the idea of Dad seeing my new place, or the fear that this idea will never actually be executed.

"Let's just see what the professionals say," I respond again, attempting to project a voice of reason, "and let's see how you're feeling next week. You know how some days you feel better than others."

My excitement quickly shifts to doubt. I refuse to get my hopes up.

The following week, I walk in to see both Mum's and Dad's jackets draped over the banister. It's happening. Dad is wide-eyed and alert as I approach.

"Well, look at you!" I wonder whether this is all just a dream.

Mum rushes in. "Now, just listen to me. There's a plan, and you've got to follow it. Otherwise, this isn't going to be able to happen."

I'm not sure if she's talking to me or to Dad. It doesn't matter. I'm more than happy to let her oversee this operation.

"We're going to have a chair on the landing so that when Dad gets up there, he can rest for a minute before going out to the garage."

"Fine by me." I'm ready to get the party started, even as I try to repress any underlying doubts I have about the whole thing.

With that, Dad grabs his walker and begins the long shuffle over to the stairs—stairs he hasn't navigated in what seems like forever. Once there, he grips the banister with one hand and his cane with the other. We somehow decide that Mum will go ahead of him on the stairs, and I will trail behind. I can only imagine the horror of the hospice staff.

I clutch Dad by his waist. I hear the gurgling in his chest as he hoists himself up, one step at a time. He feels so small, so frail. I resolve not to cry as I mentally push him up to the landing. At last, breathless, he sinks into the chair that is strategically positioned.

"Look at that!" I'm practically shouting in my amazement.

After a short break, Dad musters the strength to get himself down the two steps into the garage, where we reunite him with his walker. A few more steps, and he is in the back seat of my car. The drive out to my country estate flies by as we all ride the adrenaline wave of what just happened. Mum prattles on, excited to be on an adventure. Dad is quiet, likely exhausted by the physical and mental exertion.

"This reminds me so much of West Bend," Mum muses as we traverse the miles of farmland.

We pull into my driveway just in time for Dad's lunch, according to Mum's schedule. She thoughtfully packed everything he would need. The weather is temperate; the sun shining. My heart feels like it might burst with joy.

"Alright, Dad, you're just going to have a little picnic in the car while I give Mum the tour," I announce cheerfully.

"Sounds good to me!" Just like his own father at the narcotic farm, Dad will make do with whatever hand he is dealt. We crack the car windows and leave him to his lunch.

Mum is impressed. Sort of.

"How big is this? How many bedrooms?" She is taking mental notes to report back to her sister. I try to recite all the data she seeks. What I can't bring myself to describe for her are all the intangibles. In the few short months I've been out here, the vice grip on my heart and soul has loosened. The darkness has lifted. I sleep soundly. The commute is entirely bearable, and every single day, when I arrive back home from work, I rejoice in this new life that is all my own.

Mum is more focused on the fact that I don't have much for window dressings. "That corrugated tin is . . . interesting."

Our tastes in decorating have never jived. I am simple, casual, whimsical. She is formal, fancy, breakable.

"I don't see any pictures of me," she remarks as the tour winds down and we head back to the car.

"I still haven't completely unpacked." It isn't a complete lie.

Once back outside, I drive the car around the house and through the backyard so Dad can get a good look. In the country, it's a given that you're going to drive through your yard at some point.

"I want to get out," he says.

We brought his wheelchair along just in case. Again, he engages muscles he hasn't used in months. Remarkably, he hoists himself out of the back seat and into the wheelchair. The sun warms us as we wheel Dad a little way from the car for a photo.

"This is absolutely tremendous, M'Gil!" he proclaims, looking around.

"I know. Can you believe it?" I pinch myself repeatedly to make sure I'm not dreaming the whole thing. The darkness of the past year dissolves, and Dad is here to share in my triumph. I can't ask for more.

On the drive back, we talk about the timing for putting the bungalow on the market. I've decided on Memorial Day. Dad wants to know how much I am planning to ask for the bungalow versus how much I paid for the country estate. He's thinking about profit!

"I'm so proud of you for figuring all of this out," he remarks. "This is a really great purchase. The value will only go up in the future."

"I learned it all from you, Dad. I learned it all from you."

CHAPTER 40

Then: 1959

FEDERAL SECURITY AGENCY
PUBLIC HEALTH SERVICE

IN REPLYING, ADDRESS
MEDICAL OFFICER IN CHARGE
PUBLIC HEALTH SERVICE HOSPITAL
FORT WORTH 1, TEXAS

April 29, 1952

Mrs. Ralph Russell
3204 Goldsmith Street
San Diego 6, California

Dear Mrs. Russell:

By the time that you receive this letter your husband will have returned home after what has been, I am sure, a rather difficult period for both of you in terms of a necessity of your being away from each other, and a necessity for Dr. Russell to temporarily discontinue his practice. I believe that you will be reassured to know that Dr. Russell has cooperated extremely well in his treatment here and leaves the hospital greatly improved. Although he will undoubtedly continue to have some difficulty with his asthma which will require active medical management, it does not appear likely that there will again be either a physical or psychological need for demerol. I feel confident that your husband has the emotional and intellectual resources that will make it possible for him to again assume his responsibility without resorting to the use of narcotics.

I believe that Dr. Russell knows that we will always be willing to be of any assistance and that we will be happy to hear from one or both of you at any time.

Sincerely yours,

James W. Osberg

James W. Osberg, M. D.

Upon his return to San Diego, Papa went right back to being busy. He established a new practice, which grew to such an extent that he took on an assistant. He also continued practicing at his other clinic, as well as at the medical program at the Door of Hope, a center for low-income families, which he had established. Papa also set up a well-baby clinic for the Public Health Department as well as the San Diego Maternal and Neonatal Welfare Committee.

Auntie Ann gave me Nana's diaries so that I could try to piece together the last year of Papa's life. Unfortunately, his asthma had worsened. Auntie Ann described an oxygen tank that Papa kept in an alcove off the kitchen to help his breathing when he got home from work. Although there was never any indication that he'd relapsed, Papa couldn't seem to get a handle on moderating his professional life as he'd aspired to while at the narcotic farm. To the contrary, he seemed to be even busier. On December 1, 1959, Papa applied to be on the attending medical staff of the Donald N. Sharp Memorial Community Hospital. For this application, he provided three physician references, one of whom had been his partner in the clinic while he was at the narcotic farm.

Ten days after filling out the application and getting signatures from his references, Papa was dead.

Nana's diary told the story in succinct and devastating terms:

Sunday, December 6, 1959

Ralph had acute asthmatic attack at 7 p.m. – taken to Dr.'s Hospital about 10 p.m.

Monday, December 7, 1959

Ralph is very ill – they can't seem to break the asthmatic spasm. I have specials for him around the clock. I called Bud and wrote to Bruce and Ann – I canceled the church circle meeting to be held here – Bud arrived at 6 and went to hospital.

Tuesday, December 8, 1959

Bud is taking over – what would I do without him! Ralph is no better.

Dad's ability to support Nana and the rest of the family would serve him well the rest of his life.

Wednesday, December 9, 1959

Ralph is to be moved to Scripps Hospital – Dr. Keavey is in charge.

Thursday, December 10, 1959

Ralph died at Scripps 1:17 a.m. from cerebral anoxic damage, bronchial asthma, emphysema.

Papa's lungs simply gave out as the asthma dealt its final, vicious blow—the same frightful demise of Gentleman Brown in *Lord Jim*. He was fifty-nine years old.

Four months later, Dad took Papa's place walking Auntie Ann down the aisle for her wedding.

Less than two years after that, in August 1961, Dad married Mum and devoted the rest of his life to caring for her.

CHAPTER 41

Now: Father's Day 2018

"HOW DO YOU THINK YOU'RE DOING, RALPH?"

The latest hospice review meeting has commenced.

Andrea is shouting. It's disconcerting until I realize that it's probably the perfect volume for my parents. Dad immediately looks over at Mum. This is the norm for them. He no longer speaks for himself until her nod and smile give him permission to respond. Mum smiles back at him, encouragingly.

"Well, I think I'm doing about the same."

Same as compared to what? This is the side of Dad that I will never understand. His complete lack of self-awareness flabbergasts me. Or is it denial? Or optimism? Or delusion?

Mum jumps in; she just can't help herself. "Well, he's definitely weaker, and it's taking us so very long to get going in the morning."

Next thing I know, she is regaling Andrea and the nurse with a story about trying to move Dad from his bed to his chair and shoving Dad toward the bed as he crumpled to the floor. The cheery delivery belies her true sentiments . . . perhaps.

Andrea then turns to me. "How do you think your dad's doing, Debbie?"

I can't help myself. I tell the truth. "Dad, when I got back from vacation in March, I immediately noticed a change. Mostly, it's with your breathing and coughing. I think all your coughing is making you weaker. I also think all the nighttime thrashing makes you much weaker during the day."

I look directly at Andrea as I speak my truth. It saves me from seeing how Mum is responding to this. I really don't care. There is talk of "next steps" and "a plan." I'm the only one in this family who's ever valued plans, so I'm pretty sure that any recommendations from the professionals will be ignored.

"You know, Ralph," Andrea says, "this might be a good time to have a hospital bed brought in."

"I feel like that means I'm giving up."

As Dad responds, I think of Auntie Ann's words from over a year ago. *"It's not like he has taken to his bed."*

I decide to make a point that I fervently hope will be well-taken. "One of the things I like about a hospital bed is that it has railings and the ability to be raised and lowered, so you'll be better able to help Mum help you."

Because, in the end, that's what this is all about.

Dad's eyes well up as he stares at Mum.

Which, for some reason, causes Mum to laugh nervously and try to get him to stop. She's embarrassed by his display of emotion. She can keep him clean, fed, and presentable, but she has proven herself time and again completely incapable of listening to his fears, his grief, or anything related to his feelings. As this scene plays out in front of me, for the first time ever I do not feel the familiar rage that I would always be shoving aside. In the end, as Andrea told me almost two years ago, this is *their* journey. Whatever their relationship is now, there will not be a seismic shift in how Mum connects with Dad. His emotions are disconcerting and embarrassing to her. Her condition only allows her to connect with her own feelings.

"I just hate for this to drag on like this," Dad says. "It would be much easier to check out next Tuesday."

◆ ◆ ◆

The day before Father's Day, Dad isn't up for talking on the phone.

"Are you planning to come over tomorrow?" Mum asks.

What, does she think, I'm going to skip it?

"Of course." I keep my tone light.

"Well, Dad told me to tell you that he'd like you to bring his box of things."

Huh. Knowing Mum's aversion to Dad's box of things, it must have taken a lot for him to make that request, especially with Mum as the messenger. On the drive into town, I mentally prepare a closing argument like so many I have given to juries in my long career as a trial lawyer. Today, I will convince Dad that his life had meaning.

Mum lets me in, rolling her eyes at the box in my arms. "You won't mind if I just let you two visit, will you?" she asks.

"Of course not!" I smile brightly.

Dad's in bed. A hospital bed. It is smaller and less imposing than I expected. Mum probably isn't too put off by the aesthetics. He's dressed but appears out of it.

He's taken to his bed.

He opens his eyes as I enter the room. "You brought my box!"

"Sure did! I've been doing a lot of reading, that's for sure." I set the box on Mum's bed and take his hand in mine for the grip test. It isn't bad.

"Did you find that journal I kept during my trip to Europe on the coal ship?"

I pull out the envelope marked *Diary of Trip to Europe On Coal Ship – 6/19/53*. "You mean this one?" I ask mischievously.

"Yes!"

"Do you realize that you and I were the exact same age when we took our first trips to Europe?"

"You were twenty-five?"

"Well, close enough. My trip was also in June of the year I turned twenty-five, just like you!"

"So it was—"

I press on, "What was so interesting to me was the first part, where you had nothing to do, so you decided to write down your philosophy of life. Do you remember that?"

"I remember the long trip over, but I don't remember exactly what I wrote."

I find the passage in question. "Here's my favorite part," I say, beginning to read:

Last night I thought about "Our Town's" two points (Does anyone ever really appreciate life every minute they live), (There is something immortal about every human being). Can any great work be created in a state of satisfaction of happiness? Is personal tragedy or misfortune a prerequisite for greatness?

I think that during the course of this trip I have thought over my whole life and as I look back and reflect, I wouldn't change a minute. Even the so-called bad parts or mistakes, because many times, more can be learned from mistakes than any other way. The main thing is for life to have meaning. Maybe not an overall meaning at first, but each event has a separate meaning which can eventually be placed in some larger pattern of meaning.

My voice begins to break. I will myself to stay steady. It's as good a time as any to segue into my closing argument.

"Look at you, Dad! You'd just graduated from college and were off to see the sights in Europe! We know about the 'so-called bad parts,' but look at how you bounced back from what had happened just six years prior. You buckled down, you stayed the course, and the whole time, you were a wonderful support to your family."

He's staring at the ceiling. I'm not sure my words are resonating. I press on.

"You know—and I know—that life is a series of ups and downs, right? And now, at your age, you've seen way more than I have, but even I've had my own share of ups and downs. Everybody does. But remember when you told me way back when that I had inherited your optimism? You know what? You were absolutely right!"

He turns to me, smiling weakly. "You've always been so strong, M'Gil."

Strong acting skills, at least.

"You betcha! And you know what else I inherited from you? Problem-solving skills! Your journal is full of examples of times when you had to have your wits about you to figure your way out of a jam!"

His smile seems a little broader. Or maybe it's just wishful thinking on my part.

"I want to read a couple more parts for you. I think Paris was probably the highlight, don't you?"

"Oh, yes, that was a truly marvelous few days."

"I keep seeing the name 'Culmer.' What an odd name!"

"Oh, yes, Culmer Benson!" Dad says. "We went to high school together, and he was working in theatre in Paris. He showed me around, and we saw the sights and had the most wonderful meals. That's where I spent my twenty-fifth birthday."

Dad knew such interesting people when he was young. He remained friends with many of them through the custom of Christmas cards. I always enjoyed his stories about these people.

"One of my favorite parts was when you got the guy with the gondola to run you to the train station so you could get from Venice to Milan!"

"Did I write about that?"

"You sure did!" I flip through his journal and find the correct entry:

I went back to the gondola dock, but the gondoliers wanted 1500 lire to take me to the station. I only had 900. Just as I was about to give up a fellow came up to me and asked me where I wanted to go. I told him and also that I only had 900 lire. He said he would take me and told me to wait for him while he went for his gondola at a little gondola platform away from the main dock.

He appeared shortly and I got in. He asked what time the train left and I told him. He said we could make it. With that, he pulled out another oar, put on his gondolier's shirt, lit the light on the front of the gondola and then began to row like mad. We took all kinds of short cuts through small dark canals. I didn't know what would happen. The minutes ticked by. I had no idea where we were or how long it would take. Finally, I asked the gondolier if we were near the station. He said not to worry. A few minutes later he said we would be at the station in a few minutes. That would be ten minutes after 12:00.

By this time the sweat was just pouring down the face of the gondolier. I was overwhelmed by his kindness. Exactly five minutes later we were at the station dock. I tried to tell him how much I appreciated his effort on my behalf, because I really felt he had really put himself out to bring me all the way over there in such a hurry for only 900 lire. So, I also gave him a half full pack of cigarettes and fifteen cents in American money which then cleaned me completely out. He said he understood and away I ran and just made the train.

"I'd forgotten about that!" Dad grins, clearly relishing the memory. "I've got a couple more."

August 4 – I began to get restless wondering how I was going to get home. I hadn't heard from Dan and it was hard for me to plan anything because if I had to pay for my way home it would take nearly all I had, and I couldn't afford to go to Scotland or Ireland. . . . I decided to try to forget my restlessness by a visit to the Tower of London, followed by spending the rest of the afternoon in a record store. I wanted to get the Walton Violin Concerto, but they don't have it on L.P. and I was afraid the 78 (rpm) would get broken on the way home. I listened to it anyway.

"I've never heard of the Walton Violin Concerto," I remark sheepishly.

"Oh, it's quite something. You'll have to check it out sometime."

I continue:

On my way home I decided that if I didn't hear by the next morning, I would start exploring other means of getting home. I figured the only way for things to start happening is to make them happen.

For some reason, I chuckle. "Truer words were never said!"

"Well, what else are you going to do?" Dad responds.

In that moment, I realize that he's never lost that desire to make things happen. Even now, as his body is giving up, his spirit keeps fighting. The trip out to my place was proof.

"Do you remember how you ended up getting home?" I tease.

He slowly shakes his head, so I read:

August 6 – Today has been a day of all kinds of decisions. At American Express there was still no word for me also no cancellations on ship space, so I decided to take the big leap and get my ticket on the P.A.A. flight for Saturday. Boy how I hated to see all that money at once. I had visions of a return visit to Paris via Holland, also a little trip to Scotland and Ireland, maybe even a jump down to Stratford-on-Avon, a pair of wonderful English crepe shoes and other things. ALL DOWN THE DRAIN

Oh well, one can't have everything. I guess I should feel lucky I have the money to get back with. Well to continue, I realized that my time in London was limited so I decided to take a coach tour of the city. It was very nice and very inclusive. Then I decided to have a bite, since I had had no lunch. I saw an interesting parfait in the window of a tea shop, so decided to investigate. Evidently the girls had never made one, but they went ahead anyway and fixed me a tremendous strawberry parfait. More like a banana split, only without the bananas and with strawberries instead.

"*Mmmmmmm.*" Dad did always love his food.

I have one more passage that I want to share with Dad:

Met a funny little man from Greece who asked me the directions to someplace and when I tried to help him with my guidebook, he was very taken by the cleanness with which I spoke English. He was in London to study English but was having a hard time because of the accent and speed with which the English spoke. I spent the morning practicing conversation with him in return for which he bought my lunch. He wanted to meet me later and take me to a show but realizing that this poor little man would be prone to tiring, I told him I had other plans.

Dad doesn't remember this encounter at all.

For me, this passage reveals the soul of the man who would, twelve years later, become the husband to my mother and the father to me and my brother. It's an open soul; a generous soul; a kind and sensitive soul.

"This trip." I say. "I'm so impressed at how you navigated your way through it without always knowing whether things were going to work out or not."

"That's the thing about being young: you don't really have a sense of how badly things could go. Fortunately for me, I was able to get there and back in one piece."

I carefully consider my next statement. How to convince a man—whose first chapter had been so full of adventure, joy, and creativity— that the ensuing years, too, had meaning? Dad never wrote that memoir he contemplated in his final letter to Papa in the spring of 1952. Over the last year, I've tried to pull him out of the shadow of shame that Mum has created, if only in my own mind. I've measured his greatest accomplishments not by how much money he made or how many titles he held, but by what he meant to our family and, especially, what he meant to me. His perpetual optimism and oversized heart instilled in me a strength that I now need to recognize and utilize to its very greatest extent.

"Dad, you've been the buffer and the glue of this family for so long.

I hope you know that. I know it hasn't been easy. I hope you know just how much I appreciate everything you've done for each of us."

I pull out *Creative Careers*, the book Dad gave me for Christmas back in 1988 when I was struggling to find my way in the world after my own college graduation. I remove the little gift tag from the inside cover and hold it out to him.

"Do you see what this says? It says, *May all your dreams come true*. Dad, I'm here to tell you that all my dreams *have* come true. I know I can't really explain it, but buying the country estate may very well be the most important thing I will do in my lifetime. Even more important than all those cases I prosecuted. It represents who I really want to be, even if I'm not quite there yet. You've been my very best guide in every decision I've ever made. The new place is a dream come true. It means so much to me that you got to see it."

Dad closes his eyes, his lips curving up slightly. "Me too, M'Gil. Me too."

Sitting there with Dad, his hand in mine, a warmth settles over me as I surrender the fight. I'm ready to let him go with a full, but open heart. Dad cannot and will not abandon me because he is the very best part of me—the curious, imaginative, resilient part. I've conquered the darkness, just as he did and just as Papa had before him.

Although Papa crossed fifty-one and only made it to fifty-nine, Dad crossed fifty-one and made it to eighty-nine. Thus far, I've crossed fifty-one and made it to fifty-two.

Kevin Cronin says, "If you're tired of the same old story, turn some pages."

I'm finally ready to turn the page and begin my next adventure.

EPILOGUE

October 2020

Dad made it to his ninetieth birthday, a festive affair for which Auntie Ann and her daughter, my cousin Carolyn, flew in from San Diego. Cousin Jim also attended, as did Scott. Dad made it to his chair, and we celebrated a life well-lived. Less than a month later, he was gone, having passed quietly in his sleep. It was his final gift to Mum.

I've just crossed fifty-five and am now two full weeks post-retirement from my government lawyer gig. All the projects around the country estate that I previously could not find time for clamor for my attention. At the top of the list is cleaning out and organizing my four-stall garage. The idea of this project overwhelmed me initially, but the time for procrastination has passed. Winter will be here soon enough. I've learned that if I break something big down into smaller manageable bits, slowly and steadily, I will complete the big thing.

Today's manageable bit is hanging a tool storage rack.

I hold in my hand Dad's Black and Decker drill, from circa 1974 or so. It's corded, and the plug is not grounded. Dad bestowed this drill on me as a sort of housewarming gift over twenty years ago, when I moved into the bungalow. It served me well for all my little projects, and it never occurred to me to buy something a bit more updated.

I've marked the holes and inserted the proper-sized bit.

"Ready, Dad? Here we go!"

ACKNOWLEDGEMENTS

My heart swells with gratitude for all the people in my life who contributed, in one way or another, to this book becoming a reality. I am truly fortunate.

My editor, Elisabeth Chretien is a wizard. She took a first draft that was meandering at best and confusing at worst and gave me a roadmap to transform it into something more palatable. She asked tough questions and pushed me well out of my comfort zone. This project became a partnership, and I could not have produced the thing you just read without her.

My family of choice propped me up me in real time, as I slogged through the events depicted in this book. My Auntie Ann Simoneau, cousin Jim Verhoye, and dear friends Kristi Peterson, Linda Hendlin, and Dan and Natasha DeVoe were cherished confidents, who loved me unconditionally during one of the toughest times of my life.

I first started writing as a child, after Louise Fitzhugh's *Harriet the Spy* inspired me to keep a notebook. By the time I got to law school, creative writing was pushed to my life's back burner. In 2011 I met my friend Jess Gunderson who happens to be a brilliant writer herself. She encouraged me to start a blog, and that's how my stories first ventured out of my head and into the real world. Shortly thereafter, friend Dan DeVoe admonished me: "If you don't share your stories, it's called a diary." With that prodding, I summoned up the courage to share my blog with my friends on social media. The response was overwhelming and helped me realize that writing about my experiences and sharing my vulnerability created an opportunity to be useful to others.

My friend Lisa Pertile inspired me in so many ways: first, by embarking on that midlife pivot many of us dream of but lack the courage to execute. She's followed her own artistic passion with a singular focus and dedication that motivates me, especially when I'm in the middle of a bout of imposter syndrome. She's also been there every time I've stumbled along with this project and all the ancillary obligations it's produced. I owe her a debt of gratitude for the wonderful headshots that are my public facing image as well as her willingness to beta read the final draft.

I must also thank *all* my friends who took time to read parts of various drafts and offer feedback: Natasha, Lisa, along with Jaralee Richter, Patty Lai, Amanda Shotton, and Midge Bubany. Russell Gray provided invaluable advice as I struggled with getting my story out of my head and onto the page. You all are simply the best.

Adrienne Conzemius, court reporter extraordinaire, transcribed Dad's cassette recording from 1988. Thank you!

My friends Steve Nichols and Genevieve Dever brought their talents and skills to Debbie's Stories in ways that helped me reach so many people.

Inspiring and generous authors Nita Sweeney, Deborah Burns, Lisbeth Meredith, Julie Scolnik, Coe Sherrard, Maria Olsen and Margo Weinstein all shared their publishing experiences with me, which empowered me to advocate for myself as a debut author. Countless other authors have graciously provided information, blurbs, and resources.

Huge thanks to Victoria Twead, Jacky Donovan and everyone in the We Love Memoirs Facebook Group, my friends at Women of Words (WOW), and all my Twitter #writingcommunity friends for tips, support, and encouragement. I'm also grateful to Tricia Hedman with Ollie Media for shepherding me and the book through the San Diego media scene.

Finally, thank you to the wonderful folks at Koehler Books: John Koehler and Greg Fields, who believed in the potential of this book, my designer Lauren Sheldon, who created something so beautiful, my editor Joe Coccaro, who polished everything up, and everyone else who helped create the tangible result of something that started out as a figment of my imagination when I first opened that file folder over fifteen years ago.

◆ ◆ ◆

If you enjoyed the book, please consider leaving a review at Amazon or Goodreads or both! For more about me and my next book, please visit my website at www.debbie-russell.com

RESOURCES

At every step of the way, books enlightened, inspired, and comforted me. Here they are, in hopes one or more may do the same for you:

1) *The Narcotic Farm: The Rise and Fall of America's First Prison for Drug Addicts*, Nancy Campbell, JP Olsen, Luke Walden, (Abrams, 2008)
2) *Understanding the Borderline Mother*, Christine Ann Lawson (Jason Aronson Inc., 2000)
3) *Being Mortal: Medicine and What Matters in the End*, Atul Gawande (Metropolitan Books, Henry Holt and Company, LLC, 2014)
4) *The Mindbody Prescription: Healing the Body, Healing the Pain*, John E. Sarno, (Warner Books, Inc. 1999)
5) *The Wisdom of Insecurity: A Message for an Age of Anxiety*, Alan Watts (Vintage, 2011)
6) *The Daily Stoic: 366 Meditations on Wisdom, Perseverance, and the Art of Living*, Ryan Holiday, Stephen Hanselman (Portfolio, 2016)
7) *The Luck Factor*, Richard Wiseman (Miramax, 2003)

DISCUSSION QUESTIONS FOR BOOK CLUBS

1) How does this book affect your sense of family?
2) How do themes of shame and secrecy impact a family's history?
3) Have you ever researched your family history? Why or why not?
4) Is the author's grandfather sympathetic? How do you view his actions from December 1951?
5) The author concludes that her grandfather used narcotics to manage his stress, rather than treat his asthma. Do you agree with her opinion? Why or why not?
6) How does the author's relationship with her mother impact her actions and beliefs?
7) What do you make of the author's first therapist?
8) How does the author handle therapy? At what point do we see a transformation?
9) What role does anticipatory grief play in the book?
10) How does the author's need to control outcomes limit her?
11) How does Dr. Russell's experience provide inspiration for modern day challenges?
12) How did the author's relationship with her father affect her worldview? Have you ever had someone in your life who played a similar role for you?

13) If the author could have a conversation with her grandfather today, what do you think she would ask him or share with him?

14) What place does gratitude have in this story? What were you able to relate to that may help you find gratitude in your own life?

Ingram Content Group UK Ltd.
Milton Keynes UK
UKHW040633140723
425136UK00004B/247